Roots of Rebellion

Acknowledgements

This book bears the name of a single author but in truth is the result of a collective effort to search out the roots of rebellion in Central America. I first would like to acknowledge the patience and generosity of the many Central Americans, especially the *campesino* women and men who, in sharing their food and homes, helped me understand their hunger for justice.

Three co-workers of the Resource Center offered excellent editing and research assitance: Chuck Hosking, Deb Preusch, and Beth Wood. I also want to thank the research assistance of Mary Ann Fiske, Ed Griffin-Nolan, Camille Jones, and Jim Stansbury, and the editing work of Bernard Ohanian. The book was greatly improved by the comments of Medea Benjamin, John Cavanagh, Monica Moore, David Kaimowitz, Lydia Sargent, and Robert Williams. Grants from the Presbyterian Hunger Fund and the Sunflower Foundation made this book possible. Finally I am grateful to the dedicated folks at South End Press.

Tom Barry is a co-director of the Resource Center in Albuquerque, New Mexico. The Resource Center produces books, slide shows, and reports about politics and economics in Central America, the Caribbean, and Mexico. Readers of this book may be interested in a related slide/tape show, also entitled "Roots of Rebellion," which is available for rent or sale from the Resource Center. For more information: Resource Center, P.O. Box 4506, Alburquerque, NM 87196.

Copyright ©1987 by Tom Barry

First edition, third printing
Production by South End Press
Cover design by Jade Barker
Cover photo courtesy of Oxfam America
Copyrights are required for book production in the United States. However in
our case, it is a disliked necessity. Thus, any properly footnoted quotation of up
to 500 sequential words may be used without permission, so long as the total
number of words quoted does not exceed 2,000. For longer quotations or for a
greater number of total words, authors should write to South End Press for
permission.
Photos on chapter pages by Deb Preusch
Library of Congress Cataloging-in-Publication Data

Barry, Tom, 1950-
    Roots of rebellion.

    Bibliography: p.
    Includes index.
    1. Food supply--Central America. 2. Land tenure--
Central America. 3. Food industry and trade--
Central America. 4. Land reform--Central America.
5. Peasant uprisings--Central America. I. Title.
HD9014.C462B37   1987   338.1'9'728   87-4519
ISBN 0-89608-288-1
ISBN 0-89608-287-3 (pbk.)

SOUTH END PRESS   116 ST BOTOLOPH ST   BOSTON MA 02115

ROOTS OF REBELLION

*Land & Hunger in
Central America*

Tom Barry

SOUTH END PRESS · · · · · BOSTON

Table of Contents

List of Tables

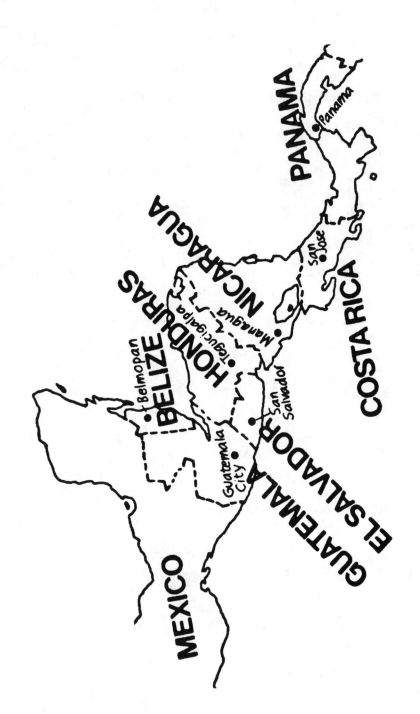

INTRODUCTION

This book looks behind the headlines and news flashes to the underlying reasons for political and economic turmoil in Central America. Each year, political violence and economic troubles worsen. But to understand the current crisis it is necessary to look behind the latest palace coup, revolution or example of U.S. intervention. The deeper crisis in Central America concerns the basic but too often ignored issues of land and hunger. It has to do with who owns the land and how it is used. The region's wealth and poverty, its history of repression and rebellion can all be traced back to the use and control of land.

Ultimately, it is up to the people of Central America to solve the difficult problems affecting their own countries. But the prominent role played by the U.S. government and transnational corporations (TNCs) in the region's politics and economy means that concerned U.S. residents can also be an important part of the solution in Central America.

The first chapter, *The Justice of Eating*, offers an overview of land use and ownership patterns followed by a description of the hunger and poverty that result from land use and ownership patterns designed to serve the interests of a small national elite and the global capitalist system. Introduced in this initial chapter is the region's two-tiered pattern of land tenure in which the best land is used by large landowners for export-oriented production while the worst land is left for peasants to grow food for local consumption. The second chapter, *The New Plantation*, focuses on the agroexport system that has dominated the region since colonial days—a system that puts coffee, bananas, cotton, sugar, and beef production for export ahead of the food needs of the local people. The region's uneven internal development as well as economic and political precariousness are examined here.

Chapter three, *The Land of the Oligarchs*, looks at the small national class that benefits from this agroexport system. Chapter four, *International Connections*, places the region's agricultural system in a global economic and political context, examining the transnational corporations that profit from the inequities of income and land distribution in Central America. The next chapter, *Chemical Craze*, investigates how this fixation on agroexport production has soaked the land and its people with U.S.-manufactured poisons that come boomeranging back to U.S. consumers.

Starting with the sixth chapter, the book looks at attempts to solve the land and hunger crisis through agrarian reform, political change, and foreign aid. *Reform or Revolution: El Salvador and Nicaragua* addresses the issue of agrarian reform, showing how revolutionary movements have pushed both El Salvador and Nicaragua to adopt land distribution programs. The seventh chapter *Reform and Rebellion: Guatemala, Honduras, and Costa Rica* reveals how the lack of meaningful agrarian reform programs has stirred peasant rebellion in these three countries. The last chapter, *Food Security: Obstacles and Solutions*, questions the value of traditional solutions—such as food assistance, population control, technological aid, rural development programs, agroexport promotion, and economic aid—that are promoted by Washington to address the region's agricultural problems. Alternative solutions that go to the roots of rebellion are presented. This final chapter concludes with the realization that national and regional food security must be achieved if peace is to come again to Central America.

The book focuses on the five countries of Costa Rica, El Salvador, Guatemala, Honduras, and Nicaragua with only passing references to Belize and Panama, the two countries located at opposite ends of the isthmus. A complete statistical overview and a series of tables on the land and hunger crisis are included at the end of the book as an appendix.

Some Facts of
Land and Hunger in Central America

Land

80 percent of farmers don't have enough land to adequately feed their families.

The number of landless campesinos has tripled since 1960.

The top 10 percent of landowners hold 80 percent of the farmland.

Small and medium-size farms producing for local consumption represent about 94 percent of existing farms but use only 9 percent of the farmland.

85 percent of best farmland is used to grow crops for export.

45 percent of arable land is used to graze cattle.

30 percent of the arable farmland is left idle.

Hunger

The average rural wage of $2 to $4 a day is not enough to pay for even half of a family's minimal food, shelter, and clothing costs.

From 35 to 70 percent (depending on country) of Central Americans are malnourished. Three out of four Central American children are malnourished.

The number of malnourished Central American children is increasing faster than the rate of population growth.

50 percent of Central Americans don't receive minimum nutritional needs.

The per capita production of staple foods like corn and beans is steadily decreasing.

Central America exports 4,620,000 tons of coffee, bananas, cotton, sugar and meat but needs to import over 750,000 tons of staple foods.

Sources: IDB, **Economic and Social Progress in Latin America: 1978**; SIECA, **Compendio Estadístico Centroamericano,** various volumes; **Latin American Studies,** Vol. 5, No. 2, 1973; Jacobo Schatan, CEPAL, **La Agroindustria y el Sistema Alimentario Centroamericano,** 1983; **Statistical Abstract of Latin America,** Vol. 22, 1982; CEPAL, **La Probreza y la Satifacción de Necessidades Basicas en el Istmo Centroamericano,** 1981.

Chapter One
The Justice of Eating

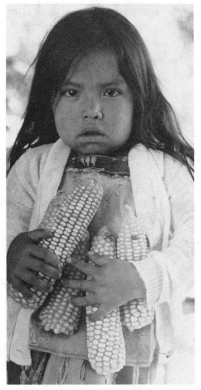

For now I ask no more than the justice of eating.
　　　—Pablo Neruda, from his poem, *The Great Tablecloth*

　　Central America is a jigsaw puzzle of countries that link North and South America. Each country has its distinct political and physical features, but all share a common colonial heritage and are affected by similar topography and climate. Recently, peasant rebellion, stagnant economies, and deepening U.S. intervention have forced Central American countries into one boiling cauldron of crisis and revolution.

　　Geologically, Central America is also a turbulent place. Earthquakes periodically rock the region; and smoking, ash-covered volanoes watch over the isthmus like fiery gods. The tropical lowlands that skirt the Pacific Ocean form the agricultural heartland of today's Central America. This broad band of fertile plains is alternately soaked by tropical rains and

1

blanched by a long dry season of blistering heat. After World War II, a network of highways, including the famous Pan American Highway, cut their way through the coastal plain, facilitating the large-scale production of cotton, sugarcane, and beef. Campesinos and small farmers* were pushed off their plots, and broad stretches of forests and swamps were cleared to make way for the expansive estates that now dominate the Pacific lowlands.

Further inland, geological turbulence has forced the earth up and the temperature down. These are the highlands, a rugged territory of mountain ranges and volcanic uplands interspersed with cool, green valleys. Rain clouds often hide the lofty peaks in Guatemala, the northernmost of the Central American countries. Here, Indian villagers living in misty villages often wear heavy wool ponchos and gloves during the winter months or rainy season.

The highlands follow the isthmus south. Intersecting mountains covered with slender pines spread over western Honduras. In El Salvador and Nicaragua, the mountains and plateaus provide relief from the steamy heat of the coastal plains. They are not high enough, however, to provide for the diversification of agriculture found elsewhere in Central America. In Costa Rica, the highlands form a broad plateau around the capital city of San José and then rise sharply again as they continue into Panama.

The cooler climate, fertile valleys, and absence of mosquitoes made the highlands the preferred place of habitation for the Spanish conquerors and settlers. To make way for their haciendas in Guatemala, the center of colonial rule over Central America, the Spanish brutally displaced Indian communities out of the valleys and deeper into the highlands, while forcing others into involuntary servitude as farmworkers and servants. The volcanic soils of the highlands nurtured the coffee plantations that still dominate rural economy and society in much of Central America.

On the eastern side of the isthmus, year-long rains drench the lowlands of the Atlantic coast. This is a sparsely populated region of rain forests, banana enclaves, and soggy port towns. If climate and topography determined national boundaries, this ribbon of tropical lowlands would be its own country. The Spanish and their descendants largely ignored the Atlantic coast, leaving the region to be exploited by British and later U.S.

---

* The term "campesino" is used interchangeably with "peasant" to designate male and female rural residents who are tied to agriculture as sub-subsistence farmers or hired farmworkers. The term "small farmers" is used to mean those farmers who own sufficient land to support their families and who rely mostly on the labor of their family members.

banana companies and other investors. English-speaking blacks (brought in from the Caribbean islands to work on the banana plantations and railroads) live on the east coast together with a small native population that makes its home on the banks of muddy waterways. Thirty years ago, the Atlantic coast was a largely uncharted barrier of dense vegetation. The region and its people often had better communication facilities with the United States than with their own national capitals. Today, the rainforests of this agricultural frontier are rapidly disappearing in the wake of new cattle ranches, timber operations, and peasant resettlement projects.

Land and Hunger Crisis

Central America is torn by political crisis. Signs of this crisis continually make the daily news: death squads, guerrilla wars, revolutions, and counter-revolutions. This political violence and the region's economic turmoil have roots sown deep in the land itself. A long-festering crisis over the use and control of land—the base of the region's economy and political power—is the principle cause of the current upheaval.

   Evidence of the land crisis—and the accompanying hunger crisis—are everywhere in Central America. Its main characteristics include the following:

* Use of the best land for agroexport production and the use of the least fertile, most easily destroyed land for basic foods production.

* An increasing number of farms too small to support a single family.

* Rapid growth of the rural landless population and increasing migration to the cities.

* Worsening malnutrition.

* Resistance by elites to reforms that would ensure better land and income distribution.

* Control of food-producing resources by a small group of landowners and corporations.

* Low food prices that keep small farmers poor and discourage increased production of basic foods.

* Escalating food imports but reduced ability to pay for them.

* Widespread and deepening rural poverty keeping internal consumer markets small, and thereby obstructing economic growth.

* Bankruptcy of agroexport economies due to declining demand, increased competition, and low export prices.

Agriculture is the main source of income, jobs, and government revenue in Central America. Heavy rains, fertile soils, and plenty of sunshine make Central America an ideal place for farming. Yet, most of the people who live here are hungry and malnourished. They wake up each morning to the problem of simple survival. Getting through the day with enough to eat is a challenge that millions never meet. Campesino families try desperately to scratch a living from postage stamp-size parcels of land on the eroded mountain slopes. During the harvest season, campesinos also labor for a couple of dollars a day on plantations, cutting cane and picking cotton and coffee.

Listless children with distended bellies, a common sight in both campesino villages and farmworker camps, are striking evidence of the hunger gnawing away at the region. These families wake up to a breakfast of reheated corn tortillas and black coffee. Going out to work in the fields, campesinos carry small stacks of tortillas seasoned with a little salt and lime for their lunch. At dinner, tortillas are often accompanied by beans and rice. Meat and vegetables are a rare treat. So poor are many Central Americans that they are increasingly substituting sorghum, a cheap cattle feed, for corn in their tortillas.

Those unable to coax a living from the land head for the closest large city, hoping to find work and opportunity. On the outskirts of a typical Central American metropolis, city lights and paved streets give way to a maze of hovels erected by a constant stream of migrants from the countryside. In 1950, only 25 percent of the region's population was urban. Today, over 40 percent reside in the cities.[1]

Most of the new city residents simply trade their rural poverty for urban poverty. The promise of industrialization has fallen flat.[2] What industries there are, have been discharging workers from the assembly line because of the deepening economic recession. Instead of steady work, the residents of muddy squatter settlements leave their cardboard and corrugated tin shacks each morning to join the growing legions of street vendors who sell everything from combs to *tamales*. Others become beggars. "With your help, I will eat today," reads the sign carried by one young girl in Guatemala City. Garbage dumps are combed for scraps of food. Ragged, barefoot children dart into restaurants to lick clean the plates of departing patrons.

Hunger inflicts an everyday kind of violence—a violence that affects both body and spirit. Its victims include malnourished children who have no strength to continue living and campesinos who are forced to choose between buying corn seed and buying medicine for their sick children. As one Salvadoran peasant observed, "You will never understand violence or non-violence until you understand the violence that happens when your children die of malnutrition."[3]

Origins of the Crisis

Hunger has not always been a fact of life in Central America. While life was no paradise for the first residents of the isthmus, hunger and malnutrition were not the problems that they are today. The director of the Central American Nutrition Institute once acknowledged that "pre-Columbian Mayans ate better than the people today."[4] Corn, papaya, and beans are among the foods that originated in the ancient Mayan culture. A major difference between the native residents and the Spanish colonizers was their contrasting attitudes over land ownership and land use. In his book about land tenure in El Salvador, David Browning wrote: "To the Indian, private and individual ownership of land was as meaningless as private ownership of the sky, the weather, or the sea."[5]

The Spanish gradually imposed an entirely different system of land use and land ownership. Spaniards and later the national elite (called *creoles*) exploited Indian labor to produce tropical crops for export to Europe. During colonization, tracts of the best land were seized for the production of indigo (a natural dye) and cacao (a tree producing seeds from which cocoa is made). The 19th century boom in coffee trade encouraged further land seizures. Indian and *mestizo* (mixed blood) small farmers saw their own land base shrink as *latifundios* or haciendas (large estates) spread across the region. At each step in this process, the confiscation of lands and the system of forced labor met popular resistance. This opposition did slow the land-grabbing of the elite classes but also gave them an excuse to continue their genocidal aggression against the native population. By the turn of the last century, most remaining communal lands were confiscated, and a system of private property dominated the isthmus. Land—a resource for the many before the Spanish arrived—was now the property of the few.

The colonial relationship, whereby the New World colony called the Captaincy of Guatemala was exploited for the benefit of the Spanish crown, set the mold for the region's modern political and economic relations with foreign nations. This center/periphery relationship persists today with the United States at the hub. As in the colonial past, the region's land and labor are exploited to produce commodities for foreign markets, and the national economies continue their precarious dependence on imported goods and food. Thus, the world's economic centers prosper, while peripheral areas remain underdeveloped. Social and economic relations within the region have also been characterized by this pattern of uneven development. National elites or oligarchs have grown wealthier and acquired ever more land while the peasantry has grown more destitute and land-poor.

A dual structure of agriculture emerged during the colonial period. Land ownership became sharply divided between very large holdings called *latifundios* and family-size plots called *minifundios*. Generally, the best lands fell into the hands of *latifundistas*. As the *latifundios* expanded, peasants were pushed onto marginal lands further and further into the highlands or other parts of what is known as the agricultural frontier.

Land use patterns reflected this system of land tenure. Because they owned such grand estates, most large landholders used land extensively rather than intensively. Portions of the estates were often devoted to indigo or cacao while other parts were devoted to cattle grazing. To tend to the agroexports and to provide for their own food needs, hacienca owners kept a crew of Indian sharecroppers (called *colonos*) on the estate in feudal fashion. Usually, large tracts of land on the *latifundios* were left idle. In contrast, *minifundios*, owned by poor campesino families, were farmed intensively. Every available scrap of land produced basic foods like corn and beans.[6] Owners of these small plots were often required to contribute part of their produce or a portion of their labor to nearby *latifundistas*.

The Modern Agroexport System

During the last several hundred years, this dual structure of *latifundios* and *minifundios* has continued to dominate the economies and societies of Central America. But there have been important changes, too. In the process of modernizing agricultural production, the *latifundios* have lost many of their feudal characteristics and become capitalist estates. Large landholders have forced the *colonos* off their plantations, finding that it is cheaper to pay seasonal workers for planting and harvesting than to maintain a year-round labor force. And instead of living on their estates, most large planters have moved into the cities, relying on foremen to manage their agribusiness operations.

As in colonial times, large plantations remain the base for most agroexport production. Before World War II, local oligarchs grew coffee in the rich volcanic uplands, and U.S. banana companies lorded over immense enclaves on the Atlantic coast. As industrialized countries stepped up their consumption after the war, Central America was persuaded to undertake a new agroexport boom. Along with the coffee and bananas, countries began to export cotton, sugar, and beef. New agroexport production was a boon to growers and governments hungry for foreign exchange and investment capital.

The suffering of campesinos, however, increased as more of their land was taken away for pastures and plantations. Each time the world market for a new agricultural commodity opens up, more Central American land is forcibly withdrawn from basic food production. At present, almost all of the most fertile land in the region is devoted to agroexport production.[7] A UN report on Central America described how export crop production "gradually pushed many campesinos onto marginal or frontier lands or transformed them into wage workers in the modern agroexport sector."[8]

In the last 30 years, the expansion of cotton, sugarcane, and beef production has resulted in the displacement of thousands of peasants and small farmers. From 1950 to 1979, acreage in cotton and sugar increased nearly ten-fold in Central America while coffee lands doubled. (Table 1) It is not surprising then, that there is so much hunger and malnutrition in Central America when one realizes that an increasing portion of the

Table 1
Distribution of Cropland by Commodity

	Arable Land*	Coffee	Sugar	Cotton	Per Capita Basic Food Cropland (hectares)
		(1,000 hectares)			
Costa Rica					
1950	353	51	23	0	.325
1979	490	83	48	12	.160
El Salvador					
1950	546	103	0	19	.220
1979	710	180	37	102	.080
Guatemala					
1950	1438	111	0	2	.450
1979	1810	248	74	122	.190
Honduras					
1950	810	63	14	0	.520
1979	1757	130	75	13	.420
Nicaragua					
1950	769	56	0	17	.630
1979	1511	85	41	174	.440

1 hectare = 2.47 acres

*Arable land includes cultivated and fallow farmland. The large increase in arable land came as a result of the clearing of more land for both agroexport and basic-food production.

Source: FAO, **Food Security in Latin America and the Caribbean**, June 1984.

region's farmland is being used to produce crops that those who produce it do not eat. As economist John Weeks observed: "In few areas of the world is such a large proportion of agricultural land devoted to products which the local population does not consume or consumes to a limited degree."[9]

At the same time that agroexport plantations cover ever more farmland, *minifundios* have been shrinking. With no new land available, the plots get smaller and smaller with each generation. Eight of ten farmers in the region do not own enough land to sustain their families, forcing them to look for seasonal jobs on the agroexport plantations. These landless or near-landless peasants are completely dependent on temporary jobs picking coffee, cutting cane, and harvesting cotton four or five months each year. But there are not enough jobs for all the unemployed campesinos. Increasing mechanization and the use of chemical weedkillers have eliminated many jobs. When prices are down and producers decide not to plant, there is no work for anyone—and therefore no money to buy food.

"We don't even have a fistful of earth to earn our daily bread," complained a Honduran campesino who had decided to join a peasant invasion of idle land.[10] The same complaint echoes throughout Central America. Land concentration and landlessness in Central America are among the worst in the world. Less than 1 percent of all farm owners control nearly 40 percent of farmland. Conversely, less than 1 percent of the total farmland is distributed among 25 percent of the region's farmers. (Tables 2 and 3) Many peasants do not even own the small plots they farm but rent the land at exhorbitant rates. During the last several decades, land tenure inequities have worsened: land ownership has become more concentrated, the number of *minifundios* unable to support a family has increased, and landlessness has tripled.[11]

Table 2
Land Concentration In Central America
(by average farm size)

	Micro-Farm 1 acre	Sub-Family Farm 5 acres	Medium-sized/ Family Farm 15 acres	Large Farm 75 acres	Very Large Farm 800 acres
% of Farms	23	55	14	6	under 1
% of Acreage	under 1	10	16	35	38

* Micro-Farm and Sub-Family Farm plots are too small to support one family.
Source: SIECA, **VIII Compendio Estadistico para Centroamericana**, 1978.

Table 3
Land Distribution Characteristics in Central America
(comparing largest and smallest farms)

Country	% of Farms (largest) (smallest)	Average Size (acres)	% Of Farm-land	% Rural Land-less	Other Description
Costa Rica	1 46	3100 4	36 2	40	65% of farms regarded as too small for one family. Landlessness tripled in last 30 years.
El Salvador	1 71	635 0.8	41 10	60	95% of farms too small to support one family. On small farms under 2 acres over 95% of land used for basic grains and less than 1% left fallow. On farms over 220 acres, 50% left fallow and less than 20% for basic grains.
Guatemala	1 78	2300 2.5	34 10	27	Four **latifundios** cover more farm-land than over 200,000 **minifundios**. Only 15% of country's food is grown on the rich coastal plain, but 25% of this fertile land is left idle by large landowners.
Honduras	4 64	over 100 0 to 5	56 9	35	The smallest 50% of farms occupy only 12% of most fertile land. Two-thirds of fertile land owned by large landowners is used to graze cattle.
Nicaragua	2 45	2100 4	48 2	32	Somoza family controlled 23% of farmland. Between 1950 and 1978, 2% of landowners increased their holdings from 40% to almost 50% of all cultivated land.
Panama	1 45	n/a 4	33	n/a	Only 10 percent of Panama's farmers have legal title; two-thirds are squatters. Over 85 percent of land surface owned by state. Just 224 private landowners account for 20% of farmland. Only 4% of farms are classified as commercial, while 35% report no cash income.

Sources: Costa Rica: 1973 figures from CEPAL, **La Agroindustria y El Sistema Alimentario Centroamericano**, 1983; El Salvador: figures from Dirección General de Estadísticas y Censos, **Tercer Censo Nactional Agropecuario**, 1971; Guatemala: 1979 figures from AID, **Land and Labor in Guatemala: An Assessment**, 1982; Honduras: figures from AID, 1974 Census contained in Honduras Working Document No. 1 May 1979; Nicaragua: 1978 figures from **La Agroindustria y El Sistema Alimentario Centroamericano**; Panama: **Tercer Censo Nacional Agropecuario**, 1971.

While peasants and small farmers cultivate every available patch of earth, large landholders have so much land that they leave vast stretches of farmland idle. Only 70 percent of Central America's arable land is being farmed or grazed, leaving 3,700,000 acres idle. Great expanses of fertile farmland are underutilized as pastureland. In Central America, where at least half the population suffers from malnutrition, there is twice as much land for cattle as there is for agriculture.[12] (Table 4) Land is a scarce resource only for the rural poor, not for the landed elite.

At first glance, the small group of wealthy landowners and the masses of landless workers and small farmers appear to be the extremes of a poorly organized society. In fact, they are complementary parts of the same unjust system. "It is a system made in the *cielo* (the heavens)," exclaimed a government agronomist in Guatemala. "The *indios* can grow corn in the mountains and then pick coffee and cotton during the other part of the year. It is a system ordained by God himself."[13]

Table 4

Land Use in Central America and Latin America
(percent of land area)

	Central America	Latin America
All arable land	11.9	8.6
Irrigated	(0.6)	(0.6)
Other cultivated	(8.0)	(5.0)
Idle arable land	(3.3)	(3.0)
Pastures	18.9	26.4
Forests	53.3	49.1
Commercially exploitable forest land	(35-40)	
Other (including urban and no longer suitable agricultural land)	15.9	15.9

Source: Derived from IDB, **Economic and Social Progress in Latin America**, 1983.

Indeed, the system has worked well for the large landholders. They can pay their seasonal farmworkers less than subsistence wages because historically these workers have had small plots of their own to keep their families fed. Keeping slaves would cost them more than temporarily hiring peasants for a dollar or two a day. A campesino family works arduously to produce the corn and beans needed to keep themselves alive, and several months each year they trek off to the plantations. Concentrated land ownership is a major attribute of the agroexport system, but this system is also based on a foundation of cheap labor and cheap food.[14]

Women and children play important roles in maintaining the two-tiered agricultural system. Women help keep the cost of labor and food low through their unpaid work. From an early age, they work tirelessly—helping with farming, tending the dwelling, going to the market, gathering firewood, rearing children, and preparing food. By their thirties, peasant women are often old and worn. Children become valued workers by age six or seven. Besides assisting with household chores, many youngsters accompany their parents to the plantations, doing their part picking coffee and cotton.

The two-tiered system of land tenure has created a society of oligarchs and peasants. While still going strong, it is increasingly showing signs of structural weakness. The narrowing land base for *minifundios* means that there is a rapidly growing sector of landless campesinos who completely depend on seasonal farm labor for their livelihood. Even those families with some land are becoming more dependent on their seasonal work on the agroexport plantations as their plots shrink with each generation. As land becomes more scarce for campesinos, they are being converted into a rural class of proletariats and semi-proletariats.[15]

This swelling workforce means that estate owners rarely have to increase wages to find farmworkers. So hungry are landless and near-landless laborers in Honduras and Guatemala that many are agreeing to work just for food. While this large supply of cheap labor keeps costs down for agroexporters, it also represents a potential political threat. As peasants find themselves without access either to land or to steady work, they are harder to control and more likely to rebel. And as their connections to the land are increasingly severed, campesinos are more likely to join in alliances with urban workers over issues of inflation, unemployment, and labor conditions. The declining production and availability of basic foods is a related problem facing the region's agricultural economy. The dual system of agriculture in Central America, which some consider ideal, is now on the verge of collapse for political as well as economic reasons.

Buying Instead of Growing Food

Because of uneven land tenure and land use patterns, Central America is now an agricultural region that does not feed its own people. Over half the labor force in Central America is employed in agriculture. Yet the region has to import food—food that could be grown locally. Since 1950, when the push for new agroexport production started, total food imports to the region have increased sevenfold.[16] The region has moved rapidly from food self-sufficiency to a precarious state of food dependency.

Per capita production of corn and beans is steadily declining in Central America. (Table 5) From 1950 to 1979, the per capita amount of land devoted to food crops dropped by 30-60 percent in Central America. The continual decline in availability of land, the low productivity of the marginal lands used for basic food production, and the rising population all mean that each year there is less food available for Central Americans.

Table 5
Per Capita Cereal Production, 1975-1981
(kilograms of cereal per capita per year)

	1975	1981
Costa Rica	156	148
El Salvador	168	144
Guatemala	179	161
Honduras	144	112
Nicaragua	159	155
Panama	150	153
Central America average	159	146
Latin America/Caribbean average	181	291

Source: FAO, **Food Security in Latin America and the Caribbean**, June 1984.

In the 1980s, imports of basic foods are expanding at an alarming rate as per capita production continues to fall. About 25 percent of all cereals consumed in Central America are produced from outside the region.[17] Even Guatemala, known for its tradition of corn production, now imports corn. A recent U.S. government study predicted that Central America's deficit for staple foods will double by 1990.[18]

The region's main food imports are corn, beans, vegetable oil, and wheat. While Central America could once again become self-sufficient in corn, beans, and vegetable oil, it will never produce all the wheat that it now consumes. Before World War II, few people ate bread in Central America. Demand for wheat flour has risen as a result of U.S. food assistance programs and advertising by the new flour mills (often U.S.-owned) located in the capital cities. The expanding market for wheat flour in Central America has been beneficial to the U.S. grain companies but has caused a severe drain on regional income. Contrary to advertising promoting consumption of wheat flour, bread represents no nutritional advantage over corn tortillas.

Increased food imports have not taken the edge off of hunger in Central America. Per capita consumption of beans and corn is declining, and there is little reason to believe that Central Americans are substituting other foods for these basic commodities. As less food is produced per capita, less food is consumed. Poor and unemployed Central Americans do not have the purchasing power to buy the imported food. The sad result is more hunger and malnutrition.

Distribution of Income

There is nothing inherently wrong with importing food. Some developed countries like Japan are net food importers yet in good economic shape with a well-nourished population. Increased food imports can be a sign of increased income and well-being. This is not the case, however, in Central America. Food imports are increasing at a time when income and consumption levels are decreasing.

There are two interrelated problems with underdeveloped countries becoming overdependent on food imports. First, these countries usually do not have enough foreign exchange (mainly dollars) to buy all the food they need. Second, only a small minority have the necessary income to buy this food. Imported food does not meet the needs of those without the money to purchase loaves of bread or cans of vegetable oil. Consequently most imported food fills the shopping baskets of the middle and upper classes.

Like land, income is also maldistributed. In Central America, the poorest 20 percent of the population receives only 2-5 percent of the income.[19] (Table 6) Between 1950 and 1980, the economies of Central America, sparked by increased cash-crop production and industrialization, grew at an annual rate of 5 percent. But the expanding economic pie in Central America was not shared equally. Barely a sliver of the new national wealth went to the lower classes. Instead, the poor of Central America became poorer and hungrier during the years of regional economic growth.

Table 6

Structure of Income Distribution and Per Capita Income Levels, by Country, Approximately 1980

(US dollars at 1970 prices)

	Costa Rica		El Salvador		Guatemala		Honduras		Nicaragua		Panama	
	%	Average income	%	Average income	%	Average income	%	Average income	%	Average income	%	Average income
Poorest 20 percent	4.0	176.7	2.0	46.5	5.3	111.0	4.3	80.7	3.0	61.9	2.7	120.0
30 % below the mean	17.0	500.8	10.0	155.1	14.5	202.7	12.7	140.0	13.0	178.2	10.0	304.0
30 % above the mean	30.0	883.8	22.0	341.2	26.1	364.3	23.7	254.6	26.0	350.2	27.0	822.6
Richest 20 percent	49.0	1165.2	66.0	1535.5	54.1	1133.6	59.3	796.3	58.0	1199.8	60.3	2710.1

Source: **CEPAL Review**, April 1984, based on official data from the countries; **CEPAL, Satisfacción de las Necesidades Básicas,** November 23, 1983.

Although average individual income in Central America is about $1,000 a year, most families live and die on much less. The per capita income of the bottom half of the population of most Central American nations is less than what North Americans spend on caring for their pets ($150-$220) each year.

Inequitable income distribution is directly related to lopsided land tenure.[20] In these agricultural nations, income flows to the large landholders while peasants and small farmers are left on the margins of the agricultural economy. Even more than other sectors of the economy, agroexport production has been notoriously resistant to any trickling down of benefits. Laboring 10 to 12 hours a day, temporary farmworkers receive a daily wage of only $1 to $3. This slim wage is less than half the amount needed to provide the basic needs of the average family.

In Guatemala, El Salvador and Honduras, 80 percent of rural families do not have enough income for basic necessities. More than 50 percent live in extreme poverty, which means that their income will not even cover the cost of meeting basic food requirements, let alone other needs such as clothing and shelter.[21] The gap between income and the price of food has dramatically worsened since 1980. Due to inflation, the real wages of rural workers have fallen 25 percent or more since 1980, putting the basic food basket out of reach for most families.[22]

Dimensions of Hunger

Hunger and malnutrition* in Central America are worse than in any other part of Latin America. Even during the 1960s and 1970s, when the regional economies were surging ahead, malnutrition among children was increasing in every country except Costa Rica.[23] Since 1980, the regional economies have sputtered to a standstill and have started rolling backwards, thereby reducing the chances for hungry Central Americans to better their lives.

After calculating the amount of food available both from local production and imports, the UN's Food and Agriculture Organization (FAO) has determined that most Central American nations come close to

---

*Malnutrition refers to the physical effect on the human body of a diet inadequate both in quantity and quality. A financially well-off person can be malnourished because of the bad quality of that person's diet, but malnutrition in Central America is commonly due to undernourishment or low food intake. Inadequate diets in Central America cause deficiencies not only in calories and proteins, but also in vitamin A, riboflavin, iodine, and iron.

supplying the minimal nutritional needs of their populations. But national averages are deceptive. While they show that the society as a whole receives enough or near enough calories and protein, these averages do not reflect the unjust distribution of food supplies.(Table 7) High-income households in Central America consume almost 3 times as many calories as low income families.[24] According to the statistical averages, available food in Honduras meets 96 percent of the country's needs. This assessment of the country's nutritional status does not indicate the severity of malnutrition in Honduras, where over 70 percent of the rural population cannot afford a minimum daily diet and where famine has recently hit parts of the countryside. Even in Costa Rica, where nutritional statistics look comparatively good, an estimated 34 percent of the population is malnourished.[25]

Adequate nutrition is out of reach for poor Central Americans. The Central American Nutrition Institute recommends that a family share a bottle of milk every day. While good advice, most families cannot afford that basic necessity. To pay for that one bottle, a farmworker in Guatemala would have to spend about 25 percent of his or her daily wage.[26] Filling your family's stomach with corn might not result in a balanced diet but most workers and peasants have little choice.

Table 7

Malnutrition in Central America

	Per capita calorie supply as percent of energy requirements	Rural Population in absolute poverty* (percent)	Average calorie deficit of poorest half of population (% of minimum need)
Costa Rica	118	40	8
El Salvador	94	70	35
Guatemala	93	60	39
Honduras	96	77	32
Nicaragua	99	57	16
Panama	103	55	—

* Absolute poverty is the inability to afford food providing minimum nutritional requirements.

Sources: IBRD, **World Development Report 1984**; CEPAL; INCAP; AID, **Country Development Strategy Statements,** FY1980-FY1986.

A recent study by the Central American University in El Salvador revealed that less than 10 percent of Salvadorans can afford the recommended minimum diet. Yet middle and high income groups were found to consume twice the calories and protein of their low-income neighbors.[27] In parts of southern Honduras where cattle compete with peasants for land, many campesinos only consume about 1000 calories a day, which is barely enough to maintain bodily functions. The fact that 1,200,000 Honduran peasants struggle to survive on the equivalent of what 200,000 better-off compatriots consume daily is just one more illustration of the hunger and injustice in Central America.[28]

Hunger and malnourishment are directly linked to skewed land distribution. Children in Costa Rica are likely to be malnourished if their families own less than four acres of land, and the children of parents with no land in Guatemala are twice as likely to suffer malnourishment as the children of those farmers who own as little as four acres.[29] Marijka Velzeboer, a consultant for the Pan American Health Organization, says, "Talking about nutrition often takes the focus off the real problem in Central America—that's the inequitable distribution of land."[30]

Hunger is a Killer

Hunger is a killer in Central America. Tiny wooden coffins piled high in *funerarias* of rural towns are a sad reminder of the high infant and child mortality rate in Central America. It is not uncommon in the rural areas for one of every two children to die before they reach the age of five.[31]

Gastrointestinal and respiratory diseases are the main child killers. It is well-documented that influenza, pneumonia, bronchitis, diarrheal diseases, and respiratory illnesses are linked to poor nutrition. While lack of medical care and sanitation are factors, hunger provides the main breeding ground for the diseases that kill most Central American children. The Pan American Health Organization identified malnutrition as the primary or associated cause of death in 60 percent of the deaths of children between the ages of one and four in poor regions of Latin America.[32]

Families have a difficult time raising healthy children in rural Central America. The health records of three-year-old children in villages throughout the region show that children are afflicted by an average of one illness every three weeks.[33] In Guatemala, even a moderately malnourished child is 3 times more likely to contract diarrheal infection than a well-fed child, and ordinary pediatric illnesses such as measles are deadly.[34] Where undernourishment precipitates disease, it also retards mental development.

In addition, malnutrition takes its toll on adults. Central Americans can expect to live about 61 years—approximately 11 years less than

residents of developed countries. Life expectancy in areas where hunger is a
constant companion, like the Guatemalan Highlands, is only about 45
years.[35]

James P. Grant, executive director of UNICEF, points to the cause
and effect relationship between land and malnutrition.

> For those who simply do not have enough to eat, the long-term
> solution lies in having either the land with which to grow food
> or the jobs and the incomes with which to buy it. Concern for
> children's health is therefore inseparable from a concern over the
> lengthening shadow of landlessness cast by the increasing
> concentration of its ownership.[36]

According to Grant, the main cause of malnutrition is neither the
absence of technological farming methods nor population growth. In
Grant's words:

> The problem is rather one of what crops are grown by whom on
> whose land and for whose benefit. And the solution lies in
> political and economic change to allow the poor to both
> participate in, and benefit from, the increase in production
> which can most certainly be achieved.[37]

Political and Economic Change

To ask for "no more than the justice of eating" in Central America is to ask
for a great deal. To ask for an end to hunger means demanding that land be
redistributed. And to tackle questions of land tenure and use means nothing
short of confronting the structures of political and economic power—both
on a national and international level. In Central America, the patterns of
land ownership have shaped both the political economy and social
relations. To change the unjust relationship that people have with land also
entails altering the relationship that the poor have with economic elites, the
government, and the military.

The land and hunger crisis has for centuries been set squarely in an
international context. Foreign demand for cheap tropical products has
dominated the economy of Central America for over 400 years. The early
colonial rule of the Spanish has now been replaced by less direct but equally
powerful forms of control. As we shall see in later chapters, foreign
corporations, mainly from the United States, assume a commanding role in
the agroexport economy through their trade and investment practices.

The U.S. government itself has a long history of intervention in the
region. It is a shameful history of protecting elites, furthering its own
economic interests, and backing repressive governments. The United

States fought its first counterinsurgency war in Nicaragua, where it helped crush a peasant rebellion led by Sandino in the 1920s. When a democratically elected government in Guatemala tried to distribute idle land owned by local oligarchs and the United Fruit company, the CIA directed a military coup. Foreign aid programs that further the agroexport system and channel resources to the elite in the name of promoting economic progress also bear responsibility for perpetuating the land and hunger crisis. Today, as this long-term crisis explodes in political violence, Washington is intensifying its economic and military intervention.

Solutions to the land and hunger crisis will not come easily, or peacefully. In Central America, asking for the "justice of eating" is not a simple plea but a call for rebellion and revolution.

Chapter Two
The New Plantation

The conquest of territory by the coffee industry is alarming. It has occupied the Highlands and is now descending to the valleys, displacing maize, rice, and beans. It has extended like the conquistador, spreading hunger and misery. Although it is possible to prove mathematically that these changes make the country richer, in fact, they mean death.

—Alberto Masferrer in *La Patria*
newspaper in El Salvador, 1929

The Spanish arrived in Central America with the ambition to become wealthy exporters. In the early years of the conquest, they looted the region of its gold and silver, forcing Indians to work in silver mines as slaves. Indigo and cacao, grown on *latifundios* with forced Indian labor, were the region's first agricultural exports. Central America never boomed as a source of raw materials for the Spanish mercantile system. Yet the Spanish conquest did forcibly place the region in a dependent role in the emerging world capitalist system.

Over time, this role as a source of largely unprocessed commodities has solidified. Local elites together with foreign traders and investors have shaped a regional economy dominated by agroexport production. Economic development in Central America has been largely export-oriented while internal development needs are routinely ignored. Most credit and infrastructure improvements benefit the large producers of export crops rather than those farmers producing for themselves and the local market.

The "conquest" of Central America by five main agroexports—coffee, bananas, cotton, sugar, and beef—has continued apace since Alberto Masferrer deplored the expansion of the coffee industry in El Salvador. Still in progress, this conquest is directed by a partnership of economic and political forces, including local oligarchs and governments, foreign investors and traders, and major foreign powers and financial institutions.

The modern plantation started its evolution soon after the region obtained its independence from Spain in the early 1800s. Coffee production for foreign markets came to dominate the economies of most Central American countries by the end of the century. Then U.S. banana barons like Minor Keith and companies like United Fruit began grabbing vast strips of land along the Atlantic coast, and the coffee republics were on their way to becoming banana republics.

Another surge in agroexport production seized the region in the 1950s and the 1960s as a new grouping of oligarchs maped out vast sections of the flat and fertile Pacific plains for cotton and sugarcane cultivation. To satisfy U.S. hamburger cravings, ranchers bulldozed forests and evicted peasants to make way for herds of cattle. This spate of agroexport activity was fueled by grants and low-interest loans from the U.S. Agency for International Development (AID) and multilateral financial institutions like the World Bank and the Inter-American Development Bank (IDB). Such foreign assistance enhanced agribusiness expansion in large sections of Central America by transforming dirt roads used by oxcarts into all-weather roads, building the Pan American Highway, paying for technical expertise, and constructing the ports from which these new agroexports were shipped to foreign consumers.

Today, just five commodities make up 85 percent of the region's agricultural export trade.[1] (Tables 8 and 9) And during the last 25 years, Central America's dependence on export earnings has been on the increase. Export revenue (from all sources) as a share of the gross domestic product

(GDP) in El Salvador jumped from 20 percent in 1960 to over 50 percent in 1980. And reliance on export production is higher in Central America than most other agricultural regions in the third world. Whereas export revenue as a share of GDP averages about 11 percent for Latin America as a whole, the corresponding figure for Central America is about 30 percent.[2]

The agroexport system is at the same time a highly unstable and unjust system. Booms and busts on the world market periodically shake the region's fragile economy. Widely fluctuating commodity prices keep these small nations constantly adjusting, like so many puppets on a string. Profiting from these fluctuations and pulling the strings of the world market are the world's largest commodity traders and transnational corporations (TNCs)—the main beneficiaries of the new plantation, as we will see in Chapter 4.

Just as the profits from agroexport production are unevenly divided on the world market between the commodity producers and the corporations that buy, process, and market those commodities, so too is the wealth unevenly shared within the producing nations. The agroexport system is built on a cracking social foundation. While it relies on millions of rural laborers to pick its agroexports, the system does not pay campesinos enough to eat or live decently. Nor does it allow them enough land or resources to feed their families with their own crops. Cheap labor and easy access to land are the main building blocks of the new plantation because they help agroexporters produce inexpensive agricultural commodities for the world market.

Table 8
Top Agricultural Exports

Belize *	sugar, citrus, wood
Costa Rica	coffee, bananas, meat, sugar, rice
El Salvador	coffee, cotton, shrimp
Guatemala	coffee, cotton, sugar, bananas,
Honduras	bananas, coffee, meat, sugar, shrimp
Nicaragua	coffee, cotton, sugar, bananas, meat
Panama	bananas, sugar, shrimp, coffee

* Marijuana, which is not included in official trade statistics is probably Belize's major agroexport.

Source: UNCTAD, **Handbook of International Trade and Development Statistics, 1984 Supplement.**

Table 9
Share Of World Trade In Top Agroexports, 1981

Column 1: Rank among third-world nations in export of this commodity.
Column 2: Percent of the nation's exports represented by trade in this commodity.
Column 3: Percent of export value which the country's trade represents among third-world nations.
Column 4: Percent of export value which the country's trade represents among all nations.

COMMODITY	EXPORTER	1	2	3	4
Meat	Costa Rica	6	7	3.3	0.5
	Honduras	10	7	2.1	0.3
	Guatemala	11	3	1.4	0.2
	Nicaragua	13	4	1.0	0.1
	Central America			8.8	1.0
Fish	Panama	21	15	1.0	0.4
	Honduras	25	4	0.6	0.2
	El Salvador	28	3	0.5	0.2
	Central America			2.1	0.8
Fresh Fruit	Costa Rica	3	23	6.0	2.5
	Honduras	4	30	5.6	2.3
	Panama	16	22	1.8	0.8
	Guatemala	17	6	1.7	0.7
	Nicaragua	32	5	0.6	0.2
	Central America			15.7	6.5
Sugar & Honey	Guatemala	12	9	1.3	0.7
	Belize	18	48	0.7	0.4
	Panama	19	17	0.7	0.4
	Nicaragua	20	11	0.7	0.4
	Honduras	24	6	0.6	0.3
	Costa Rica	25	4	0.5	0.3
	Central America			4.5	2.5
Coffee	El Salvador	4	57	5.6	5.0
	Guatemala	8	24	3.3	2.9
	Costa Rica	9	24	2.9	2.6
	Honduras	12	24	2.1	1.9
	Nicaragua	17	30	1.7	1.5
	Central America			15.6	13.9
Cotton	Nicaragua	6	26	4.1	1.7
	Guatemala	9	10	3.7	1.5
	El Salvador	17	7	1.8	0.8
	Central America			9.6	4.0

Source: Derived from data in UNCTAD, **Handbook of International Trade and Development Statistics**, 1984.

The allocation of the best land to agroexport production means that the Central American nations do not produce enough basic foods to feed their own populations, forcing them to use increasing amounts of foreign exchange to import food. The landed oligarchs staunchly defend the agroexport system precisely because it concentrates rather than distributes wealth. They rely on state security forces to maintain the uneven social order and crush periodic campesino rebellions.

The new plantation is more than just a productive entity. It is a political and economic system that is, like the old plantation of the Spanish colonists, subordinate to the economic demands and politics of global capitalism. This chapter focuses on the development of the major export crops within Central America and the unstable nature of the agroexport economy. The following two chapters look more closely at the national elite and the foreign corporations that control and profit from the new plantation.

King Coffee

Coffee is indeed king in Central America. The coffee business is the region's top exporter, employer and leading source of foreign exchange. The owners of the plantations and *beneficios* (mills where the beans are extracted from coffee cherries), continue to form the traditional oligarchy. The United States, which imports about 30 percent of Central America's coffee, is the region's top coffee purchaser, followed by West Germany.

Spurred on by an ever-increasing demand in Europe, coffee planting took hold in Costa Rica in the 1820s and by the end of the century, had spread throughout the region. In order to free up land for the new crop, 19th-century legislators in Central America enacted various laws that paved the way for coffee farmers to seize Indian lands in the fertile volcanic highlands. A law passed in El Salvador was typical. It decreed that the existence of traditional Indian communal lands, "impedes agricultural development, obstructs the circulation of wealth, and weakens the family bonds and the independence of the individual."[3] The new law required individual Indian landholders to apply for land titles and authorized the government to tax property. But the Indians were not told how to apply for land titles, and did not have the cash to pay the taxes.

With the Indians out of the way, coffee production in Guatemala increased 20 fold between 1870 and 1880, a pace duplicated in Costa Rica and El Salvador. Victims of this manic growth, a group of Guatemalan Indians told Guatemala's president: "You have ordered us to leave our lands so that coffee can be grown. You ask us to leave the land where our grandfathers and fathers were born....We want [our lands] for our corn, our animals, our wood."[4]

Rebellion and Repression in El Salvador

The "conquest" by coffee over the region's economy and society was most complete in El Salvador. By the late 1920s, coffee accounted for 95 percent of El Salvador's exports.[5] Then the Great Depression sent coffee prices plummeting, and Salvadoran plantation owners responded by firing thousands of workers and cutting in half the wages of those who remained. In 1932, tens of thousands of campesinos spurred by Communist party organizers, protested the firings and wage cuts. They seized rural villages, driving out local police, but they were no match for the country's armed forces.

With a U.S. warship waiting offshore, ready to help the government, the armed forces were joined by volunteer units of what author Thomas Anderson described as "upper-class gentlemen" in hunting down and murdering 20,000 or more Salvadorans over a period of several weeks. The victims were campesinos, particularly Indians, who were considered communists if they could not be vouched for by a landowner. In his book, *Matanza, El Salvador's Communist Revolt of 1932*, Anderson described the gruesome scene:

> Men were taken in big batches, tied together by their thumbs, and lined up along the roadsides or against the walls of the military forts and churches. They were machine-gunned and their bodies hauled off to makeshift mass graves.... The extermination was so great that they could not be buried fast enough, and a great stench of rotting flesh permeated the air of western El Salvador.

In their opposition to the worker/peasant rebellion, the merchant and planter classes firmly united; and to maintain their fragile hold on society, they called upon the military to assume an expanded and more centralized position in running the country. The 1932 massacre, or *matanza* as it has come to be known in El Salvador, quieted peasant opposition for close to 50 years. The massacre did not, however, solve the land and hunger problems caused by the coffee economy.

Domain of the Oligarchs

In El Salvador, which remains Central America's largest coffee producer (despite a decline since the civil war began in 1979), a mere 4 percent of the plantations, or *fincas*, owned by 36 families account for 60 percent of the coffee land. These same families also own the country's coffee *beneficios* and, just for good measure, have representatives in the offices of the state coffee agency.

At the other extreme, 15,000 small landowners share only 6 percent of the coffee lands. Commenting on this lopsided distribution of coffee land, William Thiesenhusen of the Land Tenure Center at the University of Wisconsin said: "There is no rationale why coffee in El Salvador needs to be produced primarily on large holdings, though I am certain I would never convince a Salvadoran producer of that."[6]

Salvadoran coffee growers have fought firmly against the U.S.-supported agrarian reform enacted in 1980 to quell growing rebelliousness in the countryside. A statement in 1980 by a coffee grower typifies the arrogant attitudes of this ultraconservative clique: "Coffee growers should not anguish over the situation in El Salvador today. There was a similar situation in 1932. If it was solved then, it can be solved now."[7]

Coffee production is also highly concentrated in Guatemala, where just one percent of the growers produce over 70 percent of the coffee.[8] And the concentration is rapidly increasing. In a recent ten year period, the number of small coffee farms in Costa Rica fell by 20 percent.

So tenuous is the position of small coffee growers throughout Central America that they are more like contract employees than independent producers. While the large coffee growers can afford their own *beneficios*, small farmers have no leverage in selling their harvest to the *beneficio* owners, since the coffee must be washed and dried prior to storage. These small growers are often forced to accept coffee prices that are 50 percent below the export value.

It is common for the exporters to purchase an unharvested crop of coffee from a small grower at below market prices in exchange for an *anticipo* (cash advance) to allow the farmer to get through the year. "We are always losing right off the top," commented a small coffee farmer in Guatemala. "The rich growers finance themselves, and they can afford to buy Cherokee trucks and to fly back and forth to Miami. But we (small coffee growers) can never get ahead."[9]

At the bottom of the pyramid of power in the coffee industry are the seasonal coffee workers. Crews of barefoot coffee pickers work from dawn to late afternoon filling basket after basket with the red coffee cherries, which are then carted in bins to the *beneficio*. In El Salvador and Guatemala, entire families labor in the coffee harvests. As one young Salvadoran mother named Julia explained: "You earn according to what you pick, so you have to bring a large family."[10]

Jorge Candelaria, a Guatemalan Indian who began picking coffee when he was ten, remembers how he and his family were shoved into trucks "like cattle" for the 15-hour trip to the coffee plantations. During the harvests, families commonly sleep outdoors under the coffee trees. Coffee pickers never get enough to eat, and are often sick with respiratory illnesses and parasites. Candelaria revealed:

> For our family of six, the plantation bosses gave us each week two to three pounds of corn, one pound of beans, and a pound of limes. They didn't even give us a little coffee. And when the coffee harvest was over, you went back to your village all pale and weak because you hadn't eaten.[11]

Victor Melendez, a 21-year old Salvadoran peasant from the Santa Ana region, remarked that, although he had been working on the coffee *fincas* since he was seven, he had never seen any of the plantation owners because they live in the cities or in Miami. He complained:

> The coffee growers have the biggest cars and houses, but many families who work on the coffee *fincas* don't even have money to buy warm clothes for their children. Many *niños* (children) die on the plantations. But all the growers want is to get the coffee crop harvested. They only thing they care about is their money while we only get about $2.50 a day.[12]

Declining consumer demand and the downward trend in prices are weakening the coffee economy. In the last 20 years, the percentage of U.S. consumers drinking coffee has dropped from 75 to 55 percent.[13] Another factor is the steady rise in instant coffee, which yields 50 percent more liquid coffee than the equivalent amount of roasted coffee beans.[14] Central American countries depend on coffee exports as their leading source of foreign exchange, yet the ups and downs of the coffee market make government budget planning a difficult proposition.

Banana Enclaves

The banana industry began to flourish around the turn of the century. Not a native plant, bananas came to Central America and the Caribbean on Spanish ships which carried seeds from Africa to the New World.[15] The banana tree adapted to its new home, as one writer put it, "with the arrogant ease of a conquistador."[16]

During most of the 1800s, the banana trade was largely the domain of growers who sold their fruit to ship captains passing through Central America. Bananas entered the world market in the late 1800s when U.S. companies began establishing their enclaves along the Atlantic coast.

Through huge government land grabs, government concessions, and takeovers of smaller companies, the United Fruit Company (UFCO) soon became the leading actor in the banana scene. Thirty years after its founding in 1889, United Fruit (or *La Frutera* as it is called in Central America) handled over 80 percent of the region's banana trade. In the 1920s, another U.S. banana company, Standard Fruit, acquired its own banana plantations in the region.

Los Pulpos

Today, bananas are the region's second largest export and are the top export crop of Honduras and Panama. Costa Rica, Guatemala and Nicaragua also export bananas. The distinctive trait of the banana business is U.S. corporate involvement in actual production. With other agro-exports, foreign companies frequently control the financing, marketing, processing, and distribution of the product while production remains in the hands of local growers. From the beginning, United Fruit and Standard Fruit have owned their own plantations as well as controlling all other steps in the commercialization of bananas.

As a result, the banana growing areas of Central America resemble corporate colonies. They maintain closer ties to U.S. ports than to the capitals of the very countries in which they have operations. From their inception, the banana concessions were developed as autonomous economic units. In exchange for land from the government, United Fruit and Standard Fruit built the region's first railroads—to connect the plantations with ports developed for the banana trade. Capital and consumption goods, needed to run the plantations and feed the employees, were imported from the United States without import taxes. The workers were paid in company scrip and shopped at company stores.[17] Many of the plantation workers were not Central Americans, but ex-slaves brought in from the Caribbean Islands.

This isolation from national life gave rise to a variety of other businesses—beverage companies, shoe stores, banks, electricity plants, plastic manufacturing plants (to bag the bananas), restaurants, and communication services—owned by the banana companies and designed to meet the needs of the companies and their workers. These subsidiary companies soon reached throughout the national economy, until United Fruit and Standard Fruit had their hands into everything. For this reason, Central Americans often refer to the two companies as *los pulpos*—the octopuses. During their heyday in Central America (1910-1940), the banana companies were law unto themselves.

The banana enclaves once covered vast expanses of Central America.

In Guatemala, for example, United Fruit owned 550,000 acres of prime agricultural land. Entire campesino communities sometimes were forced to leave their homes to make way for the advancing banana plantations. In 1916, United Fruit's company lawyer advised an UFCO manager in Costa Rica to push a community of Bribri Indians off their land because "the Indians were timid and I am sure that by insisting strongly they will abandon all pretension of ownership of the land."[18] A Bribri elder, Don Alejandro Montero, later recalled the land grab by United Fruit: "We did not realize that the Company had gotten hold of papers for all the lands. How were we going to fight back? There was no one to defend us....There was nothing we could do."[19]

Only a small percentage of the banana enclaves, however, was used to grow bananas, because the world market wasn't big enough to absorb all the fruit the land could produce. During the 1950s, just 5 percent of United Fruit's holdings in Central America were in banana production. The rest lay idle or provided pasture for cattle.[20]

The banana companies began selling much of their land to the government and local growers in the early 1950s, when the rise of nationalism (particularly in Guatemala) frightened them into thinking the land might be seized. Although the nationalist fire was doused by the U.S. government when the CIA overthrew a progressive Guatemalan government in 1954, the companies continued to divest their idle holdings for economic reasons. Their estates now cover about 250,000 acres throughout the region—only a small fraction of what they were in the past.[21]

No longer do the banana companies actually grow all the bananas exported from Central America. An increasing amount is supplied by small farmers and cooperatives that grow the fruit. Yet, while the prevalence of banana trees in Central America may be somewhat exaggerated in the U.S. public mind, banana companies are still the largest private investors and landowners in the region.

The Cotton Club

An acre of Central American soil will yield more cotton than any other non-irrigated land in the world. Before the Spanish arrived, Indians were already growing cotton for their own needs. Production as an export crop did not begin until the 1950s. But when it did, thousands of small farmers were displaced to make room for the new plantations.

Along the coastal plains of Guatemala, El Salvador, and Nicaragua, cotton plantations extend for miles astride the Pan-American Highway. A chain of billboards parallels the highway singing the praises of the latest brand of pesticides. For three months each year a legion of malnourished cotton pickers, with scarves around their heads and necks to protect them from the sun and insects, descends on the cotton fields. For their 10 to 12 hour days (often seven days a week), the workers get about $1-$2 a day and a spot to sleep under the open-air shelters on the edge of the plantations. It is cheaper to pay this unorganized regional labor force of several hundred thousand than to harvest the cotton mechanically.

The Indian families that pick cotton in Guatemala are hired by labor contractors, who employ workers for a month or more. Desperate for cash, the Indians usually get an advance from the *contratista*. Just before the harvest begins, the *contratista* loads the Indians into the back of his truck for the grueling ride to the coast. Because the contract laborers are so tightly packed in the trucks, suffocation and carbon monoxide poisoning are common. Recently, six Indians died in the back of a truck driven by the bodyguard of a cotton plantation owner. Rigoberta Menchú, a Guatemalan opposition leader, said that she, like most Indians, started working on the country's agroexport plantations when she was only a child. When she was ten, Menchú remembers

> After my first day picking cotton, I woke up at midnight and lit a candle. I saw the faces of my brothers and sisters covered with mosquitoes. I touched my own face and I was covered too. They were everywhere; in people's mouths and everywhere. Just looking at these insects and thinking about being bitten set me scratching. That was our world. I felt that it would always be the same, always the same. It hasn't ever changed.[22]

Recalling her little brother's death from pesticide poisoning, Menchu continues:

> I was both angry with life and afraid of it, because I told myself: 'This is the life I will lead too; having many children, and having them die, and having nothing to cure him with or help him live.' Working in the *finca* was one of my earliest experiences, and I remember it with enormous hatred. That hatred has stayed with me until today.[23]

Buoyed by a downtrodden, indebted labor force, the prospects for corporate profit in cotton were propitious. A global cotton boom in the 1950s attracted investors such as politicians and military men, whose principal source of income came from outside the agricultural sector. These newcomers to agriculture, along with the more forward-thinking coffee oligarchs scrambled to get in on the profits, manipulating their political connections to get cheap land and credit.

Cotton is distinctive because of its annual rotation—the only such crop among the region's agroexports. Land used to grow cotton can easily be converted to produce a different crop the next year, allowing investors to respond to world market fluctuations.

Cotton also absorbs dollars like no other agroexport crop. For every one dollar's worth of cotton, the producing countries must import as much as 50 cents in fertilizer, machinery, and pesticides.[24] This heavy dependence on imports considerably reduces the net foreign exchange earnings from cotton, and raises questions about the wisdom of taking land out of basic food production to produce cotton for export.

Making Way for the Cotton Plantations

"The introduction of cotton in the 1950s, in El Salvador is most tragic from the viewpoint of the country's displaced population," observed Central American author Dr. Edelberto Torres-Rivas.[25] The spread of cotton farming pushed small farmers out of the way, and used up the only remaining uncultivated fertile fields on the country's Pacific lowlands, precluding their use to grow basic foods. Cotton produced high levels of profit for the large landowners and investors at the cost of "a large margin of hunger and hopelessness."[26]

As with other agroexports, cotton production is highly concentrated and becoming more so. Less than 40 farms occupy about 20 percent of El Salvador's cotton lands,[27] while 15 Guatemalan families account for 45 percent of that country's production.[28] A similar level of land concentration was also the case in pre-revolutionary Nicaragua, where 6 percent of the country's producers accounted for 50 percent of the cotton production.[29]

By 1955, cotton had surpassed coffee as Nicaragua's major export and ten years later the country was the world's 10th largest exporter of the downy fiber. The best corn land soon turned into the best cotton-producing land. Even the area around Leon, once known as *el granero* (the granary), fell prey to cotton farming. Throughout Central America, when basic-food farmland was lost to cotton plantations, food imports increased dramatically. In Nicaragua, cotton exports and food imports each increased fivefold between 1960 and 1977. For the well-fed growers during the Somoza era, it was at the commercial level, not at the level of production that the cotton business in Nicaragua was most profitable. The cotton-ginning business in Nicaragua was heavily concentrated—a feature repeated throughout Central America. Unlike the coffee industry, where most export houses are locally owned, the cotton exporters in Central America are frequently branches of foreign trading companies. Foreign interests skim another hefty portion of profits from the local cotton business through the supply of machinery and agrochemicals.

Central American cotton production began dropping dramatically in the late 1970s as a result of a large world surplus, the increased use of synthetic substitutes, and low market prices. The continuing upward climb in the price of imported agrochemicals also persuaded many cotton farmers to reduce their acreage, and by the early 1980s planted acreage had dropped to less than half its 1977 level with no sign that cotton production would regain its former promise. The ones who suffer most from cutbacks in cotton production are the cotton pickers. Having neither land of their own nor work, they are without any source of food or income. The changing fortunes of the cotton industry once again illustrate the vulnerability of a society perched on a few slim pillars as well as the danger of depending on a market completely controlled by outside forces.

The Bittersweet Business of Sugar

Central America's main sugar producers are Guatemala, El Salvador, Nicaragua, Panama, and the sparsely populated nation of Belize. Sugar production is not as tightly controlled by a small number of large growers as coffee or cotton. Sugar, however, is still a concentrated industry because of the limited number of mills where sugarcane can be processed. In the case of El Salvador just three sugar mills control two-thirds of production.[30] Small growers depend on the mills, which are generally owned by leading families or by the governments themselves.

Like workers in other Central American agroexport sectors, cane cutters earn too little to adequately support their families—despite long days spent in the fields slashing down a couple of tons of sugarcane with their machetes. But one British sugar exporter in Guatemala City sees it quite differently: "The workers on the sugar plantations are generally satisfied although, as you know, we do have a communist problem in this country that sometimes causes us trouble. But I myself stay out of the politics."[31]

The Sword of U.S. Quotas

The sugar industry provides perhaps the best example of the power that importing nations can wield over countries dependent on a few agroexports. In 1962, the Kennedy administration demonstrated its displeasure with the Cuban revolution by halting all imports of sugar from Cuba, the world's largest sugar exporter. Before the embargo, Cuba had exported most of its crop to the United States.

To fill the gap created by the Cuban embargo, Washington distributed Cuba's quota among the Central American countries, and U.S. sugar imports from the region tripled in the 1960s.[32] Until recently, some 70 percent of Central American sugar exports have gone to the United States. But the fear of reduced U.S. sugar quotas hangs like a sword over all sugar-producing nations.

Like Cuba, Nicaragua's revolution displeased Washington, and the hapless land of Sandino thus finds itself the most recent victim of politically motivated sugar decisions by the U.S. In May 1983, President Reagan suddenly reduced the sugar quota from Nicaragua by 95 percent and redistributed Nicaragua's share to Honduras, El Salvador, and Costa Rica. Nicaragua complained that the sugar quota cut violated "the most elemental norms of international law and the principals of international organizations,"[33] and took its case to the council of the United Nations' General Agreement on Tariffs and Trade (GATT). The council found Washington in breach of international trading regulations that had been approved by the United States. Undeterred, the Reagan administration went on to declare a total trade embargo against Nicaragua in April 1985.

While the closure of the U.S. market to Nicaragua's sugar exports was politically motivated, economic reasons explain why other Central American nations have been hard hit recently by cutbacks in U.S. sugar imports. Responding to pressure from U.S. sugar growers, who are experiencing a bloated domestic market, President Reagan has been slashing the sugar quotas of all foreign producers. Since 1984, the quotas for Central American nations have been reduced each year so that today only 25 percent of the region's sugar production enters the lucrative U.S. market.

This new U.S. protectionism has had a devastating impact in Central America. Growers have cut back production by 50 percent, thereby increasing unemployment and depleting the national treasuries of another source of scarce foreign exchange. Other nations, like those in Western Europe, have also cut their sugar imports, but the shrinking of U.S. imports has been particularly painful to Central American nations because of the high price paid in the protected U.S. market. Central America stands to lose as much as $80 million in 1986 because of reduced U.S. quotas. Yet the worst is probably still to come.

Sugar Substitutes

Besides facing political threats, sugar producing countries ride the roller coaster of changes in both taste and technology. Ever since soft drink companies introduced high-fructose corn syrup (HFCS) into their products in the 1970s, consumption has been falling at a rate of 3 percent a year.[34] The recent decision by Coca-Cola to use a higher percentage of HFCS in its soft drinks caused the USDA to re-evaluate its estimates for sugar imports, and some experts predict that the U.S. market will be completely sealed shut to sugar imports by 1990.[35]

Dieting concerns have also hurt the sugar market, as U.S. consumers increasingly move away from sugar in favor of low-calorie sweeteners. Ironically, the short-term effect of efforts to combat a prominent major North American dietary concern—obesity—have aggravated Central America's number one dietary problem—malnutrition—as sugarcane growers cut back production and hire fewer workers. Long-term reliance on sugar exports is a dangerous proposition given the political and protectionist nature of the market and the sobering fact that sugar's 1986 price was one-tenth what it was six years earlier.

The Hamburger Connection

On a bus rumbling through mile after mile of Costa Rican pasture land, a middle-class man sighed: "We cannot afford to eat meat anymore. Almost all our beef is exported to your country, where consumers can pay higher prices. We Costa Ricans are being forced to become vegetarians."[36]

Costa Ricans are not the only Central Americans complaining about the meat-export business, which has more than tripled over the last 25 years. The ability of consumers in industrialized countries to pay more for meat has indeed reduced its availability for local consumption: as per capita beef consumption in the U.S. was increasing by 50 percent over a period of 20 years, it was dropping by 30 percent in Central America.[37] Most U.S. housecats now eat more beef in a year than does the average Central American.[38]

The growth of the meat export industry has adversely affected the local availability of basic grains. Besides shifting land away from local grain production, the industry has gobbled up much of the region's grain imports. In 1983, for instance, about 40 percent of Central America's grain imports from the United States went to feed cattle, not people.[39] In the process of squeezing out the peasantry, the cattle industry has also increased unemployment.

Between 1960 and 1980, Central American land devoted to cattle raising increased by two-thirds, the number of cattle almost doubled, and meat exports shot up seven-fold.[40] Beef has become one of the region's five top agroexports, and now ranks as the third largest export in both Honduras and Costa Rica. The cattle industry also presents an environmental threat to the region, which may lose what is left of its rainforests to the industry's avaricious quest for new pastures.

Raising cattle has become a coveted pastime for professionals, who often put on their *sombreros* to become gentlemen ranchers on weekends. An agronomist in Costa Rica noted: "There isn't a single successful lawyer in San José who doesn't have a ranch. Every ex-president of Costa Rica owns a ranch, every banker owns a ranch, and every doctor owns a ranch."[41] In contrast to small farmers, who of necessity make the most intensive use of their small holdings, the prestige rancher is often content to use his land in an inefficient and wasteful fashion.[42]

Supplying the Hamburger Chains

A shortage of cheap cuts of meat in the United States for the growing fast-food industry opened the door to the creation of a lucrative meat export business in Central America. The region was attractive to U.S. meat importers because of its cheap land, proximity to the United States, and absence of hoof and mouth disease.

Ranching has always been part of the agricultural scene in Central America. The colonial-style haciendas each had their small herd of cattle. And most towns had their own municipal abattoir where small farmers brought their steers for slaughter. Cattle were sold within the region "on-the-hoof" rather than cut and packed.

Since 1957, when the first modern USDA-approved packing plant was completed in Managua, the cattle industry in Central America has become an entirely different beast. By 1979, 28 modern packing plants in the region, many of them partially owned by U.S. investors, were preparing some 250 million pounds of beef for shipment to the United States. These plants commonly slaughter over 200 head of cattle every day, with diseased and scroungy specimens marked for "domestic consumption." Internal organs, the very parts where pesticides concentrate, are also slated for the domestic market.[43]

The boom in the beef business was promoted by an array of international forces. Within the United States, the Meat Importers Council of America formed to loosen up U.S. quotas for imported beef. Multilateral loans created a modern highway system in Central America that opened up frontier lands for grazing and facilitated the trucking of freshly slaughtered beef to ocean ports. The World Bank and IDB latched onto the cattle industry as a quick and easy way to boost the region's export-led growth and pumped multimillion dollar loans into projects that would expand beef production. In the late 1960s, a decade after the beef boom got started, a full third of agricultural credit in several Central American countries was given to cattle growers. Easy access to credit continues today. In Honduras, the government's agricultural bank in recent years has allocated less than 5 percent of its credit to basic foods production while giving the livestock industry 24 percent.

All this assistance made it possible for the industry to start sending thousands of 60-pound cartons of chilled, boneless beef to Miami and New Orleans for distribution to meat wholesalers and hamburger chains throughout the United States.

During the 1970s, about 90 percent of the region's beef exports went to the United States, accounting for about 15 percent of total U.S. meat imports. Beginning in 1979, however, the beef export trade with the United States began to slow down as U.S. ranchers lobbied to have meat import quotas reduced, in part due to declining per capita meat consumption in the United States. The USDA also started to clamp down on beef imports by rejecting shipments from Central America because of their high pesticide content.[44] Looking for ways to help the region out of its economic doldrums, the Kissinger Commission in 1984 recommended that restrictive quotas be lifted for Central American countries. But given the present protectionist spirit of Congress, cattlemen in Central America cannot rely on an expanding market in the United States.

A Question of Land Use

The cattle industry, more than any other part of the agroexport system, illustrates the distorted land-use priorities in Central America. Cattle ranches stretch across the fertile valleys and the coastal plains, with one or two head of cattle grazing on the amount of land that could feed an entire family for a year. Considering the region's serious malnutrition problem, it seems a tragic misuse of resources to allocate half the area's arable land to livestock. While the cattle industry makes wasteful use of precious land resources, it makes almost no use of the region's large pool of labor. Even by conservative estimates, coffee offers 13 times more employment per acre than the cattle business.[45] Unlike some other labor-intensive agroexport industries, the cattle business is labor displacing, not labor absorbing. With a few hired hands, a ranch owner can run a large herd.

The spread of the livestock industry has, like the growth of other Central American agroexports, encouraged large landowners to expand their holdings. Herds of cattle are often placed on areas formerly considered too remote for profitable agricultural operations, and many ranchers spread their herds over public and untitled private holdings as a way to validate their own claims to those lands.

In the last 30 years, the land devoted to pasture has increased close to three-fold. In the process, many thousands of campesino families have been pushed off their subsistence farms by the advancing cattle industry.

The expansion of the agricultural frontier not only displaced peasants but also cut into the region's diminishing forest reserves. To prepare new land for grazing, ranchers team up with their government in colonization schemes that use campesinos initially to clear the land for planting. After a couple of years, the ranchers then move onto the cleared land and the campesino pioneers must search for another spot of forest to clear.

The region's rainforest is thus being cut down at a furious pace. In the last 20 years, about 40 percent of the forest reserves have been lost, mainly to ranchers. During the first few years of grazing, two acres are needed for each head of cattle, but after five years, it often takes more that 12 acres to sustain just one head of cattle. After an additional 2-5 years of grazing, the soil is sometimes too eroded and weed-infested for any productive use.

At the current rate of destruction, tropical forests in Central America will be gone by the end of the century. The clearing of these rainforests represents a serious environmental loss not only to Central American countries but to the entire world. The dense forests of the isthmus serve as a global climate regulator and a genetic pool. Without the rainforests' absorption of carbon dioxide, the build-up of atmospheric levels could raise the world's temperature and seriously disrupt weather patterns.

In the United States, groups like the Rainforest Action Network, the Environmental Policy Institute, and the Environmental Project on Central America have recently formed to educate citizens about this impending environmental catastrophe. They are demanding that the World Bank and other multilateral institutions stop funding cattle industry and other environmentally destructive "development" projects. There is also increasing official concern in Central America. In Nicaragua, the government has proposed to create an international biosphere reserve on its border with Costa Rica, an area which has been threatened by the advancing cattle industry.

Meat or Eat

The boom in meat exports has occurred at the direct expense of food consumption in Central America. As pastures and cattle increase, land available to grow basic grains decreases. The following statistics reveal some of the beef-related causes for hunger in a few Central American countries.

* In Nicaragua, pasture land doubled from 1960 to 1978, while arable land in small farms fell by 20 percent.[46]

* Cattle-raising areas covered only one-tenth of Costa Rica's total land area in 1950 but more than one-third by 1980.

* There is one head of cattle for every two people in the region. In Costa Rica, the cattle population now equals the human population.

* Between 1965 and 1975, the per capita beef consumption in Honduras dropped 10 percent while meat exports to the United States tripled.[47]

The beef export business is, of course, not the only reason that Central Americans are not eating as much meat as they used to. If they had as much money as foreign consumers, ranchers and packing houses would gladly sell them their beef. However, to expand the domestic market for meat consumption would require income and resource distribution in Central America—measures that go against the grain of the big operators of the region's cattle industry.

Whose Advantage?

Since the days of the Spanish Armada, Central America has been a region that exports primary commodities to the world market. Little has really changed. Colonial relations have been replaced by neocolonial ones. Instead of serving Spain, today's exports are directed toward the United States. A new armada of international shipping, trading, and processing companies deals with a tiny exporting elite in Central America.

Some economists argue that Central America should concentrate on the production of agroexports like coffee and bananas because its tropical climate and abundant agricultural labor give the region a comparative advantage over industrial nations of the temperate zones. Likewise, so the argument goes, countries like the United States can manufacture cheaper and better cars than third-world nations. Manufactured products and even some agricultural products like wheat that benefit from industrialized technical capacity, can then be traded for the largely unprocessed commodities of Central America.

A major problem with this "comparative advantage" theory is the increasingly unequal terms of trade for the region's exports. Over the last two decades, unprocessed agricultural commodities have shrunk from 30 percent of the value of all world trade to less than 14 percent today.[48] Agricultural commodities are increasingly losing out to petroleum products, processed food, and manufactured products—trade items in which Central America is almost totally lacking. As the prices for Central American agroexports drop on the world market, foreign exchange earned from the sale of those agroexports to the industrial world buys fewer and fewer imports. In 1960, for instance, the income from the sale of a ton of sugar bought 6.3 tons of oil, and the income from a ton of coffee bought 37.3 tons of fertilizer. By 1982, a ton of sugar bought only 0.7 tons of oil, and a ton of coffee bought only 1.6 tons of fertilizer.[49]

In the early 1980s, cocoa prices were the same as they were in the 1940s and sugar prices at 5 or 6 cents a pound dipped below production costs. Overall during the past 25 years, the terms of trade for agricultural commodities produced in Central America have declined by 40 percent.[50] Since 1979, the deterioration of terms of trade has accelerated. It is not as if the Central American nations can simply decide to stop importing expensive goods from industrial countries. Pesticides, fertilizers, and agricultural machinery are essential ingredients in this import-dependent system.

* During the last decade the cost of pesticide imports increased sevenfold, while the amount imported only increased by half. In the 1970s, Central Americans paid about $650 for each ton of pesticides. By 1981, they were paying $3150 per ton.

* The price of imported fertilizers jumped five-fold during the 1970s, but import volume increased by only 25 percent. In 1971, Central Americans were paying $58 for each ton of fertilizer. Ten years later they were paying four times as much.[51]

* The same imported agricultural machinery which costs $1084 in 1970 soared to $4770 a decade later.[52]

Just to stay even, the Central American countries have to produce ever greater quantities of crops for export. Since most other third-world agroexporters are also trying to increase their agroexport production, the world market is becoming flooded with agricultural commodities, driving prices even lower. This arrangement suits the short-term interests of the industrial world but casts a long shadow over the continued ability of the global capitalist economy to grow. As the terms of trade are pushed ever downward by industrial nations, agroexport producing nations find it impossible to pay their external debts and have no foreign exchange to purchase imports.

The theory of "comparative advantage" parallels the needs of the developed nations and the transnational corporations. They, in fact, set the terms of trade and global trading patterns from their position of power. For Central American countries, "comparative advantage" is more myth than theory. The current global division of labor and production offer them little advantage but instead keep them in a disadvantaged state.

Dependence on the United States

With the exception of Nicaragua, Central American economies depend on U.S. agricultural trade. This unhealthy dependence on U.S. trade is the result of the long neocolonial relationship that has been forced on the region by its bully neighbor to the north. Dollar and gunboat diplomacy have put Central America in the economic pocket of the United States, representing a cheap source of commodity imports and an open market for U.S. exports.

Trade figures reveal the staggering proportions of this economic dependence. About 40 percent of all Central America's agricultural exports is shipped to the U.S. market, and over 50 percent of the region's agricultural imports comes from the United States.[53] This heavy reliance on U.S. markets wreaks havoc with the regional economy when U.S. demand for Central American products slips or when U.S. trade patterns shift. As the Central Americans see it, when the U.S. sneezes, the isthmus catches a cold.

Central American nations have a positive balance of agricultural trade with the United States, exporting 4 to 5 times as much agricultural produce as they import from their powerful Northern neighbor.[54] But this hardly means that Central America has the upper hand. The quantity of its main agroexports, although significant in regional terms, amounts to less than six percent of U.S. food imports. Instead, it is the United States that exercises the market power because Central American countries are so dependent on U.S. markets, whereas the U.S. can be more selective about its trading partners. This lopsided power balance of trade in the hemisphere has allowed Washington to reward friends and punish revolutionary countries throughout the Caribbean Basin.

No Easy Answers

Central America, formerly a colony lorded over by *conquistadores*, is now a string of agroexport republics. They are caught in a cycle of under-development that on a regional level only benefits the national elites who own the land and run the economy. Transnational corporations and traders that do business there also benefit from the region's cheap labor, unjust land tenure, and repressive political climate. There are no easy ways out of the time-hardened system that produces cash crops for export. But the quality of life for most Central Americans would improve if:

* A balance were struck between production of crops for export and production of basic foods.

* Land were more equitably distributed.

* Producing countries banded together to set higher prices for agricultural goods.[55]

* Agroindustries were developed to process raw commodities for intra-regional and domestic markets.

* Workers were guaranteed liveable wages and the right to organize.

The following two chapters more closely examine the national and international owners of the new plantation, showing that oligarchs and foreign corporations are the main obstacles to such steps to free the region from its overdependence on the agroexport system.

Chapter Three
The Land of the Oligarchs

The cause of our problems is the oligarchy, that tiny group of families which has no concern for the hunger of the people, but in fact needs it in order to have cheap and abundant labor to export its crops.

—Salvadoran Archbishop Oscar Romero,
assassinated March 1980.

Just as you cannot miss the desperate poverty of Central America, neither can you miss its wealth. Well-dressed men and women move in and out of major airports gossiping about their latest weekend shopping trips to Miami. Expensive sports cars roam the streets of exclusive residential districts, where *campesinos* cut the lawns with *machetes* because labor costs less than lawnmowers.

Inside fancy clubs like Club Guatemala, members of the social elite discuss the relative merits of various U.S. universities. Often they will fly their own planes to visit their children at UCLA, Notre Dame, or Georgetown. A former deputy director of the Salvadoran Agrarian Transformation Institute remarked, "The oligarch you see in London, in Miami, he plays golf with your cousin in Palm Beach, he has a daughter at Vassar, he has a *Playboy* subscription, he's one of the boys."[1]

Typically, members of the oligarchy speak English, dress in the latest American styles, and follow U.S. sports. They are a cosmopolitan class with tastes and business interests that lead them to frequent the major port cities of the United States. But with their armored cars and bodyguards, they seem more like wealthy hoodlums than socialites. They bankroll death squads and security forces to keep their countries "free", but maintain comfortable second homes in San Francisco, New Orleans, or Miami where they will flee in the event of revolution. A popular joke circulating in El Salvador is that the oligarchy has rephrased the popular slogan, *Patria Libre o Morir* ("a free country or death") to read: *Patria Libre o Miami*.

Origins of the Oligarchy

The Greek philosopher Aristotle wrote that an oligarchy exists when "men of property have government in their hands."[2] The Central American governments are self-proclaimed democratic republics. But the term "oligarchy" better describes the political reality of most of the region, where economic power and government are controlled by an elite.

Spain laid the foundations for a Central American oligarchy through a land grants system, in which small number of Spanish families were given control over the region's main resource—land. Together with the Catholic Church and representatives of the Spanish monarchy, these *latifundistas* formed the triad of colonial power in the 1600s and 1700s.

During the colonial era, Central America remained on the periphery of the Spanish mercantile system. Most goods exported from the region went through Mexico; and consequently the Mexican *creole* class was much wealthier than its counterpart in Central America. The region's economy was largely subsistence agriculture, either on a small scale by peasant farmers or on a much grander scale by the *latifundistas* on their haciendas.

Agroexport production was common only in the territories of Guatemala and El Salvador, where large landowners relied on forced Indian labor to produce indigo dye and cacao for export to Mexico and Spain. During the colonial years, the other areas of Central America were isolated from both the political and economic bonds of Spanish rule.

Central America won its independence from Spain in 1821, and by 1839 was divided into the separate countries we know today. The remnants of the colonial power structure, based on the hacienda agricultural economy and the old Spanish mercantile system, grouped around the Conservative Party in each country.

But independence, coupled with the expansion of the coffee economy throughout the 1800s, opened the region up to a new faction of growers and traders opposing the old elite. These new coffee producers, who gradually integrated modern trade, agricultural, and labor practices, formed the backbone of the Liberal parties, which sought to usurp the power of the Conservatives.

The Liberals were reformers who espoused a philosophy of economic liberalism. They wanted to expand the region's trade relations to countries besides Spain, especially the European powers and the United States. At home, they sought to reduce the influence of the church while pushing for economic modernization. They favored "land reforms" that confiscated church property and communal Indian land in order to open up new land for private ownership. As they expanded coffee production into the frontier areas of Central America, new roads, telegraph systems, international steamship routes, and the influx of foreign capital followed. The intense struggle between the two parties continued for most of the century with the Liberals gaining the upper hand in the 1870s. In the case of Nicaragua, the contest between the two factions of the oligarchy was still going strong in the first quarter of this century.

For the native residents, though, little changed. Work on the coffee *fincas* was no less brutal than on the traditional haciendas. Nor did the emergence of the coffee oligarchy in Central America radically change government. In some countries, Liberals simply replaced Conservatives as the new ruling class. The ascendancy of the coffee growers, an emerging merchant elite, and the Liberal parties accompanied the region's increasing integration into global capitalism. This era constituted the first period of internal economic growth in Central America. The class of oligarchs who directed this growth would hold undisputed control of the economy and politics until the next period of economic changes after World War II. At that time, a new breed of oligarchs evolved due to economic growth resulting from a new agroexport boom, industrialization, and a wave of U.S. investment. In the last 40 years, the established planter class joined together with the modern agroexporters, the military, and leading figures in industry and finance to form the modern oligarchies of Central America.

Land, Labor, and Authority

The reactionary despotism that has characterized Central America cannot be explained apart from the control of labor exercised by the large landowners.[3] The traditional haciendas and later the coffee plantations relied on the forced labor of (usually) Indian families. Forced labor was formally abolished at the end of the colonial epoch but the system continued into this century. The use of involuntary servitude to operate haciendas and agroexport plantations initially took a feudal form whereby peasants were obliged to relinquish a certain amount of their labor and produce to the large landholders. A system of coerced labor also manifested itself as debt peonage, whereby a peasant debtor was legally required to work for the creditor until the debt was repaid.

The production of coffee for the world market strengthened rather than weakened the forced labor system, according to economist John Weeks.[4] Vagrancy laws decreed by Guatemala and El Salvador in the late 1800s made it a criminal offense not to work a portion of the year as a wage laborer, thereby facilitating the incorporation of peasants into the plantation labor force. The Guatemalan law required all males (only Indians in practice) to work 150 days a year.

The actual function of these vagrancy laws was to create a cheap, docile workforce for agroexport production. "In probably no part of Latin America in the twentieth century were individual rights more grossly sacrificed to the demands of landed property than they were in Central America," writes Weeks.

The wealth of the society's upper class depended on the severe control of the region's agricultural workforce. Fear of rebellion united the commercial and agricultural elites in keeping the peasant class subservient and repressed. Nowhere else in Latin America has the labor force been so restricted and repressed by a landed elite for so long.

Changing Times

The main elements of Central America's agroexport system—large landholdings, oligarchic control, and a repressed labor force—persist, despite the broadening of the economy and modernization of agricultural production. The changes in the economy and society have occurred without substantially altering old patterns of land and labor. In fact, the oligarchy's hold on the region's land, labor, and politics has tightened with the development of each new agroexport.

The contemporary oligarch is a modern businessman who is involved not just in coffee production but in cotton, sugar, and even nontraditional agroexports like melons and cucumbers. The modern oligarch also usually has off-plantation investments in agroindustry (like cotton ginning), commerce, manufacturing, and finance. In addition, today's oligarch often maintains a foreign investment portfolio, commonly in Florida real estate.

In the 1950s and 1960s, the region began industrializing. With U.S. economic assistance, a common market and regional economic institutions were established to push industrialization forward. The larger regional market for national industries and new U.S. investment did result in industrial growth, but by the 1970s intraregional industrial trade began to stagnate.

Although Central America has made some strides toward industrialization, it continues to look to the agroexport system for its main income. The primary source of capital, even for those oligarchs with large industrial investments, still comes from agroexport production, with its attendant system of land and labor control. As such, many of the historical practices and attitudes of the landed elite still find strong expression in the economic and political life of Central America.

A major reason for Central America's failure to develop a healthier industrial sector is the lack of land reform, which most economists say is a necessary step towards enabling peasants to increase their income, thus creating a wider consumer market. From the beginning of the common market, however, the landed oligarchy insisted that industrialization would have to go forward without any program of land distribution. It is unlikely there can be another spurt of industrialization in Central America until its large peasantry gains access to land and income.

Attempts to increase rural wages, redistribute land or organize farm labor are perceived as threats to the stability of the agroexport system rather than as necessary steps in the economic advancement of the entire society. The oligarchy has historically relied on the armed forces to protect its narrow interests. But in the last 50 years, politics have become increasingly militarized as the oligarchy has ceded to the army some of its own political and economic power in the face of popular opposition. The armed peasant movement in Nicaragua led by Sandino and the worker-peasant rebellion in El Salvador inspired by Farabundo Martí persuaded the region's oligarchies to beef up their national armies. The land reform program announced in Guatemala by the reformist government of Jacobo Arbenz sent new tremors through Central America, and governments eagerly sought U.S. aid to modernize their armies in order to guard against reformist or revolutionary movements on their own soil. These two factors—fear of internal rebellion and generous military aid from Washington—have served to shape the Central American armies into important national institutions. They have become much more than the private gendarmes of the oligarchy. They now hold privotal economic and political positions in several Central American nations.

Associating for Power

One way in which the business elites exercise their power on a national scale is through their business and trade associations. These groups operate in the context of representative governments, which in most cases are merely facades for oligarchic rule. The directors of these associations are often leading figures from the country's political parties, who are chosen by the government to manage the very committees that regulate business and trade. Government officials usually confer closely with the business associations before announcing new economic measures. The power of these business groups is further enhanced by the ties that exist between the oligarchs and the security forces. The associations are forever reorganizing, but lately there has been an entire new crop of business groups that receives copious funding from the Agency for International Development (AID).

The traditional business organizations generally represent the most reactionary elements of the oligarchy. In Honduras, the National Association of Growers and Cattlemen (FENAGH) has bitterly resisted agrarian reform and its members have directed brutal assaults against campesino groups. Amigos del País and other private-sector groups have openly supported death-squad activity and military governments in Guatemala. In El Salvador, FARO, the main association of large landholders, took the question of public order into its own hands in the mid-1970s when it created vigilante groups to defend their *latifundios* against peasants trying to acquire land through the national land reform law.

In the 1980s, AID has begun trying to create a network of business organizations that are not so closely connected with the extreme right wing. It wants these new organizations to be instruments of the United States' economic and political agenda in the region. The old organizations, AID feels, are too politicized to work well with government institutions. It also says these groups are too backward-looking to adopt the modernization programs necessary to spur new agroexport projects, especially those involving nontraditional crops. In the last several years, AID has pumped many millions of dollars into the newly created business groups with the mandate that they lobby for such measures as the privatization of publicly owned corporations and more government incentives for agroexport investment. Because of the AID money now flowing through this new breed of business associations, the more traditional ones are losing membership and influence.

Rulers or Managers?

The power of this oligarchy does not exist in an international vacuum. It is part of the world market for agroexports and the international division of labor. While the oligarchy takes the first cut out of the income from agroexports, most of the profit goes to foreign corporations that control the trading, processing, and marketing of commodities. Central American growers and exporters only control a small portion of the coffee and other commodity-based industries. They have to accept the prices dictated by a world market in which they have very little influence. The fortunes of these oligarchs come not from their ability to set prices and manipulate markets but from their access to cheap land and labor as well as their monopoly on credit and government assistance. In Guatemala and El Salvador, for example, only 5 percent of agricultural credit went to basic grains production in the 1970s.

Just as the region's agroexport producers are dependent collaborators in international commodity trading, the region's industrialists are the junior partners of foreign corporations. Most Central American industry is controlled by U.S. corporations who append the national oligarchs as local partners. In El Salvador, four out of five foreign investments established after 1960 were joint ventures with Salvadoran businessmen.[5] And American Chambers of Commerce throughout Central America now include many of the region's own leading industrialists.

This international relationship benefits both the oligarchy and the foreign corporations. The corporations depend on the oligarchy to keep the laborers or peasants working for low wages. Those wages—less than one-tenth paid to workers in developed countries—guarantee the continued supply of low-priced commodities for the international market. The repressed wage-scale means that manufacturers can assemble their goods in Central America for only a fraction of what it would cost in the United States.

The oligarchy, in turn, depends on the TNCs to buy their exports and to provide them with the inputs they need for agriculture. Without the technology provided by the TNCs, the regional elite would not have been able to industrialize.

Besides being business partners, business elites are highly valued political partners for the institutions, corporations, and governments of the developed world. They serve as the front line in the international effort to stave off and repress rebellion by the disenfranchised population of Central America. In turn, these elites have learned that they can rely on U.S. military and economic intervention to protect the interests of the "private sector."

The composition of Central American oligarchies and the way they exercise power vary greatly from country to country. The differences derive from the relative amount of power wielded by four main oligarchic

players: 1) the traditional and more backward landowners known as
latifundistas, 2) the new agrarian capitalists, 3) the commercial, financial,
and industrial elites, and 4) the military high command.

The distinctive features of oligarchic control in Central America today
are that it:

* Receives most of it wealth from agroexports although it has diversified
into commerce and manufacturing.

* Relies on a police state to control labor and protect its interests.

* Uses business associations to pressure the government to meet its
self-interested demands.

* Subordinates all other social needs like that of local food production to
those of the agroexport system and private sector.

* Remains fundamentally dependent on foreign-controlled (mostly U.S.)
trade and investment, and recently on U.S. economic assistance as well.

* Obstructs agrarian and other economic reforms needed to broaden the
base of the region's economy.

* Is fundamentally unstable and headed for an inevitable but probably
violent collapse.

El Salvador: The Essence of Oligarchy

As the coffee boom took hold of the isthmus in the mid-to-late 1800s,
creole growers, like the Regalado, Escalón, and Meléndez families, broadened their ranks to include wealthy immigrants from Europe who helped
direct the country's expanding export trade. The names of these immigrants—Parker, Wright, De Sola, Schoenberg, Hill and others—are still
prominent in today's coffee industry and national politics.

By the turn of the century, coffee was El Salvador's unchallenged
source of wealth and political power.[6] The narrow interests of this one
sector were forced upon the entire nation. Governments were created by
agreements among small groups and sometimes within families. Between
1913 and 1931, for example, the coffee-growing Meléndez family
circulated three different family representatives through the national
Palace.

After the peasant rebellion of 1932, the military took direct control of
the government, although members of the coffee oligarchy continued to
define the country's political direction by retaining key cabinet posts.
There were no dramatic changes in the balance of power until 1950, when
budding industrialization and the introduction of new agroexports created
additional sources of profit.

Henceforth, industrialists and cotton magnates were to share power with the elite coffee growers. Some elements of the traditional agricultural sector were pushed aside—those landowners who still considered themselves *patrones* and balked at making the full transition to the modern plantation. In contrast, many coffee growers and other large landowners embraced the new opportunities presented by cotton production and industrial development.

Most of the internal investment for agrarian modernization and industrialization came from the accumulated wealth of the economically progressive coffee growers, who put their money into cotton plantations, textile mills, food processing plants, and industrial parks. The coffee grower and the new industrialist were often one and the same. The coffee oligarchs invested 4 times more heavily in industry than did any other economic group.[7] Today, in El Salvador, about 40 percent of the country's top 1,429 firms are controlled by the nation's 36 largest landowners.[8]

While the oligarchy has grown more diversified, the nation's wealth has remained extremely concentrated. Among Salvadoran businesses, less than one percent of the business owners appropriate 60 percent of the profit.[9] In 1931, a U.S. Army officer, struck by the sharp contrasts he saw in San Salvador, said:

> There appears to be nothing between these high-priced cars and the oxcart with its barefoot attendant. There is practically no middle class. . . . Thirty or forty families own nearly everything in the country. They live in almost regal style. The rest of the population has practically nothing.[10]

With only a few qualifications, such as the growth of a small middle class, that description matches life in El Salvador today.

The Oligarchy in the New Balance of Power

The oligarchy is monolithic neither in El Salvador nor in any other Central American country. Since the peasant/worker rebellion and ensuing massacre in 1932, most elements of the country's private elite have been united in the proposition of protecting their privileged position in society. There have always been moderate factions of the oligarchy but the most right-wing forces have been dominant until recently.

Characteristic of the mentality of the country's far-right oligarchies is the Salvadoran Association of Cultivators and Exporters of Coffee (ABECAFE). ABECAFE evoked the memory of General Maximiliano Hernández Martínez (the main perpetrator of the 1932 massacre) to justify the current wave of repression. The coffee growers noted at the outset of the current civil war, that "many years ago one of our rulers understood this very well when he made the Republic's internal security, peace, and order a primary and indispensable condition for the development and prosperity of our country."[11]

For many years, the country's main business organization has been the National Association of Private Business Owners (ANEP). ANEP advocates a free market economy, private control of all the means of production and—like most other Salvadoran business associations—has vigorously opposed land redistribution and other reforms. ANEP scoffs at human rights concerns, contending that the "primary obligation of government . . . is to maintain public order," and charging that El Salvador will "fall into bankruptcy, if we do not move sharply to the right." ANEP's influence has slipped since the start of the civil war because many of its leading members have left the country. The formation of the Productive Alliance, which protested the reformist policies advocated by the Christian Democratic Party and the U.S. embassy in the early 1980s, also diminished the influence of ANEP.

Political parties like the extreme right-wing ARENA depend on the associations for their support and direction. For example, the man who in 1985 replaced Roberto D'Aubuisson as the chief of ARENA was Aldredo Cristiani, one of the largest coffee growers in El Salvador and past head of both the coffee and cotton associations. Following the presidential victory of José Napoleón Duarte in 1984, another right-wing party called Patria Libre (Free Fatherland) formed in an attempt to build a right-wing movement that was not so publicly associated with death-squad operations. The party's international secretary is Alfonso Salaverria, who comes from one of the country's wealthiest coffee clans.

Since 1980, with the formation of a military-civilian junta and the beginning of the civil war, the power of the oligarchy has ebbed but hardly disappeared. The intervention of the United States with its counterinsurgency agenda gave the Christian Democratic Party, long an enemy of the right-wing oligarchs, an opportunity to administer the government. José Napoleón Duarte and the Christian Democrats represented the small urban middle class and those workers and peasants tired of oligarchic power and military repression but unwilling to support an armed overthrow of the system. To gain the support of these sectors and to win international and congressional suport for its counterinsurgency project in El Salvador, Washington backed the Christian Democrats' bid for power and supported a reformist political platform including a land redistribution program. With his campaign financed by Washington, Duarte was elected president in 1984, defeating ARENA's D'Aubuisson. Washington has not shunned the oligarchy, but it has tried to distance the U.S. embassy, the military, and the Salvadoran government from its most right-wing elements.

In 1982, AID created a new business organization, the Salvadoran Development Foundation (FUSADES), to represent those members of the economic elite willing to cooperate with the Reagan Administration's economic and political agenda. FUSADES has become an extra-official planning department for the Duarte government. In accord with the Caribbean Basin Initiative (CBI), FUSADES has given special attention to projects promoting new lines of agroexports.

After its brief experiment with reformism in El Salvador, Washington is again following a policy aimed at strengthening both the military and the oligarchy. It continues to support the "democratization" of the country through periodic elections, but will not permit the participation of political forces that would challenge the dominant positions of the military or the oligarchy—the two elements that Washington oddly regards as the country's strongest partisans of freedom.

Describing the relationship between the oligarchy and the military, a Salvadoran oligarch in 1980 remarked, "We have traditionally bought the military's guns and have paid them to pull the trigger."[12] For the last half century, the military remained faithful to the oligarchy. But the huge sums of U.S. military and economic aid that are flowing to El Salvador have critically affected the balance of national power. The military has grown more independent of the oligarchy in recent years—for the simple reason that the United States now pays the generals to pull the triggers.

The oligarchs, while still exercising considerable power, have themselves grown dependent on U.S. financial backing. Without handouts from Washington, many businesses would go bankrupt and the Salvadoran government would probably crumble. Yet boosted by U.S. economic aid to the private sector and confident that Washington is not going to allow revolutionary forces to succeed, the oligarchy has managed to survive the country's political and economic crises in good form. The institution of the agrarian reform program by the military-civilian junta in 1980 demonstrated the reduced power of the oligarchy; but its ability to bring agrarian reform to an early end in 1983 (see chapter 6) is a recent example of oligarchic muscle-flexing in El Salvador.

Guatemala: The Military Joins the Club

As in El Salvador, the introduction of coffee to Guatemala transformed the agricultural sector and gave birth to a powerful landed oligarchy that included many immigrant families. By the 1920s, nearly 400 foreigners, mostly Germans, commanded more than one half of Guatemala's coffee production while 1000 Guatemalans owned the balance of the coffee *fincas*. As proxy for a small clique of coffee oligarchs, Guatemala was ruled by a succession of dictators until 1944, when General Jorge Ubico was replaced by an elected reformist government.

Militarization of the Oligarchy

The old-line coffee barons who had controlled Guatemala since the late 1800s saw their economic hegemony threatened by a rising class of bankers and entrepreneurs during the reformist government from 1944 to 1954. This new power group, joined by those coffee growers sufficiently business-minded to shed their feudal attitudes, began investing in expanding sectors of the Guatemalan economy such as cotton production. A military coup in 1954 reversed many reformist features of the Arbenz government, which had come to power in 1951. Under Arbenz, peasants no longer had to carry proof of employment; unions were legally allowed to organize; and land reform was instituted. But the economic features of the reformist era—the creation of state ministries to promote export agriculture, the construction of an improved infrastructure, and the encouragement given to business organizations—survived the coup, and in fact laid the groundwork for 25 years of economic growth.

After the coup, Guatemala was ruled almost uninterruptedly by military presidents until early 1986. The influence of the armed forces spread into the country's economic life as well. Individual generals now own so many plantations and cattle ranches in the country's Northern Tranverse Strip that Guatemalans commonly refer to it as the "Zone of Generals". The army now has its own bank, a cement factory, an arms factory and a television station. Military officers live like oligarchs in the capital's military colony, Santa Rosita. ORPA, one of the leading guerrilla groups in the early 1980s, refers to this phenomena as the "militarization of oligarchic power."

Since 1979, with the spread of guerrilla resistance, the military has taken on a yet more dominant role in the civilian/military partnership. Large landholders and business owners back increased militarization, knowing that the security of the state and their own individual survival depend on a strong military. The inability of the army to crush the guerrillas, however, has sparked sharp criticism of the security forces by business moguls.

Families of the Oligarchy

About 50 economically influential families stand at the center of Guatemala's private sector. This oligarchy derives its wealth from diversified sources—commerce, agriculture, industry, and finance. With several hundred members, the families manage five banks and own some 100 of the most productive industrial firms and the largest 100 of the country's 3,000 coffee plantations.[13] Most oligarchs, like the Alejos and Herrera families, that manage large coffee plantations are also deeply involved in the cotton and cattle business.

This economic elite, led by the Kong, García Granados, Sandoval, Alejos, Arana, Herrera, and Zimeri families, accumulates riches behind a masque of terror imposed by the military.[14] Their patriarchs travel in armored cars, usually escorted by a small army of former members of the security forces. "It is as if we were ruled by the Mafia," one Guatemalan politician remarked.[15]

The agroexport sector has maintained an influential position in the operations of the military state. The real power behind the Lucas García regime (1978-82) was the García Granados family, the country's (and reputedly Latin America's) largest cotton producer. Raul García Granados, a relative of former president Lucas García, was also a founder of the country's notorious death squad, *Mano Blanca*, organized in 1966.

As author Thomas Anderson wrote, "the soldiers and landholders arranged the elections of such men as Lucas García and then saw to it that they did not overstay their hour upon the stage." Anderson further comments that "failure to consult the interests of those who control the wealth of the country, especially the export sectors, would bring down a presidency and possibly the system."[16] In 1982, the military high command called for a series of elections, deciding that a civilian government was necessary to attract foreign economic and military aid.

Guatemala's oligarchy voices its concerns through producers' associations and other business groups, the most important of which are CACIF, the main business owners association; Amigos del Pais, a smaller private-sector organization concerned with U.S. policy in Guatemala; and UNAGRO, a powerful organization formed in 1984 that brings together all the major agroexport producers.

In 1985, AID helped form another major association, Camara Empresarial, whose main function is policy analysis and recommendation. This new organization stresses the need to develop new agroexports as well as supporting AID's overall economic and political program for the country. As in El Salvador, the creation of this new business association has caused some division within the private-sector elite, but the flow of U.S. economic assistance to Camara Empresarial gives it a power beyond its membership. Guatemala's oligarchy also maintains close ties with influential foreign companies operating in the country through the American Chamber of Commerce in Guatemala, which has in the recent past expressed its unreserved support for the repressive tactics of the army.

Since the 1954 coup, a strong national security state has evolved in Guatemala. According to the British Parliament's Human Rights Commission, government forces have killed some 100,000 people since 1954. While there are disputes between the private sector and the military—primarily over the armed forces' desire to raise taxes—the entire oligarchy, from the traditional *latifundistas* to the country's powerful industrialists, has backed the military's savage handling of domestic human rights issues. This fusion of interests has created a powerful national power structure that will make the peaceful imposition of agrarian and economic reforms in Guatemala all but impossible.

Disappointingly, the election of Christian Democrat Vinicio Cerezo in 1986 portends no signs of changing the oligarchic power structure. His financial advisers are members of the business elite, and the new president consults closely with this elite group before announcing his economic policies. President Cerezo has refused to discuss an agrarian reform program that would expropriate private land, and has continued government support for the military's campaign to crush the guerrilla army and control the Indian population through such pacification programs as "development poles" and "model villages."

Honduras: The Subordinate Ruling Class

The oligarchy in Honduras never developed in the mold of the elites in Guatemala and El Salvador. The country was ignored by Spanish colonizers, and not until recently has it developed a national ruling class. Lacking a broad class of entrepreneurs, Honduras did not experience the 19th century coffee boom that modernized agricultural production and created oligarchic wealth elsewhere in Central America. The local economy's growth was further stymied by direct U.S. investment in the banana and mining industries, to a degree surpassing investment levels in other countries of the region.[17] As a result, the country's oligarchy, until recently, remained a weak economic class of traditional *latifundistas*, who grazed cattle and sharecropped their landholdings.

When the U.S. banana companies set up their enclaves on the Atlantic coast, they moved into a void left by the lack of a strong national elite. The companies quickly dominated the economy. They also became occasional kingmakers in national politics. The formation of service, finance, and manufacturing subsidiaries by the banana companies further impeded the development of an independent national bourgeoisie.

The Honduran economy did not begin to diversify until after 1950. For the first time, a national agroexport sector (including coffee growers) emerged. An industrial elite sprang up in San Pedro Sula, and a small middle class appeared in the urban areas of both Tegucigalpa and San Pedro Sula. Many immigrants from the Middle East—collectively labeled *turcos*, or "Turks"—became prominent members of the modern oligarchy in Honduras.

While the middle class was growing, a peasant and labor movement was also beginning to stir. Spurred on by the success of a 1954 general strike against the banana companies, peasants and workers throughout the country organized unions and rural associations. The lack of a united oligarchy allowed rural and labor organizations in Honduras to become sophisticated players on the national political scene. Today, these popular organizations are a strong force, modifying the power of the landed oligarchy and the military.

The year 1954 also marked the institutionalization of the Honduran military's role in national politics. A few days after the 1954 banana strike began, the character of the Honduran armed forces began changing, as a result of a military assistance agreement the government in Tegucigalpa signed with the United States. The country's first infantry battalion was placed under direct U.S. supervision, and the entire army modeled itself after its U.S. counterpart, in everything from style of uniform to rank and command structure.

The agreement with the Pentagon helped modernize, centralize and professionalize the Honduran military, which ran the government almost uninterruptedly for 30 years until 1982, when a civilian, Roberto Suazo Córdova, assumed official control. However, despite the presence of a civilian in the National Palace, the military has continued to play a leading role in the country's political life.[18] Because the capitalist class is relatively weak, the military has not been as beholden to the oligarchy as it has been in neighboring countries. This situation has enabled it to serve as an arbiter of last resort in disputes that set workers and peasants against business interests and political parties. Another indication of the independence of the military's Superior Council is that the military is not even constitutionally subservient to the civilian government.

During his campaign, rancher Suazo Córdova had promised to enforce the 1975 land reform program, a move vigorously opposed by the Honduran oligarchy's two main business associations, the National Association of Growers and Cattlemen (FENAGH) and the Council of Private Businesses (COHEP). Campesinos, hoping that the new civilian

ruler would made good on his land reform promise, were to be dis-
appointed when the president scuttled the plans for a full and rapid
implementation of the program. In 1986, José Azcona del Hoyo became
Honduras' second elected civilian president, but once again pressure from
FENAGH and COHEP has obstructed the land redistribution program.
Ranchers associated with FENAGH have taken it into their own hands to
violently attack peasants who have attempted to farm idle private lands.

Power in the 1980s

The main actors in Honduras' present power structure are the oligarchy,
the military, and the political parties. While less developed than its
counterparts in El Salvador and Guatemala, the nation's oligarchy still
exercises control over government policy affecting its varied economic
interests. This power structure includes traditional *latifundistas*, an agrarian
bourgeoisie, and a small group of industrialists based in San Pedro Sula.

For the most part, the military stands outside national economic life,
unlike in Guatemala where it has developed its own extensive economic
interests. Although it no longer occupies the National Palace, the military
high command remains, nonetheless, the ultimate national source of power
in Honduras. Unlike El Salvador and Guatemala, where the landed elite
and the military have been closely linked, the military has populist
aspirations and occasionally backs measures demanded by the country's
peasants and workers. In the absence of a strong national elite, the military
thinks of itself as the guardian of the collective interests of the nation. This
assumed role, however, has not stopped the military from jailing hundreds
of peasant leaders (at the behest of the large landowners) and repressing
leftist dissidents. As a rule, the military has been flexible in its exercise of
power, trying to coopt rather than crush popular movements. Unlike its
neighbors, though, the Honduran military and oligarchy have not yet been
confronted by a truly threatening, militant peasant movement. In such an
event, the iron fist will probably come down as hard as it already has in
Guatemala, El Salvador, and in Somoza's Nicaragua.

The power and independence of the oligarchy, the military, and the
political parties are prescribed by and contingent upon the pervasive U.S.
presence in the country. The banana giants—United Brands and Castle &
Cooke—are the most prominent foreign actors in the Honduran economy
and politics. These two companies, as the U.S. embassy's commercial
attaché in Teguicigalpa acknowledged, "have their hands into just about
everything in this country."[19]

U.S. economic power, however, extends far beyond the banana
enclaves. The country's five largest firms are wholly owned subsidiaries of

U.S. corporations. So dominant is the U.S. in the Honduran economy and politics that many Honduran scholars believe that a national state has never been able to coalesce in Honduras.[20] The recent U.S.-sponsored militarization of Honduras and the flood of U.S. economic aid into the country has made the Honduran elite still more dependent on the United States.

In the last several years, AID has supported a phalanx primarily of new business associations, almost all of which aim to promote agroexport production or export-oriented manufacturing. One AID-funded group, ANDI, published a full-page ad in a San Pedro Sula paper in 1985 criticizing a strike by Standard Fruit banana workers. ANDI said the striking workers were "threatening the investment climate" and "putting in danger the country's productive units, which are key to the nation's exports."[21] With a little help from their friends, Honduras' agroexporters thus remain an endemic obstacle to social and economic change in Central America's most impoverished nation.

Costa Rica: The Subdued Elite

With its stable democratic government, solid system of social services, and relatively large middle class, Costa Rica has long been considered the exception to every generalization about Central America. But the country's pattern of rural development in many ways parallels that of the troubled nations to its north; and it may yet face similar turmoil.

During the 17th and 18th centuries, family farms, rather than *latifundios*, dominated Costa Rica, and the colony closely resembled the type of rural democracy later advocated in the United States by Thomas Jefferson. There was no large native population, forcing Spanish settlers to limit the size of their holdings to what they could work themselves. Most of the Spanish settlers in this neglected part of Central America were not aristocrats, but rather, common people. In Costa Rica, even the governor of the territory worked his own land. The presence of many yeoman farmers and the absence of forced labor during the colonial epoch largely explain Costa Rica's democratic development.

The rise of coffee production in Costa Rica in the 1820s is characterized by scholar Mitchell Seligson as "the aristocracy's salvation and the peasantry's ruin."[22] The coffee boom dramatically altered what had been a nation of yeoman farmers. The high cost of labor was a main factor in the growth of land concentration. High wages enticed many small farmers to abandon their plots in favor of working as laborers at larger farms, since a small farmer had to cultivate more than 20 acres to maintain the standard of living enjoyed by a wage laborer. Good accessible coffee land was scarce, and therefore expensive, so many small farmers either sold their plots to larger growers or lost them when they were unable to meet their credit payments. And while medium-sized farms played a central role in coffee production, distinguishing Costa Rica from El Salvador and Guatemala, seven of ten rural families in this land of "small farmers and democrats" were landless by the late 1800s. Even so, the sector of family farms in Costa Rica has remained proportionately larger than in other Central American nations.

Costa Rica did develop a coffee oligarchy, although it was never as powerful nor as tied to feudalistic structures as elsewhere in the region. It is a diversified elite based more on local processing in *beneficios* and trading operations than on large estates. From its inception as a nation, the economic elite included a local class of merchants and growers—another circumstance that distinguished it from other Central American countries.[23]

Dynasty of the Conquerors

Although its history is more peaceful and democratic than that of its neighbors, Costa Rica shares the burden of having been politically dominated by a small number of families. Thirty-three of the 44 people who served as president of the country between 1821 and 1970 were descendants of three original settlers, and one family—that of conqueror Juan Vasquez de Coronado—produced 18 presidents and 230 national assembly representatives.[24]

In 1948, social democratic forces led by José Figueres won a 40-day civil war forming a new government that adhered to many of the principles of liberal capitalism. The social democrats ousted a government that had made stategic alliances with the country's communist party and its powerful labor unions. The new government headed by the National Liberation Party (PLN), a coalition of the middle and upper classes headed by a forward-looking faction of the oligarchy, outlawed the communist parties and dissolved the communist unions, thereby breaking the back of the country's labor movement which was based in the banana plantations. The Figueres government, boosted by the high coffee prices of the 1950s, ushered in an era of economic modernization by building infrastructure needed for new agroexport and industrial investment and by laying the groundwork for the country's extensive system of public education and social services.

As elsewhere in Central America, Costa Rican coffee barons were forced to make room after 1950 for other agroexporters and a new class of industrialists. In the last 30 years, land ownership has become increasingly concentrated due to the new agroexport boom and the arrival of individual

U.S. investors and land speculators. While large coffee producers and exporters no longer directly control politics in Costa Rica, they retain (along with the cattle ranchers) a firm grip on the agrarian economy.

In contrast to the oligarchies of other Central American nations, the Costa Rican elite has responded to peasant and worker demands with more than repression, tempering its acquisitive nature with reformism and social welfare programs. Through these reforms, the country's oligarchy has managed to conserve and expand its political and economic power by keeping the middle class and portions of the working class pacified. The absence, until recently, of a centralized and well-equipped military has also meant that class tensions have not led to the violent repression common in other agroexport nations. A well-developed government bureaucracy has helped to blunt the raw power of the economic elite, but this political bureaucracy is still subservient to the oligarchic class.

In his study, *Pressure Groups in Costa Rica*, Oscar Arias Sanchez noted that powerful organizations like the National Association for Economic Development and the National Chamber of Coffee Producers mold public opinion and direct legislation. "We shouldn't fool ourselves." he warned, "Public opinion is nothing more than the private opinion of those who have the power to disseminate it."[25]

The government apparatus controlled by the major political parties is not tied to one economic sector but instead represents the collective interests of both the rural and urban bourgeoisie. Called the "new oligarchy" by one Costa Rican sociologist, the political managers of the government bureaucracy have displaced the old "*caudillos*" (charismatic leaders). To gain the favor of the economic elite, they channel government resources and international loan money to the industrial and agrarian magnates.[26]

There is a superficial quality about democracy in Costa Rica. The two political parties—the PLN and the Unity Party—receive virtually all their funds from the country's economic elite. In their campaigns, both parties promise to improve the lot of the middle class, workers, and peasants but once in power invariably carry out a program designed in the interests of the oligarchy. Neither party counts on a strong social organization but simply rallies popular support around election time. When the populace gets tired of the "liberationists," they vote in the "anti-liberationists" of the opposition party; and so it goes, back and forth, in Costa Rican politics, with the oligarchic interests always on top.

Workers and peasants have been completely left out of the political process. While both parties have been careful to keep the middle class tranquilized with public-sector jobs, housing projects, and other government benefits, the needs of workers and peasants have been largely ignored. The oligarchy in Costa Rica has, for example, prevented the adoption of a strong labor code and a substantive agrarian reform program.

A new force in Costa Rica is the powerful private-sector organization, Coalition of Initiatives for Development (CINDE), which was recently formed with AID funds. AID is channeling most of its aid to agribusiness and other export-oriented investment through CINDE, which it calls a "one-stop investment center." Through CINDE, AID is pushing the Costa Rican government to "privatize" government corporations and increase incentives for agroexporters. The National Patriotic Committee (COPAN), a consumer organization, complains that CINDE serves as an unofficial economic planning ministry representing the interests of the right-wing and the economic elite.

As the economic crisis worsens and regional conflicts build, the political bureaucracy grows more aligned with the interests of the agrarian and industrial capitalists. Cutbacks in social services, the reduction of government price subsidies, and currency devaluations have hit workers and peasants hard. Austerity measures are also reducing the standard of living for the country's relatively large middle class.

Economic hard times are aggravated by a sharpening of the political climate mainly as a result of U.S. intervention in the region. Since 1980, Costa Rica has become increasingly militarized. The country's two police forces have been centralized under one command and are now receiving U.S. military aid and training. Several paramilitary forces have formed including the Organization for National Emergencies (OPEN) which operates under government auspices as a right-wing civil defense force. If these trends continue, they may leave Costa Rica ripe for the kind of repression and polarization experienced by other Central American countries.

Nicaragua: An End to Oligarchy

In 1979, oligarchic power in Central America received a strong blow when the FSLN guerrillas (or Sandinistas) toppled the region's number one oligarch: Anastasio Somoza. The overthrow of Somoza was one more portent of the inevitable collapse of oligarchic control in Central America.

The weaknesses that led to the fall of the Somoza dictatorship— concentrated economic power, repressive political control, and a dispossessed rural majority—are also present in other nations of the isthmus. But there were differences that made the oligarchy in Nicaragua particularly vulnerable to popular revolution. In Nicaragua, oligarchic power was personified in one family and its corrupt control of government angered even other factions of the oligrachy, creating the conditions for an unusual anti-government alliance among most economic and social sectors. Oligarchic power in other Central American countries is more diffuse and not quite so closely identified with corruption and violations of human rights.

The Somoza clan exercised absolute control over politics and government and was the country's largest landowner and investor. But the Somoza clan did not monopolize the economy. Factions of the oligarchy were tied to each of the two largest private banks: Banco de Nicaragua (BANIC) and Banco de America (Banamerica). These two groups, which emerged in the 1950s and 1960s drew their strength from new agroexport production and manufacturing industries, and accounted for nearly 20 percent of the country's gross national product. The BANIC and Banamerica groups were coalitions of businesses and families formed as a defensive response to the Somoza clan's unrelenting aggrandizement and political control.[27]

Besides these three elements of oligarchic power in Nicaragua—the Somoza clan and the BANIC and Banamerica groups—another faction of the business elite coalesced around the Superior Council of Private Enterprise (COSEP) in the 1960s. This was an umbrella organization of the country's various business and agricultural groups. It represented the middle bourgeoisie and those individual oligarchs not already incorporated into the three major clusters. It was this group that was cultivated by Washington through the Agency for International Development (AID) as the best-suited successor to the Somoza dynasty. Many members of COSEP considered themselves reformers. They advocated political and capitalistic economic reforms that would improve their own standing as well as forestall a leftist revolution.

After the 1972 earthquake, a broad non-violent opposition movement began to form in Nicaragua. The middle and upper classes were indignant at Somoza's embezzlement of relief and reconstruction funds. Two opposition coalitions formed—the Democratic Liberation Union (UDEL) and its successor the Broad Liberation Front (FAO)—to challenge the Somoza dictatorship. The 1978 assassination of anti-Somoza newspaper publisher Pedro Joaquin Chamorro catalysed new opposition to the regime among the upper class. Although wary of the Sandinistas, the bourgeois opposition led by figures associated with COSEP began supporting the guerrillas as a way to get rid of Somoza.

Soon after the Sandinistas marched into Managua, the economic base of the oligarchy was dismantled. The new government expropriated the property of Somoza and his associates and nationalized the BANIC and Banamerica. These measures were expected even by bourgeois members of the anti-Somoza opposition as part of the spoils of the civil war. COSEP disaffection with the FSLN grew, however, as the victors also nationalized the import/export trade and made it clear that the bourgeoisie could not expect a major political role in the revolutionary government. The Sandinistas insisted that the revolution they led was going much further than removing the country's patriarchial oligarch from power merely to facilitate COSEP filling the void. As FSLN founder Carlos Fonseca had written in the 1960s, "The question is not only to bring about a change of the man in power, but to overthrow the exploiting class and achieve the victory of the exploited."[28]

Counterrevolutionary sentiment budded in the business community in the year after the Sandinistas' triumph. The FSLN directorate promised to maintain a mixed economy of public and private-sector business, but many COSEP members demanded a stronger voice in determining economic policy and a more influential political position in general in the new society. In 1980, Jorge Salazar, the vice-president of COSEP and the head of the Union of Nicaraguan Growers joined a counterrevolutionary plot to topple the Sandinistas. Learning about the anti-government conspiracy, secret police killed Salazar during a police stake-out. Since then, a steady trail of Nicarguan growers and businessmen have left Nicaragua to lend their support to the contras. All three directors of the political directorate of the armed counterrevolution—Alfonso Robelo, Arturo Cruz, and Adolfo Calero—come from the country's economic elite.

Inside Nicaragua, COSEP, along with the Catholic Church hierarchy, has been a center of anti-Sandinista sentiment since 1980. Jorge Salazar is hailed by COSEP as a martyr for democracy and capitalism. Policy blunders on the part of government ministries have increased the disaffection of large producers with the revolution. The main reason for the bourgeois opposition, however, has been the Sandinistas' commitment to popular welfare over narrow business interests. Feeling politically and economically upstaged, even though they continue to control most agroexport production, most large businessmen and growers have refused to make new investments and have slackened production in order to stagnate the economy and create popular discontent.

It is the apparent hope of COSEP members that this popular discontent will grow into an anti-Sandinista movement that they will be able to control. Over the border, the U.S.-financed contras also hope to capitalize on popular dissatisfaction with the economy. They reason that Nicaraguans will tire of the endless pressures of their besieged struggle to survive, thus providing less resistance to the counterrevolutionary drive to reinstate oligarchic power in Nicaragua.

State of the Oligarchy

Despite diversification of agriculture and the move toward industrialization in Central America over the past several decades, the essential nature of oligarchic control has changed very little. The traditional elite has not disappeared; it has adapted. The semifeudal estates evolved into modern agribusinesses, and the landed oligarchs joined with merchants and the dependent bourgeois to form an integrated modern oligarchy. While adapting to global capitalism, the oligarchy has filtered the new developments through its own repressive and anti-democratic style of social and political domination.

In recent years, the position of the agroexport elite has been bolstered by the policies of the International Monetary Fund (IMF) and AID. The IMF and AID have stepped up the pressure on Central American countries to produce more exports that will earn foreign exchange, in order to pay back foreign debts, further exacerbating the spiral of oligarchic oppression.

As oligarchic control continues in Central America, the land and hunger issues become ever more serious. The oligarchy has teamed up with the military and has received the backing of the United States in confronting popular challenges to its essential power. The election of civilians in Guatemala, Honduras, and El Salvador has done little or nothing to reduce the economic and political power of the oligarchy. In Costa Rica, the elite has grown more resistant to popular pressure in the face of economic hard times, and its interests are now backed by stronger security forces. The ouster of Somoza was a severe blow to oligarchic power in the region, and only in Nicaragua are the issues of agrarian reform and food security being seriously addressed. But backed by the United States, the reactionary despotism of the Somoza era threatens to reassert itself. As long as the narrow interests of the oligarchy prevail in Central America, broad national development will lose out to exploitation, and social progress will be sacrificed on the altar of stability and social order.

Chapter Four
International Connections

By retaining a tight grip on global marketing and financing, transnational corporations retain the power to determine the conditions under which raw materials are supplied and priced.
            —John Cavanagh and Frederick Clairmonte,
                                    The Transnational Economy

Central Americans from the barefoot canecutter to the smartly dressed coffee oligarch are part of the network called agribusiness. Agribusiness, a term coined by Dr. Ray Goldberg of the Harvard Business School, is the seed-to-customer chain that links the peasants of Central America to the World Trade Towers in New York City.

This three-part chain actually starts before a single seed is planted, with what is known as the pre-production phase. Seeds, pesticides, and farm equipment are acquired, genetic research carried out, and financing arranged. Actual farming and harvesting make up the production phase, while the processing, shipping, insuring, trading, and retailing of the finished product constitute the post-production phase. Control over this world-wide agricultural network rests primarily with transnational corporations (TNCs). TNCs, also called multinational corporations, are companies with either assets or production facilities in more than one country.

Historically, foreign investors in Central America have operated under the protection of their home governments. When a loan was not being repaid on time or if a government took measures that threatened the profits of investors, foreign governments often used their military or economic clout to force a settlement favorable to the financier or investor. Although Washington no longer sends in the Marines when U.S. investors complain, corporations can still count on the U.S. government to stand up for their interests abroad. Washington does this by threatening to withhold aid to foreign countries, refusing to sign international commodity agreements that do not benefit U.S. TNCs, and by using its economic and military assistance programs as leverage to ensure that other governments adopt trade and investment policies conducive to U.S. corporations.

Bananas: The Fruit that gave TNCs a Bad Name

From behind his desk at the American Chamber of Commerce in Guatemala City, Chamber director Cecil Wilson says, "United Fruit developed this country. It did many truly great things for Guatemala. I know, because I worked for the company for many years."[2]

In the center of the country's fruit growing region, a hundred miles from Guatemala City, sits a town whose very name signals the local reality. But almost 80 years after its founding, Bananera still lacks paved roads, sewers, and proper housing. Workers leave dilapidated wooden homes each morning for the old railroad station, where they board trains bound for the banana plantations now owned by Del Monte—which bought United Fruit's Guatemalan holdings in 1972.

Across the street from the station, a 20-foot white concrete wall blocks off a section of Bananera most residents have never seen. Guards stand at the gate protecting "barrio gringo," the separate domain of company officials, replete with manicured lawns, luxurious two-story homes, tennis courts, baseball fields, and swimming pools.

TNC Tentacles

In the last few decades, the TNCs have come to dominate most branches of agribusiness. They have created oligopolies in all three parts of the agribusiness chain. An oligopoly occurs when capital concentration in an industry has reached a point where the sector is dominated by a few very large corporations. Through their economic and political powers, these giant corporations can determine output and prices.

In Central America, TNCs focus on the pre- and post-production phases of agribusiness, leaving most of the actual farming to local growers. Only in the production of bananas, beef, and nontraditional crops (like winter vegetables and flowers) is there substantial foreign investment in the direct production of agroexports.

Low profit margins and high risks account for the relative absence of TNCs in the on-site production of export crops like cotton, coffee, and sugar. The TNCs have found that they can effectively control the production phase through contracting arrangements as well as through their dominance of the pre- and post-production phases. TNCs like General Foods and Nestle have become giant food corporations without owning a single cocoa or coffee plantation.

Because of this control of agribusiness, the TNCs grab a disproportionate share of the income from agroexport production. Of every $100 consumers spend on tropical products in their final form, agroexport countries get only $15.[1] The $85 balance goes mainly to the TNCs like Monsanto and John Deere that sell agricultural inputs, ones like Sea-Land and Coordinated Caribbean Transport (Transway) that control shipping, companies like Cargill and Volkart that handle most world commodity trade, corporations like General Foods and RJ Reynolds that process and distribute the commodities, and finally those like Safeway that market the goods.

* Six TNCs control 60 percent of world coffee sales.

* Three TNCs control 75 percent of world banana sales.

* Fifteen TNC traders control 90 percent of world cotton sales.

* Four TNC traders control more than half the world's sugar sales.

* Two TNCs control more than half the world's wheat trade.

* Two TNCs control more than half the world's production of farm machinery.

* Eighteen of the top 25 U.S. food processing companies do business in Central America.

Banana Style Development

In an attempt to entice U.S. investment in the early days of large-scale banana production in Central America, the region's governments granted economic and development rights to United Fruit and Standard Fruit. These rights, known as concessions, helped the banana companies build an empire from Guatemala to Panama.

A typical example is that of Honduras, where United Fruit was granted the right "to engage in all the businesses conducted by entrepreneurs engaged in shipping, by land and sea; planters; farmers; traders; contractors; importers and exporters; dock supervisors or any other business which may increase the value of its properties." The contract allowed the company to operate "railways, wharves, bridges, viaducts, telegraph and telephone lines, and telegraph stations."[3] Once United Fruit controlled the transportation and communication system, it could effectively discourage competition from local growers.

During the first half of the century, the power of the banana *pulpos* went unchallenged by either governments or unions. Lords of corporate fiefdoms, company managers ran their banana plantations and assorted subsidiary businesses without concern for the internal development needs of their host countries. The *pulpos* built roads and railways from company town to company plantations while the rest of the country did without paved roads and rail transportation.

A letter written by a United Fruit official during that time set forth company objectives in Honduras:

* To obtain implacable contracts in order to avoid competition from other firms and/or to overrule them and make them receptive to the rules laid down.

* To impose the commercial philosophy of the firm on the country and, in particular, to make use of its unscrupulous political leaders by offering them posts and titles.

* In general, all the corporation's strategies must strengthen its power and further its progress, impose its discipline and methods of work, but at the same time it must operate in such a way as not to expose its ambitions for dominance.[4]

In Guatemala, United Fruit's control of banana production on the Pacific coast was based on a 1936 contract signed with dictator Jorge Ubico, a man the company had previously encouraged the Guatemalan oligarchy to support for president. The prestigious Washington law firm, Sullivan and Cromwell (whose executive partners included future CIA director Allen Dulles and future Secretary of State John Foster Dulles), negotiated the deal. In the grand giveaway style of these early banana contracts, Guatemala granted United Fruit a 99-year lease to vast expanses of land and exempted it from virtually all taxes and duties. [5]

Banana Companies Go Modern

The 1950s were tumultuous years for the banana companies and the producing countries. In the early part of the decade, the administration of President Jacobo Arbenz of Guatemala became the first Central American government to confront United Fruit. The Arbenz government objected to the company's control of Guatemala's major port and its only railroad, and began building a highway that would reduce the importance of the railroad. As part of its agrarian reform program, the Arbenz government nationalized and then redistributed 100,000 acres of idle company land.

United Fruit responded by lobbying the Eisenhower administration to overthrow the Arbenz government, which had been democratically elected. The company also mounted a cold-war publicity campaign against the Arbenz government, highlighted by the film *Why the Kremlin Loves Bananas*—which linked the expropriation of company lands in Guatemala to the "evils of Communism." The movie, described later by a United Fruit executive as "the Disney version of the episode," was produced by the company's chief public relations officer, whose wife served as President Eisenhower's private secretary. The campaign worked. A CIA-directed coup in 1954 threw Arbenz out of office and replaced him with a right-wing military officer, who quickly returned the expropriated lands to United Fruit.

But United Fruit faced other threats to its banana empire elsewhere in Central America, including the successful 1954 strike in Honduras against both United Fruit and Standard Fruit. Despite intervention by the Honduran military on behalf of the companies, the workers held firm and won important concessions, including the recognition of their right to organize a union. About the same time, Costa Rican workers struck United Fruit after the company fired more than 100 workers for taking part in a May Day demonstration. The Rural Guard declared a state of siege in the banana region and proceeded to crush the Costa Rican strike.

Deciding that the old style of business had grown too risky, the banana corporations began to remodel the banana enclaves in the late 1950s. Besides selling off much of their land, they moved to reduce their risk by adopting new labor policies and production strategies. They started cooperating with moderate labor unions, and enlisted the help of the Inter-American Regional Labor Organization (ORIT) and its successor the American Institute for Free Labor Development (AIFLD) to train

The Top Bananas

United Brands

United Fruit became part of a new corporation, United Brands, in 1969. The company is one of the world's largest producers, processors, and distributors of food products. United Brands produces Chiquita brand bananas in Panama, Costa Rica, and Honduras. Its other activities in Central America include telecommunications, meat exporting, transport, and data services. For the regional market it produces beer, vegetable oil, processed fruits, plastic, and boxes. In the United States, United Brands ranks number two in the banana industry, number three in meat packing, and number seven in food processing, and is the 92nd largest US corporation.

Castle and Cooke

Founded in 1851 in Hawaii, Castle and Cooke's banana operations are managed by its subsidiary Standard Fruit, whose brand name is Dole. Specializing in agribusiness, the company also owns breweries, pineapple and African palm plantations, a canning company, banks, shipping and transport operations, and factories that produce soap, plastic and boxes. Standard Fruit has plantations in Honduras, Costa Rica, and (until 1983) Nicaragua. The largest banana company in the United States, the third largest tuna company, and the top pineapple firm, Castle and Cooke ranks number 343 in the list of top US corporations.

RJ Reynolds

The largest US tobacco company, RJ Reynolds is also well known for its Del Monte food subsidiary. Del Monte produces bananas primarily in Costa Rica and Guatemala and in 1984, entered into an agreement with the Honduran government to produce bananas with local growers. Other Central American operations include shipping and vegetable canning. Del Monte is the number one U.S. manufacturer of canned fruits and vegetables. Although it is the smallest of the Central American banana companies, RJ Reynolds ranks far ahead of the other two in overall sales. In 1984, it was the nation's 32nd largest corporation. Its 1985 acquisition of another food behemoth, Nabisco Brands, made it the largest food and consumer-products corporation in the United States.

and pay the labor organizers. The companies also dramatically reduced their workforces: in the early 1950s, the banana companies employed about 70,000 workers in Central America, but today only about half that number work for the TNC banana growers.[6]

Meanwhile, with the help of mechanization, the use of herbicides, and the development of better strains of banana plants, the TNCs boosted profits by making production more efficient. Productivity per worker has increased four-fold over the past two decades, and the companies have almost tripled their banana production per acre. This increased productivity has not, however, led to corresponding increases in wage rates. The wages of those still working on the banana plantations have barely kept up with inflation, let alone reflected the increase in worker productivity.[7]

The banana companies also began reducing their risks by diversifying into cattle, pineapples, and African palms (to produce vegetable oil). In addition, the banana TNCs have expanded their investment in food processing for the regional market.[8]

Contracting Associate Producers

The principal change in the banana enclave has been the gradual switch to contract farmers, called "associate producers" by the companies. When the banana companies began selling their lands, they sought out small farmers to buy them. The companies then contracted with these "associate producers" to grow bananas. More recently, the banana companies have been turning banana lands over to state companies, which then sell the fruit back to the TNCs.

United Fruit began contracting associate producers in the 1950s by leasing 45-acre sections to selected employees it called "old faithfuls." United Fruit, and later Standard Fruit, exercised careful control over these associates. Each year, the companies set the volume of production, the quality, the time of delivery, and the price they would pay for the bananas. The contracts specified that associate producers could neither increase nor diminish their banana crop without company authorization, and they were not permitted to sell their land.

The arrangement was ideal for the TNCs. It allowed them to foist off most of the risk of banana production: If a hurricane were to strike, the local producers would suffer the losses more than the TNCs.[9] Not only could the TNCs count on a certain quantity and quality of bananas from the producers every year without risking anything themselves, they also benefited from their position as the suppliers of credit and pesticides to the producers. And the move toward associate producers was a smart one politically, because by turning over some of the production to local growers, the TNCs reduced the pressure for more national control over the banana enclaves. Most importantly, the contract arrangement meant the *pulpos* had no local labor problems to contend with.

Explaining the trend toward associate producers, an official of Standard Fruit in Costa Rica said: "Standard is not very interested in having its own production since the costs of production increase day by day." He added that damage from hurricanes, tree disease, and flooding also "encouraged Standard to quit cultivation in certain areas and leave it in the hands of Costa Ricans."[10]

In Central America, the TNCs' associate producers now account for about one-third of the banana production of the three corporations.[11] Yet, even with more land in the hands of associate producers, the banana TNCs remain the region's largest private landholders.

The Producers Take On the TNCs

In the early 1970s, skyrocketing oil prices hit the Central American nations hard. The value of their own exports, especially bananas, stayed at the same low level. Inspired by the success of the Organization of Petroleum Exporting Countries (OPEC), the banana producing nations of Central America, along with Colombia, formed the Union of Banana Exporting Countries (UPEB) in 1974 and a marketing organization called Comunbana in 1977.

Until the 1973 founding of UPEB, the transnational companies paid only one or two cents tax on each box of bananas exported. They paid no import, property, or income taxes at all. The countries of the nascent UPEB agreed to push for a $1 export tax on each 40-pound box of bananas.

The TNCs flatly refused to discuss a price-fixing plan, rejected UPEB's demand for a $1 export tax, and threatened to close down or substantially reduce operations in any country that imposed the higher taxes. Fear of the *pulpos* caused the Central American nations to back down. A typical showdown occurred in Costa Rica, which went ahead and implemented a $1 per box tax, only to reduce it to 25 cents shortly after Standard Fruit threatened to leave the country.

With producing countries still trying to impose higher taxes and the TNCs still resisting, a turning point emerged. In 1975, shortly after United Brands president Eli Black committed suicide by jumping from the 44th story of New York City's Pan American Building, federal investigators discovered that he had authorized a $1.25 million bribe to the Honduran government to ensure that the country would not levy the proposed export tax. Honduran President Oswaldo López Arellano resigned due to the controversy.

Table 10

Bananas are Big Business

Just three TNCs—United Brands (United Fruit), Castle and Cooke (Standard Fruit), and RJ Reynolds (Del Monte)—control 90 percent of the region's banana production and virtually all marketing of the fruit.[12] United Brands counts on the region for over 60 percent of its bananas.[13] These three conglomerates supply 60 percent of the world banana market and 90 percent of the US market.

Bananas make big money for big corporations. For United Brands, bananas—the fruit Chiquita made famous—are 5 times as profitable as other food sales. For RJ Reynolds, bananas account for only 7 percent of corporate sales but 17 percent of profits.

Domination of World and US Markets By Banana TNCs

	% of World Market	% of US Market
United Brands	28	36
Castle and Cooke	21	38
Del Monte	12	17
Combined Control by 3 TNCs	61	91

Source: CEPAL, "Bargaining Postion in the Banana Industry," 1982

The affair, which came to be known as "Bananagate," forced the companies to lift their pressure on the banana countries. Prices paid to small growers went up, and new taxes were imposed. While they didn't reach their collective goal of $1 per box, the producing countries nonetheless enjoyed a tremendous jump in revenues. Earnings within the region from banana export taxes increased from $1 million in 1972 to $80 million by 1980.[14]

In the early 1980s, the transnationals again took the offensive. When storms in 1982 curtailed production, the TNCs demanded a sharp reduction in export taxes. After lowering the taxes, the Central American countries discovered that company profits were in fact booming. Renewed corporate threats and the closure of a few banana plantations, however, persuaded the banana-producing nations to make new concessions to the TNCs. In recent years, Central American countries have bowed to company pressures and substantially lowered taxes, in some cases eliminating them altogether. Today the countries are in a position not much better than when they founded UPEB more than a decade ago.

Nicaragua is the only country operating independent of the banana TNCs. The Sandinista government negotiated an agreement with Standard Fruit in 1980 whereby the company would buy all the country's bananas. But one day in 1982 the company unilaterally broke the contract. When Nicaragua found an alternative outlet in the United States, Standard argued that Nicaragua was upsetting the market. The 1985 trade embargo against Nicaragua forced the country to find new markets in Europe.

The Banana Republics of the 1980s

The Kissinger Commission report on Central America, issued in January 1984, noted that while United Fruit once had an "ugly American" image, the company "is widely regarded as both a model citizen and model employer." But while economic diversification in Central America over the last several decades may have reduced the dominance of the banana TNCs and somewhat limited their arrogance, it remains difficult to consider them model citizens. They constantly threaten to withdraw their operations whenever asked to pay higher taxes or wages—and when they do conceed to higher taxes, they turn the situation to their advantage by passing on disproportional price increases to banana consumers.

Neither do the banana workers and their unions consider the banana TNCs to be model citizens. In Costa Rica, two striking workers at a United Brands plantation were killed by the police which the company had ordered in to break up the strike. In Honduras, the banana companies have teamed up with the government and AIFLD (the U.S.-financed labor organization for Latin America) to break up the progressive unions. In one case, Standard Fruit agreed to keep a plantation open only if the union disbanded, which it did in an arrangement sponsored by AIFLD.

And the region derives meager benefits from the presence of these model citizens. Bananas undergo little processing after they leave the packing sheds of Central America, meaning that there are less jobs available and no spin-off industries. Of the retail price in consuming nations, only 14 percent is returned to Central America—mostly in the form of wages and taxes.

The remaining 86 percent goes to the foreign corporations that grow, ship, ripen, distribute, and retail the bananas.[15] Shipping companies alone (subsidiaries of the banana TNCs) charge as much to transport the bananas to U.S. docks as the entire economic benefit of the fruit to the isthmus. The TNCs claim that the relatively simple process of ripening also costs more than the entire production process in Central America.

UPEB still hopes to impose a $1 per box tax and to expand its marketing agency, Comunbana, which sells bananas directly to foreign markets without any TNC involvement. The association is lobbying within the United Nations for a World Banana Agreement that would impose an import quota system in the principal consumer nations. Such a system would theoretically make producing nations less vulnerable to threats that the companies will shut down or cut back production. Given the opposition to the scheme by TNCs and the United States (which imports 80 percent of UPEB bananas), there is virtually no hope that an international banana agreement will be reached.

There remain many obstacles to a more beneficial relationship between banana TNCs and producing countries, including the lack of unity among the banana producers themselves. The producers also need some sort of international backing for their demands, but that support would appear to be hard to come by given the trends toward protectionism and competitiveness in world affairs. The banana firms have fomented a lack of unity among UPEB nations by successfully pitting producer nations against each other, and threatening to abandon production in countries where governments refuse to reduce taxes or labor unions become too militant.

A state of oversupply in the world market is also working against the banana countries. Increased productivity and disease-resistant plants have allowed banana companies to produce more bananas with fewer plantations and fewer workers. The banana corporations have shut down several plantations in Central America, citing the high costs of production and the world banana surplus. Fears of more shutdowns haunt governments, who are then willing to reduce banana taxes and make other concessions to keep plantations open.

But neither the lack of producer unity nor the condition of the world market are enough to explain the weak bargaining position of the banana-exporting nations. The main obstacle is the firm control maintained by the three TNC *pulpos* over all phases of the banana business. Without real control over banana production and marketing, most Central American nations remain shackled with banana republic images.

Coffee: Oligarchs and Oligopolies

The coffee industry's fortunes are closely linked to tastes and trends in the markets of developed countries. Coffee traders found a seemingly boundless market of enthusiasts in 19th century Europe: "When one drinks coffee," the great French writer Honore de Balzac declared, "ideas come marching in like an army." In this heady atmosphere, Central American coffee nations had no trouble selling all the coffee they produced. But Central American growers now experience coffee surpluses most years, as over 50 countries compete with the region's nations to meet the needs of a faltering market.

Coffee remains the leading commodity traded in the world after petroleum.[16] All production is in the third world, yet most coffee is consumed in the developed world. Together, Central American nations supply about 15 percent of the world's coffee exports, and El Salvador, Guatemala, and Costa Rica rank among the world's top ten coffee exporting countries.[17] The United States—where the average consumer drinks about two cups every day—imports about 3 times as much coffee as any other nation. The United States and West Germany are the leading importers of Central American coffee.[18]

Unlike the banana industry, where the TNCs have direct (although declining) involvement in production, the coffee TNCs stand entirely outside the production process. They exercise their control through trading, roasting, and marketing. For millions of coffee growers and thousands of coffee exporters, the handful of TNCs are the only connection to the billions of coffee drinkers around the world.

The Traders

Two types of TNCs control the coffee industry: commodity traders, and roasters. Central American exporters sell most of their green coffee to commodity trading TNCs based in New York, London, Tokyo, and Switzerland. These TNC traders, in turn, act as intermediaries selling the coffee beans to TNCs that roast and market processed coffee.

Until recently, most commodity trading companies were family firms, but many trading companies are now being acquired by huge financial-services corporations and large conglomerates. These giant firms deal in many trading items to avoid the pitfalls of wildly fluctuating prices in a single commodity in any given year. Mergers, takeovers, and bankruptcies are making small- and medium-sized trading companies a thing of the past.

The multi-commodity traders boast tremendous warehousing capability and maintain extensive global financial and marketing connections.

Their highly sophisticated networks allow them to buy and sell commodities with a speed and flexibility that gives them great influence over the trade of coffee, sugar, cotton, tobacco, cocoa, and other commodities. Because they buy and sell vast quantities of unprocessed commodities, the trading companies define the structure of the international market and can manipulate both prices and supplies.[19]

The Processors

Most of the largest roasters·also do some of their own buying from exporters, without involving multi-commodity traders. Procter & Gamble, for example, buys part of its green, or unprocessed, coffee directly from Guatemalan export houses.

But whether it's sold to multi-commodity traders or directly to processors, most of Central America's coffee leaves the isthmus without being processed. Only the preliminary step of extracting the green beans from the red coffee cherries is done in local shelling facilities, or *beneficios*.

Until the 1950s, small and medium scale firms did the bulk of coffee processing in North America and Europe. Since then, coffee has become a highly concentrated industry dominated by globe-trotting corporations, none of which is based in a coffee-growing country. In the United States, for example, the number of roasters has dropped from 260 in 1960 to just 40 in 1980.[20]

Six large roasters—General Foods, Nestle, Procter and Gamble, Consolidated Foods, Standard Brands (RJ Reynolds), and Jacobs of Switzerland—account for 60 percent of world sales. And just two TNCs, Nestle and General Foods, manufacture 75 percent of all the world's instant coffee.

But even for the largest coffee TNCs, coffee is just one part of their food processing business. Nestle, for example, is also the world's largest chocolate company. General Foods and Consolidated Foods rank among the world's top ten in soft drinks. Coca-Cola, the world's fifth largest processor of instant coffee, also ranks first in soft drinks and seventh in the tea industry. [21] Nestle and General Foods have annual sales higher than the gross domestic products of any Central American country; in fact, the sales of General Foods are seven times that of Costa Rica's annual budget.

Ironically, most Central American coffee drinkers gulp down the instant variety. Beans of inferior quality stay in the country, where they are made into coffee crystals and heavily promoted for local consumption by Coca-Cola and Nestle.

Splitting the Coffee Bean Profits

The Central American laborer who painstakingly picks each red coffee cherry off the bushes receives only a minuscule part of the final retail price of coffee. Working over 10 hours a day for a grand total of $2.50 or less, laborers harvest as much as 200 pounds of coffee cherries—or about 70 pounds of processed coffee—each day.

Coffee is one of the few commodities to be regulated by an international organization. Wide fluctuations in price and supply encouraged both producers and consuming countries to support the founding of the International Coffee Organization (ICO) in 1962. Through a series of International Coffee Agreements, the ICO attempts to stabilize coffee prices by stipulating export quotas for producing countries.

Because both producers and consumers are involved, the ICO is not a producers' cartel like OPEC (Organization of Petroleum Exporting Countries). The equal division of voting power between the two blocks in the ICO promotes a myth of fairness and mutual cooperation. But the voting power of two dozen consuming countries is equated with twice that number of producers. Further weighting based on relative volume within each block results in the U.S., as the world's largest coffee importer, controlling twice as many votes in the ICO as do all the Central American nations combined.

While the producing nations recognize that the International Coffee Organization has brought them some benefits, they argue that the organization caters to the interests of the coffee TNCs and the coffee drinkers in the industrial world. The UN's Economic Commission on Latin America (ECLA) agrees, noting in 1982 that "the effectiveness of the international coffee agreement was hindered by the opposition of the industrialized countries and by pressure from the TNCs which dominate the industry."[22]

As in the other commodities, the main coffee corporations and traders take advantage of (and manipulate) fluctuations in supply and price caused by weather and consumer demand. They buy coffee at low prices, store it, and then sell it at high prices. The largest corporations can thus circumvent the purpose of international agreements.

Over the last 30 years, the real price for coffee received by Guatemalan exporters dropped more than 10 percent.[23] Coffee's share of the value of all world exports fell by one half during the 1970s. Despite this downward trend in international market prices, retail prices are steadily rising. With their tight control of the coffee market, the TNC roasters can raise the price when the cost of their coffee is actually falling.

Coffee prices for ICO producers began to rise in late 1985, as a result of a drought in Brazil. Higher prices did bring some relief to the foreign-exchange starved nations of Central America but small ICO quotas and the high quantities of coffee sold at low non-quota prices diminished the benefits of the price increase.

In recent years, Central American producers have had to sell an increasing amount of their coffee on the open world market at prices sometimes 50 percent below the ICO standard. This expanding non-ICO market has resulted from overproduction by third-world producers desperate for foreign exchange.[24]

Both the number of producing countries and the total quantity of coffee production is expanding as other third-world nations also desperately try to earn more foreign exchange. Since 1982, the International Monetary Fund (IMF)—in response to the debt crisis—has encouraged countries to export even more. This, in turn, further pushes down prices as international supplies expand. The state of overproduction and the expansion of the open world market threatens the stability of the ICO, and some consumer countries like the United States are hinting that they may increase non-ICO purchases and possibly withdraw from the ICO.

While the producing countries are stepping up their production, consumers in the industrial nations are drinking less coffee. In the last 20 years, U.S. coffee imports have declined by almost one-third. In the United States, the percentage of coffee drinkers precipitously declined from 75 percent of the adult population in 1962 to 55 percent in 1983. Many have kicked the habit for health reasons. Still other consumers have decided that a cup of coffee is simply getting too expensive. Another additional threat to exporting nations is the growth of substitutes and additives.

In 1972, Latin American coffee countries joined together in an attempt to match the bargaining power of the huge corporations. The members of the Bogota Group, as it was called, tried to market their own coffee, but quickly met combined opposition from the coffee TNCs and the U.S. government. General Foods and others charged that the producers had artificially boosted prices.[25] The TNCs threatened boycotts. Finally, the U.S. government refused to sign a new international agreement in 1980 unless the producers' group disbanded. Reluctantly the Bogota Group backed down, leaving the coffee producers once again subject to the control of importing nations and TNCs.

In another blatant example of U.S. government enforcement of TNC interests, the United States prevented the creation of an international coffee stockpile to be regulated through the International Coffee Organization.[26] Such a stockpile, promoted by the United Nations, would help producing nations improve their long term price position.

Coffee trades on poverty. The most lucrative parts of the coffee business—shipping, trading, processing, and distribution—are securely in the hands of the TNCs who are based in countries where there are no coffee trees. The tremendous wealth that comes from the coffee bean has not filtered back to the hundreds of thousands of small growers and coffee pickers of Central America.

Cotton, Tobacco, Cocoa, and Sugar Trade

According to UN economists, cotton producers in the third world are subject to "wildly oscillating prices with their accompanying injurious impact, particularly for countries that depend on cotton as a major source of export earnings and development finance."[27] Increased use of synthetic cloth also threatens countries that depend on foreign exchange from cotton sales. Only low production costs, extremely favorable climatic conditions, and the meager wages paid to farmworkers allow Central America to maintain its tenuous share of the world cotton market.

Just 15 multi-commodity traders control 85 to 95 percent of the world's cotton trade. They include: Bunge and Born (U.S.), Cargill (U.S.), Ralli Brothers (UK), Volkart Brothers (Switzerland), and Toyo Menka Kaisha (Japan).[28] Large transnational traders control the cotton export business through their representatives in Central America. These traders buy cotton produced in Central America and then sell it to major textile firms.[29]

Before the Nicaraguan revolution, only three of the country's 16 export houses were not affiliated with transnational trading companies. Today, the Nicaraguan government manages the cotton export trade.[30]

The leading TNC banks also profit from the international cotton trade. These banks finance as much as 85 percent of the cotton trade conducted by trading companies based in the United States.[31]

Some commodities produced in Central America, like tobacco and cocoa, fall under even tighter TNC control. Six TNC trading companies, led by Universal Leaf Tobacco[32], account for about 90 percent of all world tobacco purchases. These trading companies then sell the tobacco to TNC cigarette manufacturers, including the four that dominate the world market: British American Tobacco (BAT), Philip Morris, RJ Reynolds, and American Brands.

Similar control over the world's cocoa trade is exercized by trading and processing TNCs. Six trading TNCs, including firms like ACLI International and Volkart which also dominate coffee trading, appropriate 70 percent of the global market. The two leading cocoa traders are Gill and

Duffus (UK) and S. & W. Berisford (West Germany).The chocolate processing industry, in turn, is controlled by Nestle, Mars, Hershey foods, Cadbury-Schweppes, and Standard Brands (subsidiary of RJ Reynolds).[33]

Four Central American nations—Belize, Costa Rica, Guatemala, and Honduras—export cocoa. Yet because the region does not process its own cocoa, Central America pays more to import chocolate than it earns from exporting cocoa beans. In 1983, Central America exported $1.4 million worth of cocoa to the United States, but imported from the U.S. $2.4 million worth of processed chocolate products.

The world's sugar market is dominated by four TNC traders: Sucre et Denrées (France), Tate and Lyle (UK), Englehard Phillips (U.S.), and EDF Man (UK).[34] Other TNCs like Gulf and Western, U.S. Sugar, and Amstar then refine the raw sugar. Central Americans see this sugar coming back to their region in concentrates for the region's soft drink factories, which are owned by yet another set of TNCs.

The Beef Business

Transnationals play a larger direct role in the beef business than they do in most other agroexports. Their involvement extends from cattle raising to packing houses to the supply of feed and veterinary products.

To supply U.S. fast-food appetites, several TNCs and many individual U.S. ranchers have turned to Central American pastures. The banana companies converted vast extensions of their idle land holdings into ranches. Even before the beef-export boom, some of their land was already being used to raise beef for the plantation workforces. Seeing a new opportunity for profit, the three banana companies began raising cattle for export in the 1950s.[35]

A consortium of U.S. corporations called the Latin America Agribusiness Development Corporation (LAAD) has also found a home on the range in Central America. After food-processing, the beef business is the consortium's largest area of investment. LAAD-financed herds roam the range in Costa Rica, Honduras, and Guatemala.

Some TNCs prefer to contract with local ranchers rather than have their own ranches. Burger King, a subsidiary of Pillsbury, contracts with Costa Rican ranchers to produce 6 million pounds of beef—enough to supply 2 percent of its hamburger needs in the United States.[36]

From the beginning of the cattle boom, U.S. firms have had financial interests in the packing houses. These slaughter houses, where cows are slaughtered and packed, are the source of the greatest profits in the Central American cattle industry. Most of them are backed by a mixture of domestic and international capital. Among the U.S. firms with investment in Central American packing houses are Borden, United Brands, and International Foods.[37]

Foreign firms, usually from the United States, also provide many of the supplies needed by the beef industry, including such items as frozen semen, boxes, refrigeration equipment, animal feeds, grass seed, and medicine. Ralston Purina, Weyerhauser, Crown Zellerbach, Fort Dodge Labs, WR Grace, and Cargill number among the main industry suppliers with operations in Central America.[38]

Phases of Agribusiness in Central America (Selected TNCs)

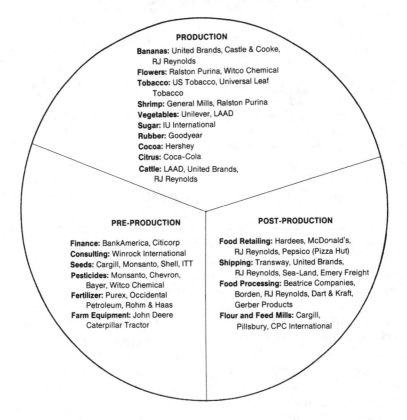

PRODUCTION

Bananas: United Brands, Castle & Cooke, RJ Reynolds
Flowers: Ralston Purina, Witco Chemical
Tobacco: US Tobacco, Universal Leaf Tobacco
Shrimp: General Mills, Ralston Purina
Vegetables: Unilever, LAAD
Sugar: IU International
Rubber: Goodyear
Cocoa: Hershey
Citrus: Coca-Cola
Cattle: LAAD, United Brands, RJ Reynolds

PRE-PRODUCTION

Finance: BankAmerica, Citicorp
Consulting: Winrock International
Seeds: Cargill, Monsanto, Shell, ITT
Pesticides: Monsanto, Chevron, Bayer, Witco Chemical
Fertilizer: Purex, Occidental Petroleum, Rohm & Haas
Farm Equipment: John Deere Caterpillar Tractor

POST-PRODUCTION

Food Retailing: Hardees, McDonald's, RJ Reynolds, Pepsico (Pizza Hut)
Shipping: Transway, United Brands, RJ Reynolds, Sea-Land, Emery Freight
Food Processing: Beatrice Companies, Borden, RJ Reynolds, Dart & Kraft, Gerber Products
Flour and Feed Mills: Cargill, Pillsbury, CPC International

Nontraditional Exports

For hundreds of years, Indian farmers of the western highlands of Guatemala have grown corn and beans on the mountain slopes. The U.S. Agency for International Development (AID) is now urging these and other campesinos in Central America to switch to snow peas, broccoli, and brussels sprouts. These vegetables have no local market, because the Indian population's food choices are limited by both tradition and income, and lack of transport precludes reaching the tiny urban middle class market. As Rigoberto Montaño, a leader of an AID-sponsored agricultural project in San Marcos, says, "The only people who buy brussels sprouts at the marketplace in San Marcos are the Mormons and the evangelists that come here."[39]

AID is not proposing nontraditional agricultural production as a way to meet the food needs of Central Americans. Rather, it sees nontraditional crop production as a way to stabilize national economies and improve the deteriorating conditions in rural areas. The United States also supports agricultural diversification because it increases the need for U.S.-manufactured agrochemicals and it offers an opportunity for new U.S. investment.

While the regional AID office acknowledges that vegetables and flowers do not solve the food needs of Central America, it points out that they "generate hard currency needed to repay debt."[40] The promotion of nontraditional exports is also designed to increase the integration of the small- and medium-sized farm sector into a global capitalist economy, as well as to keep the agroexport system alive for big operators faced with declining prices and shrinking markets for traditional export crops. AID says that Central America needs a "long-term stragtegy that relies heavily on increasing nontraditional exports." The region needs to be more "outward looking,"[41] AID suggests.

So AID has invited Indian farmers to grow vegetables for the winter market in the United States. U.S. companies are offered handsome subsidies to freeze, process and ship the produce northward. "What would be ideal," said an AID consultant in Guatemala, "is if all the Indians started growing vegetables in the highlands and the maize and beans were grown on the South Coast."[42]

Encouraged by AID, members of the San Marcos cooperative grow brussels sprouts and snow peas for Hanover Foods, a U.S. frozen foods processor. Hanover rejects 30 percent of the San Marcos produce on the grounds that it doesn't meet U.S. standards, and because brussels sprouts are not marketable locally these vegetables are dumped. The farmers receive about $12 for every 100 pounds of brussels sprouts the company eventually buys. The cooperative members estimate that if brussels sprouts sell for 70 cents a pound in the United States (about twice that if frozen), their vegetables are being sold for prices 6 to 12 times higher than they are receiving.

"Nothing remains for us after we pay for transportation and the fertilizer and the insecticides the company requires us to use," according to Manuel García, a spokesperson for the group. "We just aren't making any money so we're now thinking about going back to the coast to work on the cotton and sugar estates."

Even if the nontraditional crops do bring a certain amount of foreign exchange into the country, they do little to solve the problems of hunger and declining per capita food production. The more farmers use their land to grow tropical flowers and winter vegetables, the less land is available to grow beans and corn. Yet an AID official in Costa Rica persists: "We're moving the campesinos away from being prisoners of basic crops." And in Honduras, AID's David Gardella declares that small farmers have to change over from basic foods cultivation "because you never know what the price is going to be" for corn, beans, and rice.

Dear Señor Presidente

A Guatemalan cooperative, the Kato-Ki ("we help ourselves" in the Mayan dialect), was hit hard by its first international business deal. In 1983 a Los Angeles vegetable dealer, Larry Elmer, persuaded the Indian farmers of the AID-funded cooperative to abandon their centuries-old practice of growing corn to feed their families and instead plant Chinese snow peas for him to export. The U.S. Embassy and the AID Mission loved the idea. But just as the cooperative prepared to deliver 100 tons of snow peas, the Los Angeles dealer abandoned his business interests in Guatemala.

The U.S. Embassy said it could not compensate for the losses of the cooperative of small farmers because it could not get involved in private business dealings. What were the farmers to do with 100 tons of wilting exotic vegetables that have virtually no market inside the country? "Snow peas are not, shall we say, in the family diet," noted cooperative president Magally Díaz de Xoyon. "It's not like corn, from which you can make many things." The cooperative's 300 members, as well as over 2,000 landless peasants they hired to work for them, had to go without corn for the winter.[43]

Government Connections

The Latin American Agribusiness Development Corporation (LAAD) is a driving force behind nontraditional agribusiness in Central America.

LAAD keeps a low profile, but it is hardly a small-time operation: it has received more than $50 million in low-interest loans from AID since its founding in 1970. Its 16 shareholders are among the world's largest banks and TNCs: BankAmerica, Borden, Cargill, Castle & Cooke, Ralston Purina, and Caterpillar Tractor. The company's portfolio covers 201 businesses throughout Latin America, of which 146 are located in Central America. The 58 LAAD affiliated companies in Guatemala represent over one-fourth of all LAAD investments.

LAAD's stated purpose is to increase the employment and income of the rural poor in Latin America.[44] While its success in meeting that goal can be questioned, its ability to bring in profits for its shareholders cannot. In 1984, LAAD's profits rose a record 23 percent.

Virtually all LAAD's businesses in Central American produce export crops rather than locally consumable foods. In Costa Rica and Guatemala, several LAAD-financed projects, like the American Flower Company, grow ornamental flowers and ferns for U.S. customers. LAAD also channels investments into processing plants for winter vegetables and into the meat-packing business. In 1983, LAAD received $6 million from AID for its Central American operations. The company then loaned or directly invested this AID money in eight companies, including two shrimp export firms (both in Panama), one flower company (Costa Rica), two sesame seed companies (both in Guatemala), one cardamom exporter (Guatemala), a frozen chicken business (Panama), and a meat-packing plant (Honduras).

Although the Reagan administration's Caribbean Basin Initiative (CBI) specifies that governments are to move toward food self-sufficiency, little has been done in Washington to foster food security in the region. Instead, President Reagan created the Agribusiness Promotion Council in 1982 specifically to encourage U.S. investment in export agriculture. Dr. Ray Goldberg of the Harvard Business School was appointed chairman of the council, whose members include executives from LAAD, Cargill, Merrill Lynch Coffee, Sugar & Cocoa Inc., Winrock International Research Center, and Archer Daniels Midland.

But nontraditional export agriculture even seems to be a faulty proposition to some experts paid to promote it. "It is a utopian solution that evades the need for land redistribution and more campesino organizing," admitted Noel García of the Inter-American Institute for Agriculture Cooperation (IICA).

> It is just rhetoric to talk about diversification. Imagine the small farmers in the Highlands with less than two acres starting to grow strawberries for the United States! They don't even have

enough land to feed their families let alone take the chance of selling their produce to unsteady U.S. markets."[45]

Food in TNC Packages

Supermarket shelves throughout Central America display many of the same packaged products available to U.S. consumers. Of the 25 top U.S food processors, 18 do business in Central America.[46] Nestle has subsidiaries in every Central American nation. Del Monte, Heinz, Philip Morris, Beatrice, Borden, Carnation, and General Mills are as familiar to wealthier Central American shoppers as they are to U.S. food buyers. Most of these TNCs, however, assume Spanish-language names when they market their dry milk, tomato sauce, canned vegetables and other products to Central Americans.[47]

TNCs gained a strong hold on the region's agroindustry in the 1960s when the banana companies invested in the processing of cooking oils and margarine. However, they did not start from scratch but generally bought out locally owned businesses. United Brands, for example, acquired 77 percent of an already established cooking-oil factory in Nicaragua.[48]

But the relatively recent arrival of food-processing TNCs to the isthmus has not helped alleviate malnutrition, since promotion of better nutrition is not a priority for the food giants. Generally, the products which TNCs market have less nutritional value than the traditional diet. And some food corporations actually act as nutrition-subtractors. RJ Reynolds, for example, removes nutritious bananas from Central America while it peddles candy and soft drinks to the people who work on the banana plantations.

The food processors make little effort to incorporate locally available food into their processed products. A study of agroindustry in Costa Rica, for example, revealed that food processing companies (which account for one-half of that country's total industrialization) "could produce entirely from national materials with the exception of wheat flour, but instead import considerable quantities of fruit and fruit concentrate, vegetable oil, fish, and cattle feed." In fact, the Costa Rican study found that one-half of the value of the processed foods exported by Costa Rica to the rest of Central America came from food and materials that Costa Rica imported. Over 80 percent of this imported value came from the United States.[49]

While they offer the entire North American diet to the upper classes, TNC food processors bring junk food to the poor. An estimated 10 to 15 percent of the money spent by the region's poor buys soda and other "entertainment" food like popcorn and chips.[50] A report issued at an international advertising conference called, "Marketing for the Non-Affluent", advocated playing on the status needs of the poor: "Even if income in towns and rural districts appears to be extremely low, discretionary expenditures are nevertheless made in ways that would be called from our point of view wasteful spending."[51]

A recent study by the United Nations on the worsening nutritional crisis in Central America condemned this type of profiteering. Speaking of the TNCs and their advertising firms, the UN report stated:

> There are only a few companies and people which exercise a decisive influence over the culture of these countries, and the behavior of a vast segment of their population, imposing in this way social, political, and cultural values of other countries that are very foreign to Central Americans.[52]

Need for a New International Economic Order

Since the early 1960s, underdeveloped nations around the world have sought a new relationship between countries that produce primary commodities and the industrial nations that buy them. Questions are being asked: "For whom are we producing all these crops?" and "Why do export countries receive so little of the profit from agroexports?" Proponents of a New International Economic Order say that international agreements are needed to stabilize commodity markets, regulate the conduct of TNCs, give third world countries greater access to the markets of industrial countries, increase access to world capital markets and debt relief, and increase the flow of foreign aid to the underdeveloped world. Among the advocates for a NIEO are economists and government planners in the industrial world who warn that North-South economic relations have to be reordered if global capitalism is to keep expanding.

Little progress, however, has been made in establishing this proposed reordering of the global economy. Instead, conditions have worsened for third world economies, as is readily evident in Central America. Yet even if a NIEO were to be put in place, such an economic restructuring would do little to change conditions for the poor. Whatever benefits accrued would flow to the state and economic elite of each country, or in other words the same national power structure that maintains the current inequitable division of land and income. To make any difference for the poor, economic remodeling has to be accompanied by substantial political changes as well. And it is the poor majorities in Central America that need to be in the forefront of economic and political reordering.

But instead of a new international economic order to improve the position of the South in relation to the North, the world economy has become further skewed toward the industrial world in the last couple decades. Most noticeable has been the unbridled expansion of TNCs and a tightly controlled global financial market. TNCs now control a global network of supplies and markets that creates immense profits. Each region's elite collaborate with the TNCs to extract the area's wealth, at the expense of peasants and workers, who are incorporated into the system as subsistence laborers. While this global agribusiness system makes good business sense for the TNCs, it fails to address the needs of most Central Americans.

The TNCs encourage reliance on imports, without helping the third world meet the challenge of food self-sufficiency. Rather than foster more basic foods production, they promote the cultivation of traditional export crops like coffee and nontraditionals like snow peas and carnations.

Neither geography nor climate dictates that Central America must grow crops to please the palates of foreign consumers. But the Spanish conquistadors and now the TNCs have imposed an agriculture system that does not meet Central America's need for either better food security or broad-based economic development.

Chapter Five
Chemical Craze

In view of the challenge posed by world hunger, emotional attacks against conscientious agricultural chemicals research are attacks against humanity.

—Bayer's *Annual Report, 1981*

An early morning bus ride through the cotton-growing area of Central America provides a stinging glimpse of everyday reality. As the bus passes plantations, its windows film over. Most of the passengers, knowing what to expect, close their eyes, slow their breathing, and cover their nose and mouth with a scarf. Those riders caught unaware feel their eyes begin to smart, their lungs involuntarily constrict, and a bitter chemical smell starts to clog their noses.

Visitors to the area will likely rush off the bus to change clothes and to wash their stinging skin with soap and water. The local population is not so fortunate; their exposure to agricultural chemicals for the day has only begun. They will toil long hours in the fields, drenched with chemicals that crop dusters sprayed earlier that morning. Three out of four farm workers have no running water in their homes to wash off the day's accumulation of pesticides. Many bathe in irrigation canals or streams contaminated with still more agrochemicals, or try to wash off with water stored in a discarded pesticide drum.

The term "pesticide" refers to any chemical used to control insects, weeds, rodents, plant diseases, fungi, or worms. Insecticides are the most commonly applied pesticides in Central America, but herbicides (weed killers) like 2,4-D, nematicides (worm killers) like DBCP and carbophuran, and fungicides like dithane and benomyl are also common.

There are four main chemical categories of pesticides: organochlorines, organophosphates, carbamates, and pyrethoids. Organochlorines, like DDT, though now banned in the United States because they persist in foodstuffs and accumulate in body tissues, are still used in Central America.

Several thousand Central Americans become ill as a result of pesticide poisoning each year. These official figures understate the true dimensions of the problem, for a variety of reasons. In the first place, poisoning statistics only include data from those who receive social security payments—about 15 percent of the population. Many growers maintain their own clinics to prevent public health officials from detecting the seriousness of the situation. And many seasonal farmworkers, return to their home villages, where there are no clinics, when they become ill. Even those victims that live near medical facilities seldom seek treatment and those who do often find that hospitals are unable to prescribe treatment because they don't know to which chemical the victim was exposed. Determining which toxin is to blame is a tricky proposition: often many chemicals have been mixed together or containers have only the brand name and not the generic name of the toxin. And there is little information about the indirect effects of heavy pesticide use—often the spray from crop dusters runs off or mists into rivers that flow past villages a great distance downstream.

Finally, when farmworkers die from pesticide poisoning, their deaths may go officially unnoticed, because many poor Central Americans do not die in hospitals and are never registered with the state.[1] "We treat only a small percentage of poisoning victims," says Rosa Maria Silva, a medical intern working in a hospital in Escuintla, Guatemala.

> Generally, we don't get patients unless they are on the edge, because they are worried about the medical costs. Unfortunately, many of the cases we get die—about two or three a week

sometimes. One reason is that we don't have the proper care and medicine available. But it is also because there is not much you can do once the worker's get the chemicals into their blood.

The living conditions of Central American farmworkers make them particularly susceptible to pesticide poisoning, according to the International Labor Organization (ILO). "Well nourished, comfortably housed workers, enjoying adequate rest and hygiene," the ILO says, "are less vulnerable to toxic chemicals than persons who are burdened with malnutrition, disease, and fatigue."[2] The dangers also rise with the temperature, because hot weather increases skin absorption and makes pesticides more volatile—adding to both skin and respiratory exposure.[3]

The peddlers of pesticides do not take the time to warn farmworkers about the attendant dangers of their products or to offer training in the safe use of these poisons. Instead they propagate pesticide use as a panacea for all pest problems. This lack of information and training has resulted in the careless use of pesticides by farmworkers and small farmers. The right of farmworkers to organize is a prerequisite to "safe" (or at least safer) contact with pesticides. Without this right, Central American campesinos do not have the power to demand more protection and training regarding pesticide application.

Rural people have integrated deadly chemicals into their daily life. Workers take pesticides home to spray around their own homes. Campesinos reason that if one chemical is good, then two or more are better. Trying to deal one death blow to all insects, small farmers create so-called chemical "cocktails" from the most heavily advertised pesticides. Agricultural laborers stir chemicals with their hands because "it's faster," and spray herbicides from backpacks while walking shirtless and shoeless through the fields.

Gilberto Galindo, manager of a cotton plantation in Guatemala, said, "The insects here have grown stronger, and it is due to the heavy use of chemicals. Not only are the insects stronger than the chemicals, but we now have problems with new kinds of insects that are attacking our crops." Asked for his solution to this dilemma, Galindo could only respond, "We have no alternative but to spray more."[4]

Most workers employed on the cotton farms live within 350 feet of the plantations.[5] In the morning they don the same pesticide-dampened work clothes they wore the day before, as the drift from the crop dusters sprinkles down on their breakfast table and their food. In many rural communities, agrochemical distributors are the largest businesses, and the corner store sells pesticides—pouring small portions into old liquor bottles for their customers. Plastic bags that once held agrochemicals become raincoats, and empty pesticide containers are used to haul water. In Costa Rica, an entire village recently became ill after eating flour that was transported on the same truck as a pesticide delivery. Farmers wear caps emblazoned with popular chemical brand names like Tordon and Gramoxone.

While most farmworkers recognize the logos and brand names on the caps, they are unable to read the instructions and warnings on the labels of the pesticide cans. Over 75 percent of the laborers in cotton production cannot read.[6] In Guatemala, the Indian migrant workers on the South Coast can neither speak fluent Spanish nor read Spanish or English language directions.

Protective gloves, boots, and masks are seldom made available to workers by owners or managers. Even if they were, most workers would find the extra clothing—which was designed for use in temperate climates—almost impossible to wear in extreme tropical heat. Many campesinos, not having the proper protective gear, try to ward off the toxic effects of pesticides with home remedies such as eating limes.[7]

Watch What You Eat

Central America's main victims of pesticide use are the farmworkers and residents of these agroexport countries. But the absence of controls either by pesticide exporting countries like the United States or by most countries that import pesticides has created what authors David Weir and Mark Schapiro have called a "circle of poison."[8] North American consumers who buy coffee, vegetables and other pesticide-laden crops from Central America are caught up in this circle, as explained by Alexander Bonilla, director of the Costa Rican environmental organization ASCONA.

> The TNCs are sending us great quantities of pesticides that are outlawed in the United States and Europe. As a result, we are exporting contaminated oranges, meat, and mangoes back to consumers in those countries.[9]

Employees at the U.S. Embassy and U.S. AID Mission in Guatemala City have recently begun to pay closer attention to what they eat. Some, in fact, have cut meat and milk out of their diets completely, as a result of a 1984 AID-funded environmental survey. The report noted the existence of extraordinarily high levels of pesticides in Guatemalan milk and meat, and acknowledged that "there exist regulatory services for the exports— but not for internal consumption. So those amounts that are rejected for exportation are consumed internally." The environmental survey pointed out that although DDT is officially banned in Guatemala, "it continues to appear in meat . . . and is believed [to come] in as contraband."[10]

The contamination of Guatemalan milk and meat is another sad result of the massive use of chemical poisons on cotton fields, which are located in the same region as the country's principal livestock ranches. Besides their exposure through air and water, cattle also are herded onto the cotton plantations to feed on the pesticide-saturated cotton stalks after cotton picking is done for the season. Insecticides in milk are not regulated despite evidence of contamination. According to the Social Security Institute's Dr. León Muniz, "In Guatemala, food can have all the insecticides in the world, yet still be sold in the market."[11]

Pesticide Profiteers

Neither national nor international regulations have succeeded in bridling the power of the handful of TNCs—primarily Bayer, Ciba-Geigy, Shell, Monsanto, and Du Pont—that dominate the pesticide business.[12] Governments of exporting nations like Britain and the United States can regulate the TNC business at home, but have little control over any foreign activities of the TNC subsidiaries. Thus if their home countries prohibit the use of certain pesticides, the TNCs can still manufacture the chemicals for export.

Central America provides a major market for banned or heavily restricted pesticides produced in the United States: an estimated 75 percent of the pesticides applied in Central America are either banned, restricted or unregistered in the United States.[13] For example, nearly 90 percent of U.S. exports of the heavily restricted pesticide methyl parathion goes to Central America.[14]

"Our countries are the trash heaps of the industrialized nations," said Costa Rican environmentalist Alexander Bonilla. "When a product is no longer utilized in its country of origin because of high toxicity, it is exported to some underdeveloped country like ours."[15]

In several cases, manufacturers have moved their entire production operations to third world countries. Not only do they avoid export regulations by formulating their chemicals in places like Guatemala, but TNCs also enjoy reduced costs. A report by Shell in 1981 explained: "Formulation can often be carried out with relatively unskilled labor and in some areas seasonal labor can be employed."[16]

The promotional teams of chemical companies frequently reach more growers than the government's own agricultural extension services. Advertising pays for the magazines of associations of small farmers and coffee growers, as well as the agricultural section of the daily newspapers. These ads emphasize the wonders of the latest chemical concoctions. In Guatemala, Dow Chemical claims that its Lorsban pesticide "guarantees a good harvest," but does not warn farmers of its toxicity. Boots, a British firm, advertises Mitac as providing a "high degree of security for the . . . environment," despite the fact it has been cited in Britain as being harmful to fish. Monsanto offers an extremely toxic herbicide called Roundup with the following notice printed on the can: "Follow detailed instructions on attached labelling." The notice and instructions, however, are printed only in English.

Buyer Beware: The Export of Pesticides

The Natural Resources Defense Council has called the loose regulation of pesticides in the United States "a national scandal."[17] Over 90 percent of the pesticides on the market in the United States have not been fully tested as required by the Environmental Protection Agency (EPA). When it comes to pesticides in U.S. food imports the situation is worse; between 30 and 50 percent of coffee imports show traces of chemicals like DDT, lindane and BHC, which are totally banned in the United States.[18] In addition, the General Accounting Office (GAO) estimates that 60 percent of the chemicals used on imported food are not even detected by Food and Drug Administration (FDA) testing.

The position of the Reagan administration became clear when the president, during his first month in office, revoked an executive order issued by President Carter that improved the notification procedures governing export of restricted pesticides. The Reagan administration has also repeatedly ignored or rejected GAO recommendations for improved testing of food imports, better notification process, and the systematic monitoring—rather than random testing—of all imports. It has also done little to prevent foreign growers from using U.S. economic aid to buy banned pesticides.[19]

In 1982, the Reagan administration shocked the UN when the United States cast the sole vote against a UN resolution called "Protection Against Products Harmful to Health and Environment." The resolution, which passed 146-1, called for countries importing pesticides to be provided with complete information on the pesticides, "with a view toward safeguarding the health and environment of the importing country." Two years later, after a leak from the Union Carbide pesticide plant in Bhopal, India, killed more than 2,000 people, the United States once again cast the lone dissenting voice on a UN panel seeking improved international pesticide control. The U.S. delegate to the panel, Dennis Goodman, said the vote reflected President Reagan's belief that the proposed $89,000 expenditure on a book listing banned and restricted pesticides was "wasteful."[20]

The Environmental Protection Agency is required by U.S. law to notify recipient governments when restricted pesticides are being exported by U.S. firms. Typically the agency sends such notice well after the shipment has arrived in the destination country. The notification says only that a certain chemical has been restricted; it does not include information explaining why the chemical has been restricted or what the associated environmental and human risks are.[21]

Often, these notices never reach the appropriate government officials. One U.S. Embassy official admitted to a GAO investigator that he "did not routinely forward notification of chemicals" to the government "because it may adversely affect U.S. exporting."[22]

Blame It On the Boll Weevil

Over the last 30 years, pesticides have become an integral part of cash-crop production in Central America. In the 1950s and 1960s, cotton growers welcomed new pesticides in their war against the only serious cotton pest at the time, the boll weevil. Foreign manufacturers flooded the Central American market with organochlorine pesticides like aldrin, DDT, endrin, and dieldrin. As a result, Central America became the world's highest per capita user of pesticides.[23]

By the mid-1960s, however, the region's crop production began to decline. In their crusade against the unholy boll weevil, the growers had destroyed a system of indigenous biological control by killing good bugs along with the bad. After repeated pesticide applications selected for a boll weevil resistant to the chemicals, the determined past found itself unencumbered by its erstwhile natural predators.[24]

The experience of Nicaragua during its cotton and chemical boom is a typical case. In the 1950s, the country's cotton economy expanded dramatically. Plantations spread; in the agricultural region around León, cotton production increased more than fourfold while acreage devoted to corn and beans was cut in half.[25] After small food crop growers were successfully evicted from their land, and with the Somoza regime offering state financing to large growers, the only obstacle to increased cotton production and profit seemed to be the weevil.

Through the government's Cotton Experiment Center, President Somoza invited chemical firms to test new products, including such highly toxic pesticides as endrin, dieldrin, kepone, leptophos, and lindane, on Nicaraguan soil. Bayer tried out its methyl parathion, a mixture closely related to a nerve gas used in World War II. Dozens of Nicaraguan farmworkers died after working with the chemical, and hundreds more were hospitalized. Nevertheless, Somoza personally approved methyl parathion for unrestricted application.

By the early 1960s, the number of chemicals in use in Nicaragua had jumped in a ten-year period from less than 5 to 70. The average number of pesticide applications rose from five to 30 per growing season. Cotton production quadrupled, and Nicaragua became the world's 15th largest cotton producer. It was also the globe's leading per capita pesticide user, and thousands of pesticide poisonings were recorded each year.

As the campesinos were dying, the hated boll weevil was growing resistant to the toxins. By 1965, this evolving resistance combined with the emergence of new cotton pests—as pesticides killed off natural predators—to result in declining yields.[26]

Concerned by the foreign exchange crisis resulting from decreasing cotton production, the Somoza government asked for international assistance in the late 1960s. Under the auspices of the United Nations, foreign consultants led by Dr. Louis Falcon of the University of California at Berkeley introduced the region's first Integrated Pest Management (IPM) program.[27]

IPM combined the use of pesticides with other, more ecologically sound means of pest control, including: 1) biological controls that encourage a pests' natural enemies and release sterile male insects to reduce breeding; 2) physical controls like hand-weeding, placing obstructive bands around trees, or using light to attract night-flying insects; 3) so-called "cultural" controls, such as ridding the fields of stubble where insects nest during the off-season; 4) use of resistant plants, and 5) setting economic damage thresholds and determining the level of pest infestation to avoid the expense of unnecessary spraying.

The program was initially successful, reducing pesticide applications and improving production. In the final analysis, however, this early IPM program was undermined. The Somoza government did not follow through with an education campaign necessary to encourage widespread participation. TNC chemical companies, threatened by the prospect of a drop in sales, waged heavy promotion and advertising campaigns to discourage reliance on the IPM program. Nicaragua reverted, instead, to its former pattern of ever stronger and more frequent chemical applications. Just two years before the Sandinista's 1979 revolution, a UN report estimated that insecticides were causing environmental and social damage of $200 million a year in Nicaragua.[28]

Pesticides on Banana Plantations

The phenomenal growth of pesticide use in Central America has not been limited to cotton production. The introduction of improved varieties of bananas in the 1960s, for example, required the systematic use of pesticides on plantations. Worm killers like DBCP and weed killers like 2,4-D—a component of Agent Orange—have resulted in the large-scale poisoning of banana workers.

In Costa Rica, the use of DBCP on Standard Fruit's banana plantations has been linked to sterility in at least 500 banana workers.[29] One study by university scientists in Costa Rica showed a direct relationship between the hours of exposure by the workers to the chemical and the percentage of sperm. According to another official survey, 23 percent of banana workers experienced head pains, 19 percent dizziness, and 13 percent faintness. An excess of burns and conjunctivitis (an eye inflammation) among banana workers has been attributed to lack of goggles, no protection of genital zone and no protection from leaking back applicators.[30]

Standard Fruit continued to import the highly toxic worm killer DBCP under the brand names Nemagon and Fumazone to Central America for more than a year after its use was suspended by the State of California in 1977 following confirmation of widespread sterility at the DBCP manufacturing plant in California. In mid-1986, Standard Fruit workers filed a suit against Dow and Shell Oil on the grounds that they continued to export the deadly pesticides to Costa Rica after their use was banned in the United States. In Nicaragua, Standard Fruit continued to apply DBCP on its banana plantations until a government decree prohibited its use in 1980. Two other chemicals used on banana plantations, benomyl and dithane, are also suspected of causing increased sterility among Central American banana workers.[31]

Plantation owners and corporate officials are often unaware of the complications which result from pesticide practices. A United Brands foreman in Panama, commenting on pesticide practices, complained.

> If you get careless and forget to rotate them, the next thing you know the damn Indian's bleeding at the nose all the time and you gotta pay for his sick care for the next couple of weeks.

Generally banana workers with the least seniority or members of minority groups are chosen for the task of applying pesticides. In Panama, for instance, managers play on racial antagonism between Panamanians and the Guaymi Indians, who migrate from the mountains to work for the Chiriqui Land Company of United Brands. Some non-Indians believe that the skin of the Guaymi Indians is thicker than their skin, and consequently not affected by pesticides or fertilizers. While there is no scientific basis for such a belief, the task of applying pesticides nonetheless falls to the Guaymis. The results are seen in Panamanian cities, where Indian men blinded by the pesticides beg on street corners.[32]

Pesticide-Resistant Mosquitoes Spread Malaria

The Kissinger Commission noted in 1984 that Belize, Guatemala, Honduras, and El Salvador "are currently experiencing a serious resurgence of malaria and dengue fever."[33] In Guatemala, for example, reported malarial infections during 1981-83 were 11 times higher than those of a decade earlier.[34] Nearly 17 million Central Americans now live in malarial zones, and over 200,000 people fall victim to the disease each year.

Unfortunately, the Kissinger Commission report neglected to point out any connection between the resurgent malaria epidemic and the use of pesticides. According to the Central American Institute of Technology (ICAITI), the region's malaria rates are "clearly related to the percent of surface that is planted in cotton."[35] ICAITI found that pesticides applied to cotton have resulted in mosquitoes resistant to the chemicals used in malaria eradication programs. The institute concludes that every two pounds of insecticide added to the Central American environment generates about 100 new cases of malaria.[36]

Spraying the Environment

Farmworkers, rural families, and consumers are not the only victims of unregulated pesticide use in Central America. The pesticides kill a broad spectrum of living things, including those insects beneficial to the corn and bean fields on which peasant families depend for food. From 50 to 75 percent of the pesticides applied by crop dusters never reaches the target crop, but instead drifts and settles over wide expanses of agricultural land, waterways, and villages.[37] The pesticides contaminate livestock grazing in nearby fields and fish living in lakes or rivers.

Many pesticides do not break down after the crop dusters leave; DDT residues, for example, require decades to disintegrate. Understandably, rural residents throughout Central America are concerned about the environmental damage caused by the chemicals. Costa Ricans say that the heavy use of herbicides has all but extinguished the armadillo, fish, and crocodile population along the Guanacaste River. Along the banks of the Guayape River in Honduras, small farmers charge that pesticides from cotton production have killed all the fish along a stretch of the river that runs through the Olancho province.

In El Salvador's coastal bays and estuaries, massive numbers of fish die twice a year—initially when heavy rains wash pesticides from the soil into streams and rivers, and later at the beginning of the dry season when growers begin aerial spraying of cotton.

Local Regulation on the Books

Most Central American countries have laws regulating the distribution and use of pesticides. Enforcement, however, is rare. At a hospital in Escuintla, the heart of the cotton region in Guatemala, an intern who treats pesticide poisonings said, "I suppose there are laws to protect the workers, but . . . I have never heard of a *finca* owner paying a penalty."[38]

According to environmentalist Alexander Bonilla, laws regulating pesticides are "not enforced" because "through their many connections in our government, the TNCs always get their way. They find the many cracks in the laws through which they can import and sell their chemicals. Our pesticide legislation is just a pile of paper."[39]

This state of affairs is not unusual in the third world, according to Dr. Harold Hubbard of the World Health Organization. "One of the reasons that LDC (less-developed) countries don't do anything about the pesticide problems," explained Dr. Hubbard, "is that the people who use pesticides, the people who import pesticides, and the people who regulate pesticides are the same people. It is a tight little group in each developing country."[40]

In Central America, the tight little groups—including national oligarchies and TNC subsidiaries—don't look kindly on those who raise the issue of pesticide contamination. Right-wing elements consider charges of pesticide misuse to be a strategy to incite poor farmworkers, and have issued death threats in both Guatemala and El Salvador against people expressing public concern about the dangers of insecticides. In Guatemala, death squads kidnapped a doctor who had reported on the harm inflicted by chemicals on that country's agricultural workforce.[41]

Leftist guerrillas have recognized that reckless pesticide use is a prominent concern of agricultural laborers. The Guerrilla Army of the Poor (EGP) in Guatemala has burned crop dusters to show their concern for farmworker issues.

Central American governments, meanwhile, tend to ignore farmworker complaints partly for fear of sparking worker/management confrontations. In Panama, a doctor with the National Health Service in the banana-growing region has said that reports of chemicals causing sterility "had to be hushed up" as a "sacrifice for the good of the national economy." In Guatemala City, a representative of the Registry and Control of Plant Health put it this way: "The job of our inspectors is to investigate complaints, but there are no worker complaints because the workers fear repression."[42]

In Costa Rica, the law requires that companies submit samples of their products for analysis. But the country has no laboratory capable of testing the chemicals. The Department of Plant Health therefore limits itself to reviewing documents submitted by the companies after a bit of library research. Nowhere in Central America are field tests conducted before approving chemicals for use.

In 1985, the Pesticide Action Network (PAN) launched a campaign to create more awareness about increasing international pesticide abuse. The campaign focused on 12 pesticides called the Dirty Dozen. According to the international network of citizens groups, the pesticides that "kill far more than pests" are:

parathion	chlordane/heptachlor
2,4,5-T	HCH/Lindane
paraquat	EDB
DDT	camphechlor (toxaphene)
chlordimeform	poentachlorophenyl (PCP)
aldrin/dieldrin/endrin	DBCP

Anwar Fazal, director of the International Organization of Consumers Unions (IOCU), has warned that the Dirty Dozen pesticides "are mainly used on export crops—such as bananas, coffee, tea, cotton, and rubber, and therefore return to consumers in Europe, the United States, and Japan as residues in food or commodities in a circle of poison." The Dirty Dozen can be found on the shelves of farm stores throughout Central America.

Nicaragua: Good Bugs, Bad Bugs, and the Contras

In the cotton-growing region of Nicaragua, farmworkers stooping over cotton plants straighten up occasionally to make notes in pads they carry in their back pockets. These insect counters in the front lines of Nicaragua's new Integrated Pest Management (IPM) program are keeping track of the kind and number of insects that they find.

By paying more attention to the ecology of insect life, Nicaragua's Ministry of Agriculture is trying to cut the country's use of expensive, harmful, and environmentally-destructive pesticides by at least 50 percent. "It's like a huge battle," said a member of a cotton cooperative near Chinandega, "with the good bugs fighting against the bad bugs. Our job is to make sure the good ones win."[43]

The war against bugs has been hampered by a more serious war, waged by the U.S.-backed counterrevolutionaries, or *contras*, against the Sandinista government. When workers count insects in the cotton fields of Nicaragua, they often wear rifles slung over their shoulders to protect themselves and their communities from *contra* attacks. Sean Sweezy, a consultant working with the country's IPM program, has called the *contra* war—which has caused over $75 million in agricultural damage since 1979, and in which 10 agricultural technicians have been killed by the *contras*— "the main obstacle to the IPM program." According to Sweezy, "the sabotage of agricultural services has been a definite strategy by the *contras*."[44] The war has also cut into the IPM program by limiting the number of available vehicles and technicians; in 1984, 13 of the 40 inspectors had joined the army and the program could count on only two trucks.

Even so, the IPM program is saving Nicaragua several million dollars each year in foreign exchange, and its success has encouraged the government to convert all cotton production to IPM methods.

Sandinistas Try New Approach

The Sandinistas have taken other concrete steps to reduce the massive use of pesticides that characterized the Somoza era. The government prohibits the use of chemicals that are banned in their country of origin. The Ministry of Agriculture has undertaken an ambitious campaign to educate workers about the dangers of pesticides. Nicaraguan law now requires all instructions for pesticide use to be in Spanish, and all pesticide containers to sport color-coded labels for illiterate workers. A medical laboratory complex has been developed to test blood samples for pesticide exposure, and those workers whose blood shows a high level of toxins are given new jobs with less pesticide exposure.

The government has also moved to stop pollution and worker exposure at the U.S.-owned Pennwalt-Hercules chemical complex, the largest pesticide factory in Central America. Beginning in the mid-1960s, the company poured 40 tons of mercury waste into Lake Managua over a 15-year period. Inspectors in 1980 also found that one-third of the workers at the plant were suffering from mercury poisoning. The government, now a part owner in the plant since taking over Somoza's interest in the company, has insisted that the pollution of the lake stop and has instituted safety standards to protect workers.

Stopping the Pesticide Treadmill

Like Bayer, which calls criticisms of the pesticide industry "attacks against humanity," other transnational corporations also emphasize the choice between agrochemicals and hunger. But in Central America as throughout much of the third world, pesticides have little to do with either producing food or solving the problem of hunger. Of the 11 pounds of pesticides used per capita in the region annually, only a few drops are applied on food crops for local consumption. Almost 50,000 tons of chemicals are sprayed annually onto cotton, coffee, bananas, flowers, and nontraditional vegetables—cash crops for export.[45]

The widespread use of pesticides is not inevitable, but rather the result of extensive advertising by chemical companies and the lack of government regulations. The success of the IPM program in Nicaragua, according to Sean Sweezy, "demonstrates that the force for stopping the pesticide treadmill can be organized within any country." However in most Central American countries the political commitment to implement pest-management and pesticide-education programs is lacking—even as officials acknowledge the risks of failing to reduce the use of pesticides. "We have entered a battle to the death with the pests," a government research team in Costa Rica has noted, "without having ever evaluated correctly the strength of the enemy. Because of their capacity to develop different ways of resistance, they have a good possibility of winning the battle if we continue in the same way."[46]

Chapter Six
Agrarian Reform and Revolution: El Salvador and Nicaragua

*It is only a question of time before a decisive choice must be made
between the political costs of reform and the political risks of rebellion.*
—Robert McNamara, president of the
World Bank, 1972

Socialist revolutionaries, military governments, peasant movements,
U.S. presidents, and capitalist entrepreneurs have, at various times, all been
part of the chorus for agrarian reform in Central America. Agrarian reform
includes the redistribution of land, and access to the credit and technical
assistance needed to develop the redistributed land. Such changes can result
in either individual, cooperative, or state ownership.

The nature and effect of agrarian reform programs vary greatly according to: 1) which class interests are in control, and 2) what are perceived to be the country's major economic and political problems. Depending on those factors, land reform can be used as an instrument of revolution or counterrevolution. It can be used to pacify the rural population or to empower it. Agrarian reform can be applied to strengthen the agroexport economy or to alter it.

Agrarian reform became an issue in Central America during the 1800s. Colonial and semifeudal property relations were challenged by a faction of the landholding elite that advocated the principles of "private property." This new breed of coffee growers and merchants yearned to break up communal landholdings of the Indians and the estates of the Catholic Church while introducing capitalist principles into agrarian life. This drive to commercialize and modernize the agricultural economy was organized by the Liberal parties of that era. The proposed agrarian reforms were jointly opposed by the peasantry, the church, and the traditional landed aristocracy.[1] But the force of history and the spread of coffee production eventually broke the resistance of those grouped around the Conservative parties.

It was not until after World War II when the region became enveloped in a new surge of agroexport production that agrarian reform again became a major issue in Central America. Until then, a major problem facing agroexporters was the scarcity of farmworkers. To address this problem the oligarchy and the state conspired to displace the peasantry, thereby creating a new source of wage labor while at the same time increasing the land available for agroexport production. The rapid growth of the agroexport economy in the post-war decades, however, created economic and political problems which recent agrarian reform programs have attempted to address. No longer was there a shortage of labor. Instead, booming agroexport production sparked soaring landlessness and declining food production. The ability of growers to produce competitive agroexports rests on their access to cheap labor. While there was now plenty of surplus labor, landless farmworkers could not support their families on the dollar or two a day they received for their seasonal labor.

An aggravating factor was the rise of food imports. Growing landlessness meant that the peasantry was no longer able to produce enough corn and beans to meet the basic needs of the society. Forward-looking government planners and members of the economic elite recognized the need for increased food production to reduce spending of scarce foreign currency on food imports. But low market prices for basic foods and the low purchasing power of most consumers discouraged large growers from switching to production for the internal market. It was felt that by settling campesinos on idle and uncleared frontier lands, an agrarian reform program could assist the country's economic growth by producing cheap food for the nation and by providing subsistence for seasonal farmworkers. Agrarian reform was also a way to open up more land for capitalist production by ridding the agricultural economies of the remaining pockets of precapitalist land tenure, and incorporating idle and underutilized land into agroexport production.

Besides the economic justifications for agrarian reform, a pressing political reason exists for land redistribution programs—the need to ease social tension caused by growing landlessness and rural poverty. In the 1950s, displaced peasants and progressive intellectuals began pressing for agrarian reform programs that would make idle land available to landless campesinos. Others in government and business argued that agrarian reforms were needed to modernize the agricultural economy and spur economic growth. They said that a reform sector of small landholders would expand the market for consumer goods and thus enhance industrialization.

The agrarian reform program announced in 1951 by the Jacobo Arbenz government in Guatemala responded to demands of landless campesinos by expropriating idle landholdings of United Fruit and the country's oligarchy. But it was more than political pressure that moved Arbenz to redistribute uncultivated land. He regarded the program as a necessary step to modernize the agricultural economy. The Guatemalan oligarchy and Washington, however, viewed the land redistribution program as a frontal assault on private property rights and labeled it "communist." More alarming to them than the land expropriation was the upsurge of peasant organizing that accompanied the program. Local oligarchs, Washington, and United Fruit all saw this blossoming of rural organizing as a major threat to the entire agroexport economy and its dependence on a cheap, repressed labor force.

The overthrow of Arbenz in 1954 terminated the agrarian reform program in Guatemala while providing a stern warning to other Central Americans advocating agrarian reform programs. In 1959, the revolution in Cuba renewed discussion in Washington and throughout Central America about the political necessity for agrarian reform. Government and military elites feared that the Cuban example would stimulate rural revolutionary movements within Central America, where conditions resembled pre-revolutionary Cuba.

A Reaction to Revolution

Agrarian reform was a main thrust of the Alliance for Progress program announced by President John F. Kennedy in 1961 and subsequently endorsed by the Organization of American States. The Punta del Este charter, which officially established the Alliance for Progress in August 1961, called for:

> ... programs of comprehensive agrarian reform, leading to the effective transformation, where required, of unjust structures and systems of land tenure and use; with a view to replacing *latifundia* and dwarf holdings by an equitable system of property so that, supplemented by timely and adequate credit, technical assistance, and improved marketing arrangements, the land will become for the man who works it the basis of his economic stability, the foundation of his increasing welfare, and the guarantee of his freedom and dignity.

The kind of agrarian reform programs promoted by the Alliance for Progress occurred within the framework of the established political economies of Latin American countries rather than challenging those structures. Instead of encouraging the landless to organize for land reform themselves, the Alliance asked the oligarchs to voluntarily redistribute their land. Kennedy advised the Central American elite to "lead the fight for those basic reforms which alone can preserve the fabric of your own societies." He warned that those who make peaceful changes impossible "will make violent revolution inevitable."

The Cuban Revolution and the resulting Alliance for Progress provided the political impetus for the agrarian reform programs established during the 1960s and 1970s in Central America. Governments instituted land redistribution and rural development programs funded by U.S. economic aid as safety valves to reduce rural tension. By promising agrarian reform, Washington and national governments took a major rallying point away from both revolutionary and reformist opposition groups. Cooptation of peasant movements was one of the political aims of U.S.-supported agrarian reforms, as was the creation of a conservative petty bourgeoisie in rural areas.[2]

Streamlining the Agroexport System

While political stabilization has been the prime reason for most recent agrarian reform programs, there were also compelling economic reasons for land redistribution. Agrarian capitalism had not completely squeezed out semi-feudal land tenure and labor relations. There were still pockets where land was left idle and sharecropping prevailed, and some reform programs targeted these traditional *latifundios* for expropriation.

Agrarian reform made political and economic sense as a way to further strengthen agrarian capitalism and stabilize countries economically and politically. But oligarchs were not as amenable to land redistribution programs as President Kennedy and his advisers had initially hoped. Joining them in opposition to agrarian reform were U.S. corporations like United Fruit. This combined resistance to the reformist programs proposed by the Alliance for Progress effectively blocked everything but token land redistribution programs in most Central American countries. The inviolability of "private property" became the war cry of the oligarchs, and those supporting land redistribution were painted as communists or communist sympathizers.

Oligarchs and right-wing forces in Central America did not accept the argument that agrarian reform was needed to preempt agrarian revolutions. Instead, they saw reforms that met peasant demands for land as inherently destabilizing. They argued (and still do) that reforms open the door to more radical peasant organizing. What was needed to block revolution, they said, were tougher national security measures, not reforms.

Long on Rhetoric

Only a year after the Alliance for Progress was announced, the reformist rhetoric was toned down. Agrarian reform was still on the development agenda; but the emphasis was placed on transformation rather than expropriation, and on redistributing government, not private lands. Washington also dramatically stepped up its police and military training programs for the region, a sure sign that it too considered repression, not reform, the best insurance against revolution.

The Alliance for Progress proved to be long on rhetoric but short on action. After finding the ruling elites virulently opposed to land redistribution, Washington substituted for "agrarian reform" less threatening terms like "rural development" and "agrarian transformation." AID-sponsored titling projects simply gave farmers legal title to land they already farmed rather than expropriating idle private land for redistribution to the landless. Instead of tackling the politically sensitive issue of inequitable land tenure, the Agency for International Development (AID) funded programs to "colonize" isolated government-owned frontier lands with landless campesinos. These projects left the skewed patterns of land tenure and land use intact. Also left unscathed was the region's political economy, whose main characteristics were agroexport production and authoritarian rule.

Despite their limited scope, agrarian reform programs instituted in Central America with AID support during the 1960s and 1970s met some of the original political and economic objectives of the Alliance for Progress. Programs to resettle landless campesinos in the agricultural frontier, for example, did ease some rural tension over landlessness. These colonization projects also served to open up new areas for agricultural production, both for basic foods and agroexports. This was especially true for the cattle industry, which used resettled peasants to clear forests for pastures. Agrarian reform, however, never went beyond colonization programs, except in Honduras where a strong peasant movement pushed the military to adopt a stronger agrarian reform program that redistributed idle private, as well as public, lands.

The agrarian reform programs of Nicaragua and El Salvador were announced when the hegemony of the United States and its elite allies in Central America was seriously threatened for the first time. Somoza, Washington's most reliable ally in the region, had fallen; leftist revolution threatened in El Salvador; and a rural guerrilla movement in Guatemala had achieved surprising strength and popular support. Throughout Central America, the agroexport economy was showing severe signs of strain. After a long period of economic growth, the region's economy found itself stagnated in the late 1970s due to declining commodity prices, world recession, and soaring oil prices.

The social consequences of the three-decade agroexport boom were also threatening the region's precarious stability. By 1979, landlessness was becoming particularly serious in Nicaragua and El Salvador, countries where at least 40 percent of the rural population were without land. The rise of this large proletarian sector in the countryside and the parallel increase in the urban unemployed population, created a favorable environment for revolutionary organizing.

Since 1979, both El Salvador and Nicaragua have instituted agrarian reform programs. Both reforms occurred in a revolutionary context—one to prevent a revolution and the other as the result of one.

El Salvador: Reform and Pacification

Since 1932, the year of the *matanza*, a social time bomb has been ticking in rural El Salvador. Memories of the bloodshed and repression quieted peasant organizing for almost three decades. But, by the early 1960s, rapidly increasing landlessness—mainly the result of land-grabbing by the cotton and cattle industries—provoked new rural discontent and peasant organizing. In 1965, the land and hunger crisis in rural El Salvador was further aggravated when many traditional *latifundistas* used the new minimum wage law as an excuse to evict thousands of *colonos* living and sharecropping on their expansive estates. The country's high population density and its lack of an agricultural frontier of uncleared lands made the crisis in El Salvador particularly explosive.

Until 1969, there was land for the taking in the agricultural frontier of Honduras, and many Salvadoran campesinos migrated across the border. But the cattle and cotton industries were also expanding in Honduras, and Honduran leaders soon began calling for the expulsion of the Salvadorans. The illegal immigrant issue plus disagreements in trade practices sparked tension between the two countries, culminating in the infamous and deceptively named 60-hour Soccer War. Resulting ill-feeling in Honduras forced tens of thousands of Salvadoran families back into El Salvador. Returning peasants erected shanty towns in San Salvador and camped on the edges of plantations, creating new pockets of social unrest.

In the early 1960s, progressive elements within the Catholic Church encouraged peasants to form cooperatives and confront economic injustice. From this base within the church, campesinos began organizing to challenge oligarchic control. They demanded more land, better wages, and an end to repression. Two peasant associations, the UTC and FECCAS, stood at the forefront of this incipient rural rebellion. The military government refused the two associations legal status and coordinated a campaign of paramilitary violence against their leaders and supporters. There was, however, one peasant organization that did initially receive government support. That group, the Salvadoran Communal Union (UCS), was created and funded by the American Institute for Free Labor Development (AIFLD) and AID. By sponsoring the moderate UCS, the U.S. government hoped to attract campesino support away from more militant groups.

In an attempt to reduce rural tension, President Arturo Molina announced an agrarian reform plan in 1976, which was to be implemented jointly by the UCS, the military, and the newly created Agrarian Transformation Institute (ISTA). Molina considered the reform program a form of life insurance for the oligarchy. The distribution of a small portion of underutilized land, he argued, would dissipate the growing revolutionary movement and guarantee the oligarchy's hold on national power. The project targeted less than 4 percent of the country's agricultural land and offered generous compensation terms to the landowners.

But the oligarchy would tolerate no land redistribution, however slight. Two landowners' organizations, ANEP and FARO, led the private sector's opposition to this first reform program. Their opposition took the form of vicious anti-communist propaganda accompanied by a sharp increase in death squad violence. Shortly after he announced the program, Molina canceled it. In 1977, the oligarchy and hardline conservatives in the military replaced Molina with his defense minister Carlos Humberto

Romero in a fraudulent election. Romero subsequently unleashed a campaign of repression against the rapidly expanding popular movement of workers and peasants. There was no more talk of reforms until 1979.

Washington Backs New Land Reform

While watching the building momentum of revolutionary forces in Nicaragua, Washington became concerned about the possibility of imminent revolution next door in El Salvador. Circumstances were different in that oligarchic power was not concentrated in one family in El Salvador; and a broad multi-class alliance, like that which existed in Nicaragua, was not challenging the Romero regime. Yet the country's stability was slipping fast as popular opposition grew to Romero's repressive regime. In October 1979, only several months after the Sandinistas overthrew Somoza in Nicaragua, a small group of young officers ran Romero out of office, setting up a military/civilian junta to run the country. The upstart officers decided that the only way to stabilize the government was through an agrarian reform government that met some of the popular demands. The junta called for agrarian reform as part of a "profound transformation of the old economic, political, and social structures which do not offer the majority of the population the minimum conditions in which to develop as human beings."

Lack of U.S. support for Romero made the 1979 coup possible. But neither could the new junta count on full U.S. support—a fact that contributed to its early demise in early 1980. Washington, while in favor of a reformist government, wanted one in which it could call the shots. And the Carter administration feared that the reforms proposed by members of the October 1979 junta might open the door for revolutionaries. In fact, the progressive members of the junta had little real power. While army moderates and civilian progressives nominally controlled the government, true power remained in the hands of the hardline officers and the oligarchy. Consequently, the reform program was not able to move forward, and the progressive junta members resigned out of frustration.

Washington, meanwhile, was waiting in the wings to form a junta government more to its liking. After several failed attempts, a military/civilian junta backed by the United States took power in March 1980. The junta, which included hardline military officers, was headed by Napoleón Duarte, who led the center-right wing of the Christian Democrats. Within several days of embracing Duarte, the junta announced a three-phase agrarian reform program. Although opposed by the oligarchy, the land redistribution plan enjoyed the support of the country's military high command.

From the outset of the U.S.-designed counterinsurgency war announced by Duarte, the main components of its pacification strategy were to: 1) shift the balance of power away from the highly reactionary landed oligarchy; 2) create a political power base for a "centrist" government, and 3) prevent the radicalization of the peasantry.

The Three Phases of Reform

From its inception, Duarte's agrarian reform was a top-down program controlled and financed by the United States. The decrees instituting the program were hastily drawn up with little discussion or consultation. A 1980 internal AID document acknowledged that the land reform proposal "could prove troublesome because it was decreed without advance discussion except in very limited government circles, and we are told it is considered by key Salvadoran officials as a misguided and U.S.-imposed initiative."[3]

The program was divided into three categories of land appropriation and distribution. Phase I targeted estates with over 1200 acres and covered 10-15 percent of the country's arable land. The Phase I land was to be redistributed to cooperatives formed among the former full-time employees of the expropriated estates. Phase II was directed at holdings between 220 and 1200 acres and covered about 20 percent of the nation's farmland. It was called the "heart of the reform" because it was aimed at the economic base of the oligarchy. Due to strong opposition by the landowners, Phase II of the program was quickly dropped. Phase III included all rental lands under 17 acres, accounting for another 10 percent of the farmland. Under the law, peasants cultivating these rental properties were eligible to apply for title to the land. Potentially, 40-45 percent of the nation's land was to be redistributed.

Soon after the reform was announced, it was hailed by AID and the U.S. embassy as a bold step to change unjust land tenure and improve the lot of the poor. In 1980, AIFLD consultants Roy Prosterman and Mary Temple claimed that the program would become "the most sweeping agrarian reform in the history of Latin America when fully implemented."[4] The amount of land scheduled for expropriation and the number of potential beneficiaries (300,000 campesino families) did make the program seem a major shakeup in the country's land tenure. In the U.S. Congress and in foreign capitals, news of the land reform proposal was taken as strong evidence that the new government was serious about its promises to undermine oligarchic power. A massive publicity campaign about the reform instilled hope that life was finally improving for the rural poor. With a bottomless budget from AID, AIFLD deployed hundreds of "promoters" to organize rural support for the reform and for the new "democratic" government.

Land Reform as a Pacification Program

The Salvadoran agrarian reform was designed by U.S. experts, financed by U.S. economic aid, and carried out by U.S. organizers and technicians. The first large shipment of military aid to El Salvador arrived the month the program was announced, a big inducement for the military to support the land redistribution. Determined U.S. support for the program and a flood of U.S dollars into the economy smothered most opposition to the program from the oligarchy. The promise of full compensation for their holdings in cash (25 percent of value) and bonds (75 percent) somewhat mollified angry landowners.

The AID Mission in San Salvador directed the program and considered it primarily as a tool of political stabilization. The Salvadoran land reform, it said, is "a political imperative to help prevent political collapse, strike a blow to the left, and help prevent radicalization of the rural population." The two main thrusts of this strategy were the creation of a sector of conservative small farmers and a network of cooperatives organized by AIFLD.

Phase III, which gave campesinos title to rented plots, was designed not to improve the life of these peasants but to give them a proprietary interest in the country. This phase was tacked onto the program at the last minute by AID. It was quickly put together for AID and AIFLD by Roy Prosterman, a land reform specialist who had no direct knowledge of Latin America. The basic concept of his Phase III plan was to turn over small parcels of land to 117,000 peasant families, giving them an economic and political stake in the U.S.-backed government.

Prosterman had designed an almost identical program for AID as part of the U.S. rural pacification campaign in Vietnam. In fact, he gave the Salvadoran program the same label he used for his Vietnam land reform program, "Land to the Tiller." A 1968 congressional report, to which Prosterman referred in his later writings about agrarian reform, called the Vietnam reform effort "an essential element of the pacification program", adding that "the resolution of the present [Vietnam] conflict may well hinge on the success of pacification."[5] Having failed in Vietnam, Prosterman saw a second chance in El Salvador to "turn the tables" on the guerrillas.[6] Most Phase III properties were in the poorest parts of the Salvadoran countryside; areas where the guerrillas had the most control. It was his belief that the beneficiaries of the Land to the Tiller program would become more interested in cultivating their new landholdings than in supporting revolution.

While the underlying goal of the agrarian reform was predominantly political, AID considered the political and economic implications of the reform to be closely interwoven. Discussing the Phase III program, one AID official exclaimed, "There is nothing more conservative than the small farmer. We're going to be breeding capitalists like rabbits."[7] Initially, AID (like Prosterman) was convinced that, with technical assistance from AIFLD and other quasi-private organizations, the Phase III beneficiaries would become an economically important sector of farm owner/operators that would boost the production of basic grains and be tightly integrated into the capitalist agricultural economy. It soon became obvious, though, that most Phase III lands were too poor to support one family let alone produce large marketable harvests.

Phase I properties were turned over to peasant cooperatives which were organized by AIFLD representatives. AIFLD attempted to use these cooperatives as its base for a "democratic" peasant movement. Cooperative leaders received technical as well as ideological training from AIFLD, and many of them were put on AIFLD's payroll. Phase I lands were turned over to cooperatives instead of subdividing them for individual beneficiaries because AIFLD was concerned about the loss of production efficiency that would result. Nonetheless, the eventual subdivision of Phase I estates was discussed early on by Prosterman and other advocates of small owner/operator farms. Prosterman and Temple wrote in 1980 that "experiments with subdividing and smaller-scale cultivation will probably get underway in early 1981."[8]

AIFLD, which had been in charge of rural pacification efforts since the mid-1960s, was given the leading role in coordinating the critical pacification work of the 1980s. Using UCS as its base, AIFLD developed a social infrastructure in government-controlled rural areas to build peasant support for the reform process. It also organized land reform beneficiaries to support U.S.-backed "democratization" and counterinsurgency initiatives. Peasant organizations created by AIFLD were especially prominent in the 1980-84 period when widespread repression obstructed organizing by independent groups.

AID recognized that the political objectives of agrarian reform would not be achieved simply by distributing land. Peasants in the reform sector had to be given at least the illusion of power and participation in the reform process. AIFLD did this through a "massive information campaign" that flooded the countryside with radio and written propaganda about the important place that campesinos had in what the army called the "new El Salvador."[9] Subsequently, during the election campaigns of 1982, 1984, and 1985, AIFLD hired "promoters" to spread its counterrevolutionary ideology, while encouraging rural residents to participate in the "democratic" process.

Reform by Repression

Military and paramilitary violence were the hallmarks of the country's agrarian reform, especially during its first few years. The military had three reasons to support agrarian reform: 1) their cooperation with the reform program was a condition for continued U.S. military aid; 2) the pacification logic of the reform was something that they themselves recognized, and; 3) they saw it as a way to extend their control of the countryside.

The day after the land reform decree was announced, the military-civilian junta also declared a state of siege. Bolstered by shipments of new U.S. military aid, the counterinsurgency campaign began in earnest. The process of land redistribution, was viewed by the military as a good opportunity to demonstrate their control in rural areas and to eliminate peasant troublemakers. The State Department's John Bushnell justified the massive troop deployment in rural areas on the grounds that "the redistribution of land would not be possible if it wasn't for the security provided by the Salvadoran army to the new property holders."[10] Within El Salvador, however, there was no evidence that campesinos welcomed the increased military presence. For most of them, agrarian reform quickly became synonomous with army terrorism.

The bloodletting frequently occurred following the election of cooperative leaders. Local commanders waited to see who the peasants considered their best representatives and then moved in for the kill. In some cases, the army used its power to protect the interests of the landowners and block the transfer of Phase I and III lands to the claimants. One instance of landlord/army collusion involved a community of 300 potential claimants of Phase I lands. Due to threats, only 40 families applied for title; of those, 27 were murdered by soldiers and the rest gave up their claims.[11]

Still, most of the violence surrounding the implementation of the agrarian reform occurred within the context of counterinsurgency. "The army thought that by making the agrarian reform, people were going to love them to pieces," observed Leonel Gomez, the former assistant of the agrarian reform institute who left the country in 1981 after receiving death threats.[12] Instead local commanders found that the reform bred feelings of self-determination and independence from the old power structure of colonels and oligarchs. This dangerous attitude was corrected by torturing and assassinating the boldest campesino leaders in the reform sector.

In addition to direct military repression, the reform "beneficiaries" were also victims of paramilitary violence by death squads. Some death squad killings were apparently ordered by vengeful oligarchs. Small right-wing groups like the Committee of Individuals Affected by the Reform encouraged vigilante action with statements like the following: "Property is the extension of a person's life and of God. It is our duty to conserve it, guard it, and avoid at all costs that ignorant people, delinquents, or terrorists deprive us of this sacred right."[13] The AIFLD-sponsored campesino union and AIFLD officials themselves were victims of the wave of official violence which killed 10,000 civilians in 1980 alone. Two AIFLD officials were assassinated by a death squad, and over 90 UCS organizers were killed during the first three years of the program. When asked about the violence associated with the land reform, Tom King of the AID mission in San Salvador responded: "We don't go around counting the dead. Body counts are not our business."[14]

Agrarian Reform in Ruins

To justify its ever-increasing aid requests for El Salvador, the Reagan administration often pointed to the alleged success of the agrarian reform program. Yet behind the administration's wall of favorable propaganda was an ill-conceived, blood-soaked program. By 1984, it became increasingly difficult to hide the program's failures.

An internal audit by AID's Inspector General showed that the land reform was riddled with financial problems and warned that the future of agrarian reform in El Salvador was "bleak." Another report in 1985 concluded that Phase I cooperatives "cannot possibly meet their land purchase payments."[15] Things had not improved by 1986 when yet another AID evaluation found that reform beneficiaries were saddled with a debt of close to a billion dollars.

AID's own evaluations of the agrarian reform consistently concluded that Phase I cooperatives suffered from massive debt, no working capital, large tracts of unproductive land, labor surpluses, and weak management. According to AID's Inspector General, there was little hope that these cooperatives would ever become financially viable. This was because they had been given poor land, no technical assistance, and were paying high interest rates to compensate former landowners (many of whom left El Salvador to live in Miami). About 45 percent of the Phase I land was non-productive and "most of the remaining land was of poor quality."[16]

Phase I fell far short of the initial projections. Over 65 estates originally scheduled for appropriation were left untouched as a result of sweetheart deals secretly arranged between politicians, military officers and wealthy landowners. By 1986, only 160 cooperatives had received definitive titles—less than half the number initially estimated. And many of those cooperatives were in economic disarray or had dissolved. In 1984, the Salvadoran Army began discussing a plan to resettle refugees on Phase I estates.

Phase III beneficiaries faced equally dim prospects. Six years after the reform began, only 18,000 of the 117,000 potential beneficiaries had been granted titles. Others had been given provisional titles, but AID in 1986 projected a maximum of 45,000 potential beneficiaries of Phase III. Close observers estimated the final number of beneficiaries much lower. At least one-third of those who received provisional titles were not working the land because they had been "threatened, evicted, or had disappeared."[17]

Both Phase I and III have been undermined by the absence of credit, technical assistance, training, and popular participation. Over 90 percent of the recipients of Phase III lands reported they had received no technical help.[18] Major decisions about the management of the Phase I cooperatives were being made by ISTA officials and appointed administrators with no input from co-op members. "Essentially the co-ops are run much the same as they were before," commented Marion Brown of the Land Tenure Center. "Before you had an absentee landlord; now you have an absentee administrator."[19]

Peasants have become neither food self-sufficient nor economically independent through their participation in Phase III. Most of these parcels cannot sustain continuous food production and need to be left fallow for a year or two before replanting. Yet beneficiaries are tied to the land for as much as 30 years (the time given to compensate the government for the land).[20] Former tenant farmers are thus paying for land they cannot farm each year. Consequently, Phase III beneficiaries have been unable to raise their income above the poverty level of $225 a year. Laurence Simon of Oxfam America observed that the planners of the agrarian reform obviously did not consider land use patterns. "To do so would have required a commitment to rural development instead of pacification or counterinsurgency."[21]

It was not as if AID was unaware of the problems with Phase III; they simply chose to ignore negative assessments of the program, even from their own consultants. A 1981 evaluation by AID consultant Dr. Norman Chapin concluded that if cultivated every year most Phase III plots "would be converted into sterile desert." The same report went on to discuss more than agronomic issues. "It is difficult to imagine," Chapin warned, "how [the land reform] can be implemented in El Salvador's current climate of violence and civil disorganization."[22] It was not, however, the value of agrarian reform as a development tool that propelled the land redistribution program forward. AID continued to fund the program, because of its value as an instrument of political stabilization and counterinsurgency.

Requiem for Reform

The 1982 election victory of Roberto D'Aubuisson's ARENA party dashed campesino hopes that the promises of the reform would be honored. Taking control of the Ministry of Agriculture and the land reform agency, ISTA, ARENA was able to block further redistribution and obstruct technical assistance and credit programs. When the Constituent Assembly passed a new national constitution in 1983, there was no mention of "agrarian reform." Instead, the constitution emphasized that the government "recognizes, promotes, and guarantees the right of private property" and "will promote and protect private initiative." Without specifically dismantling the land reform, the new constitution guaranteed landowners the right to rent out their property—a thinly veiled attack on Phase III. Another provision raised the maximum size for private holdings to 605 acres and gave landowners until January 1987 to sell off property above the 605 acre limit—enough time to rearrange title ownership among family members in the event that the limit is ever enforced.

The presidential victory of Duarte in 1984 temporarily revived hope among campesinos that land reforms would once more gain momentum. But those hopes were soon dashed as Duarte seemed more concerned about building support among the elite than in consolidating worker and peasant backing. Duarte's failure to enforce all phases of the agrarian reform and to increase government assistance to the reform sector caused many peasant leaders to join the popular opposition to Duarte. Even Duarte's Deputy Minister of Agriculture felt that the agrarian reform had run its ill-fated course. "This is a future without promise," he demurred. "Land will go back to the owners, and the people will be kicked off."[23]

Evaluated in purely political terms, land reform in El Salvador was partially successful—certainly more so than the program instituted by AID in Vietnam. At the critical stage when Washington was rapidly escalating its involvement in El Salvador, the agrarian reform convinced congressional representatives and many U.S. citizens that the Salvadoran government was indeed proceeding on the path toward democracy and social justice. As a result, massive sums of U.S. military and economic aid flowed into the country and kept the government and the economy afloat. "The agrarian reform has done a lot to take the heat out of the massive drift of the campesinos to the violent left," one government official told *Time*.[24] As slim as the benefits of the land reform were, many campesinos did feel that things were changing for the better.

Agrarian reform did not seriously weaken the oligarchy. In fact, the landed elite grew more determined and united in the face of the perceived threat to their land holdings with the implementation of each phase of the reform. They succeeded in postponing and substantially weakening Phase II, excluding many Phase I estates from expropriation, cutting short the Phase III reform program, and impeding the flow of government services to reform beneficiaries. In a gambit aimed at increasing his popularity among peasant associations, Duarte in late 1986 promised to press forward with Phase II in 1987. The announcement was greeted with predictable fury by business associations like ANEP and the Salvadoran Coffee Growers Association.

Even in the unlikely event that Phase II is finally enforced, the redistribution will have little impact on the rural poor. Most landowners have already sold off or arranged title transfers for property over the 605 acre minimum. "We're not talking about much land anymore," observed AID's Tom King in December 1986. By threatening to expropriate holdings over 605 acres, the government has succeeded not in increasing the small farm sector but in creating a large sector of 150 to 605-acre agroexport estates.[25]

Instead of choosing to extend its base among workers and peasants, the U.S.-backed Christian Democrats since 1984 have offered the oligarchy larger concessions and assurances against further reforms. Right-wing groups, like the ARENA party and the ANEP business association, have regained the initiative and demanded that Phase I estates be re-privatized. Given the government's unwillingness to provide necessary credit and technical assistance to beneficiaries, many Phase I estates and Phase III plots may now revert to their former owners. AID also backed off from its earlier commitment to the agrarian reform. Instead of placing its rural development funds into the reform sector, AID since 1984 has directed an increasing sum of economic aid into agribusiness operations controlled by the very oligarchs who opposed the agrarian reform so vigorously. Moreover, it encouraged former Phase I landholders to use their compensation bonds to set up agroindustries on the lands held by floundering cooperatives. Beginning in 1985, AID also permitted the Salvadoran government to use local currency generated from U.S. food aid and Economic Support Funds (ESF) to compensate landowners.

AID has now dismissed the possibility that there can be any significant improvement of rural social conditions through land reform even though land concentration in El Salvador remains among the worst in Latin America. "Hope for El Salvador's economic and social problems," says AID, "rests largely on the development of light industry, agroindustry and non-farm sources of employment."[26]

In summary, the Salvadoran land reform program has the following major weaknesses:

* The reform was instituted because it was a politically expedient way for the Salvadoran government to gain a base of support in the countryside and was never really intended to empower campesinos politically or economically.

* It never redistributed the country's best land, and much of the land distributed was unable to sustain the beneficiaries.

* The program only "benefited" the full-time employees of large estates and the renters of small plots, thereby excluding the large landless population of seasonal farmworkers and those small farmers with plots too small for subsistence.

* It was a top-down model imposed by agencies of the U.S. government in which there was no room for popular decision-making about the reform's directions and ultimate goals.

* Cooperatization of Phase I estates was forced on peasants by ISTA and AIFLD and the coopertives were really run not by elected leaders but by government-appointed administrators.

* It was implemented in the context of extreme repression and a civil war.

* It failed to provide its beneficiaries with necessary credit, technical help, and markets, while leaving them with a debt that they cannot pay off.

A Dead-End Reform

Agrarian reform is all but dead in El Salvador. The two phases that were implemented were watered down so much that they had little effect. After six years and over $300 million in U.S. economic aid, the agrarian reform was less than the "sweeping transformation" originally projected. Only 8 percent of the rural poor have received definitive title to redistributed land.[27] Another 15 percent have claimed land, mostly under Phase III, but most of these potential beneficiaries will probably never receive title, given the government's and AID's reduced commitment to the program. Even the most optimistic estimates of the total number of families affected by the reform fall far short of the original promises. AID had initially projected that between one-half and two-thirds of the rural poor would benefit. By late 1986, however, it was clear that at most, only a quarter of the rural poor would receive land, with 10-15 percent being a more realistic estimate.

Few among those that did "benefit" from the program actually experienced any improvement in their standard of living, and many were worse off than before (not to mention those cooperative leaders murdered by the army). Most of the beneficiaries—both individuals and cooperatives—are buried in debt and plowing lands that are among the worst in the country. While those peasants in the reform sector are obliged to pay for their land, AID has used its economic assistance programs to compensate former landowners, many of whom do not even live in El Salvador. In the end, El Salvador's agrarian reform neither significantly challenged the oligarchy nor improved life for the powerless.

Nicaraguan Reform: A Revolutionary Experiment

The Sandinistas instituted an agrarian reform program immediately after their July 19, 1979 victory over the Somoza forces. The program has since gone through two major stages that increased its scope and responsiveness to peasant demands for land. In the process of extending the reform, the Sandinistas have made critical decisions not only about the country's agricultural priorities, but also about the political and economic direction of the entire Nicaraguan society.

No longer guerrillas but government leaders, the Sandinistas faced an array of perplexing questions about the nature and direction of the country's political economy. What is the correct balance between agro-export production and production for internal consumption? Does agribusiness have a role in a revolutionary society? Are there alternatives to the agroexport economy for underdeveloped countries like Nicaragua? Should small owner/operator farms be discouraged because small farmers tend to be politically conservative? Should the emphasis be on state farms that can take better advantage of mechanization and economies of scale? Is it possible to maintain low food prices while raising the prices paid to growers? These questions have all played a part in determining the nature of agrarian reform in the Nicaraguan revolution.

The Agroexport Boom and the Peasants

Agroexport production was ravishing Nicaragua when the FSLN began its protracted struggle against the Somoza regime. Matagalpa, a center of early FSLN operations, was the country's most important corn- and bean-growing area. But the beef-export boom in the 1960s quickly converted the farms and forests of Matagalpa to pastures, displacing thousands of peasants. The province was designated a counterinsurgency zone, landless peasants were rounded up by the National Guard, and colonization projects funded by AID and the Inter-American Development Bank (IDB) resettled displaced peasants in the agriculture frontier of the adjoining Zelaya province.[28] Somoza's Agrarian Institute boasted that the colonization projects augmented the food supply and "prevented communism."[29]

After 1950, the agroexport sector in Nicaragua was the fastest growing in the region. Cotton, sugar, and beef production doubled and then tripled. In the mid-1970s, Nicaragua accounted for roughly half of the region's cotton exports and a third of its beef exports.[30]

Not only in Matagalpa but also in León and Chinandega, peasants vigorously resisted the expansion of agroexport production onto their land. Official records show over two hundred "land invasions" from 1964 to 1973, but these attempts by peasants to recover their land were rapidly crushed by the hated National Guard. As a result, landlessness soared in rural Nicaragua, and Managua began to swell with immigrants from the countryside.

After the Vatican Council (1961-65) and the Medellin Conference in 1968, progressive clerics began preaching to campesinos about the political implications of the gospel. The Jesuits established the Educational Center for Agrarian Advancement (CEPA), which, besides teaching campesinos agricultural techniques, spread the message that peasants had a right to land. A related development that sparked increased peasant organizing was the decision of the Catholic Church to form a lay ministry. In the "base communities" created by lay Delegates of the Word, social justice issues were frequently discussed. Escalating repression forced many Delegates to operate clandestinely.[31]

Many of the early supporters of the FSLN were church activists. Several key CEPA activists helped FSLN cadres organize the Committees of Agricultural Workers in 1976. Two years later, these regional Committees joined together to form the Association of Rural Workers (ATC). Three days before the Sandinistas took power, land reform began in Nicaragua. With the area around León in the hands of the guerrillas, peasants led by the ATC occupied several plantations belonging to the Somoza family. That show of peasant militance on July 16, 1979, is now commemorated as National Agrarian Reform Day.

Land of Somoza, People of Sandino

Before the 1979 revolution, the FSLN guerrillas referred to Nicaragua as "the land of Somoza, the people of Sandino." Augusto Cesar Sandino had led a peasant rebellion against U.S. Marines in Nicaragua from 1927 to 1933. He was assassinated in 1934 on the orders of Anastasio Somoza Garcia, the father of the country's last dictator. Probably more than anything else, the triumphant arrival of the Sandinistas in Managua on July 19, 1979 meant that Nicaragua was no longer the "land of Somoza."

Agrarian reform had been on the Sandinista agenda since the late 1960s. The FSLN promised to bring an "agrarian revolution" to the Nicaraguan people by expropriating capitalist and feudal estates, distributing land to peasants, creating jobs for unemployed farmworkers, and exempting "patriotic" landowners who collaborated with the guerrilla struggle.[32] The "authentic agrarian reform" proposed by the Sandinistas went far beyond the land-titling and colonization projects sponsored by AID and Somoza's Agrarian Institute.

As its birthright, the new government assumed control over all property of the Somoza family and its close associates. More than 20 percent of the country's cultivated land (about 2 million acres) suddenly became the property of the revolutionary government. Three categories of property were expropriated: 1) all farms owned by the Somoza family and its "cronies," 2) lands that had been confiscated by Somoza-linked banks, and 3) abandoned and idle property.

During its first two years, the Sandinista government concentrated on the development of agroexport plantations left behind by the Somocistas. Of the expropriated estates, over 90 percent was maintained as state-owned farms with the remaining portion going mostly to newly formed production cooperatives of former sharecroppers. Wages were increased, and land rents were sharply reduced. A wide range of social benefits, including agricultural credit for the rural population was instituted.

The initial agrarian reform fell far short of the "agrarian revolution" that the FSLN had promised when it was a guerrilla group. Rather than subdividing the Somoza estates into small or medium-sized farms or turning the plantations over to cooperatives, the new government elected to run the estates as state farms. In doing so, they opted to continue the country's reliance on large-scale, capital-intensive agroexport production. The peasantry was generally considered an inefficient sector of the agricultural economy. While there was a dramatic increase in agricultural credit available to small landholders, virtually no land was distributed to individual farmers for basic food production. While the Sandinistas have attempted to shape their own model of development, they have done so largely within the social and economic structures established by the dominant agroexport system. Nicaragua's agrarian reform until recently has been cautious not to disrupt the country's dual structure of agriculture wherein the dominant sector produces almost entirely for external markets.

Agrarian Reform Widens Scope

Landless and near-landless campesinos soon grew frustrated with the slow pace of the Sandinistas' agrarian revolution. In February 1980, over 30,000 peasants organized by the ATC rallied in Managua demanding that a more sweeping agrarian reform be instituted. Although the cries for land continued, the government waited another year before broadening the land reform.

Political and economic considerations caused the delay. A multi-class alliance had brought the Sandinistas to power, and the new leaders were anxious not to further weaken this alliance by threatening capitalist producers with expropriation. The government also did not want to precipitate a decline in agroexport production by passing a new land reform law. Furthermore, it was concerned that a stronger agrarian reform might endanger the country's sources of external financing.

Land reform took a cautious step forward in July 1981. A new agrarian reform law targeted underutilized properties over 850 acres on the fertile Pacific coast and over 1700 acres elsewhere. Land productively used was not subject to expropriation.

The law, while extending the scope of the reform, was fundamentally conservative. It guaranteed "the rights to private property over the land to all those who employ it productively and efficiently." Expropriation occurred only after judicial proceedings (which were decided in favor of the land owner in one third of the cases).[33] Landowners with holdings under the 850-1700 level risked expropriation only if they were: 1) decapitalizing by selling off farm machinery and cattle, 2) intentionally underproducing, or 3) collaborating with counterrevolutionary forces. By early 1985, the new law had affected about 10 percent of Nicaraguan farmland.

The 1981 law was not an attack on large landholders or private property, as the anti-Sandinista opposition maintained. The reform, for example, did not touch Nicaraguan Sugar Estates, a private company with thousands of acres of sugarcane fields and over 10,000 employees. In the government's eyes, Nicaraguan Sugar Estates and others like it were "patriotic producers" because they continued to produce at pre-revolutionary levels. Rather than focusing on land tenure patterns, the government attempted to mold the economy through its control of import/export trade and its power to set price levels. The Sandinistas called their approach to agrarian revolution a "mixed economy under popular hegemony." While insisting that all marketing and pricing be government controlled, the government encouraged large capitalist farms and ranches to increase their production. "More than control of the means of production," explained Minister of Agriculture Jaime Wheelock, "we are interested in controlling the economic surplus in order to distribute justly the nation's wealth."[34]

The 1981 reform was not an assault on capitalist agriculture but an attempt to rid the country of the vestiges of precapitalist land tenure. It was intended to serve as an inducement to growers of the non-reform sector to produce more efficiently. Growers who had slowed down production out of disagreement with government control of marketing and pricing faced the threat of eventual expropriation. While it was hardly the draconian measure that government opponents claimed, the 1981 agrarian reform did increase counterrevolutionary sentiment among the economic elite. Capitalist growers complained that the country was moving away from economic pluralism and toward socialism.

The ATC and the Union of Growers and Ranchers (UNAG), an association of small- and medium-sized producers, were instrumental in developing the new law and promoting its enforcement. Unlike the 1979 agrarian reform, land in the reform sector went more to cooperatives than to state farms.

One of the first title-granting ceremonies under the 1981 agrarian reform was held at the San Albino Mine in the Segovia hills. Sandino had worked at the U.S.-owned mine, and it was here that he organized his first guerrilla band. Thousands of peasants, among them older men who had fought alongside Sandino, walked for miles on this sun-baked Saturday from all the villages in Nueva Segovia province to witness the historic occasion. Minister of Agriculture Jaime Wheelock told the gathering that the Sandinista agrarian reform was the result of a long struggle for the rights of peasants that began at that very location with Sandino. One wrinkled veteran of Sandino's war against the U.S. Marine occupation of Nicaragua said that he had defended Nicaragua against the Yankees once before in the hills of Segovia, and was "ready to do it again."[35]

Besides distributing underutilized land and decapitalized farms to peasant cooperatives, the Ministry of Agriculture also began an ambitious titling program to give peasants legal title to the land they had been farming. The titling program focused on border areas in the hope that those peasants with a land title to their name would be more committed to the revolution. The strategy worked. Recipients of land titles and beneficiaries of redistributed land have been more willing to support the Sandinistas and defend the country against *contra* attacks. One such beneficiary is Victoriano Gonzalez, who farms his land with a rifle slung across his back. "I was born in a family that had no land, and my sons were born without land," says Gonzalez. "Now, my grandsons are being born on their own land. They have a future."[36]

Problems with the Reform

Still, the 1981 agrarian reform proved only a stop-gap measure. More land was made available to the peasantry, and the law did persuade large growers to make more productive use of their land and to refrain from decapitalizing. But, the ATC and UNAG were not satisfied with the extent of the law and were angered by the Ministry of Agriculture's (MIDINRA) continued reluctance to distribute land to individual peasants.

In 1985, peasants began to take the agrarian reform into their own hands by invading lands of large, usually anti-Sandinista growers. Most of the land invasions took place in the densely populated province of Masaya on the Pacific coast. The agroexport boom, especially the expansion of cotton production, had created a large landless population in this fertile region. To date, agrarian reform had only scratched the surface of the problem of landlessness in Masaya, which during the civil war had been a major source of Sandinista support. The government's apparent unresponsiveness to peasant demands for land frustrated landless peasants and sparked the series of land invasions. "The reform law passes through the clouds, it doesn't touch anybody," observed one Masaya peasant.[37] By the end of 1985, there were almost daily demonstrations and petitions for land here.

These militant demands for land persuaded MIDINRA to step up its land redistribution program. Masaya was declared a special agrarian reform zone, and MIDINRA began expropriating land (with compensation) to respond to the peasant rebellion. As a result of this new attention to peasant demands, almost as much land was redistributed in 1985 as had been distributed between 1981-1984. Not only was more land redistributed but half the land was going to individual campesinos. This was a marked change from previous years when virtually all the redistributed land went to cooperatives. Another significant change was the reduced emphasis given the state sector. Only 40 percent of the land distributed in 1985 came from negotiated sales and expropriations of private property, while the remaining 60 percent was drawn away from the state sector.

One victim of the government's recent, more radical approach to land redistribution was Enrique Bolanos, the president of the Superior Council of Private Enterprise (COSEP). After MIDINRA agreed to turn over

Bolanos' land to peasant occupiers in 1985, he declared: "All Nicaraguans who have something here and have not lost it will lose it, because that is the system, the ideology, the doctrine of the ones running the country."[38] The other side of Bolanos' complaint is that many other Nicaraguans who have never had anything are, for the first time, landowners because of the Sandinistas.

By late 1985, MIDINRA had exhausted the expropriation possibilities of the 1981 law. Large landholdings over 850 acres in the Pacific coast and over 1700 acres in other regions had covered 36 percent of the farmland before the revolution but had declined by 1985 to 11 percent of the country's farmland—most of which was being fully exploited. If it were to distribute more land, MIDINRA would need either to broaden the agrarian reform or to redistribute state farmland. It decided to take both steps. One MIDINRA representative estimated that the state sector would decline from 19 percent to 10 percent by the end of the decade.

The land invasions in Masaya happened at the same time that the government was reevaluating its entire strategy of agricultural development and agrarian reform. The government's concentration on capital-intensive, mainly agroexport production and its relative inattention to the demands and needs of peasant producers were being reconsidered in the light of the following factors:

* Reduced peasant support for the revolution and signs of increasing support for the counterrevolution, particularly among campesinos in isolated areas.

* Continued disintegration of the alliance betweeen the government and more capitalist producers and the integration of many large growers into the counterrevolution.

* The inability of the government to manage the state sector efficiently.

* A worsening foreign exchange crisis that prevented the country from importing the inputs needed for large-scale, "modernized" agricultural production.

* A declining per capita production of basic foods.

Agrarian Reform Responds to Peasant Pressure

In February 1986, the 1981 agrarian reform law was abolished and replaced with one that had a more radical and pro-peasant profile. The new law removed the limits set by the 1981 reform, making estates of all sizes subject to expropriation if they were underutilized. It also gave MIDINRA the power to expropriate property "for public use or social interest" even if that land was being farmed efficiently. Upon announcing the new law, President Daniel Ortega cited the "peasant's greater need for land and the U.S. war of aggression." He promised, "The land will be given away until there is not one single peasant in Nicaragua without land."[39]

The first stages of Nicaragua's agrarian reform—the 1979 expropriation of Somoza property and the 1981 land reform law—did not constitute an agrarian revolution. Instead, they were essentially attempts to strengthen the agroexport system, albeit in the interests of a government committed to workers and peasants. In contrast, the 1986 agrarian reform law was a step toward a redefinition of the agricultural economy. Adding to its impact were other pro-peasant measures, including the complete liberalization of basic food marketing and the political strengthening of UNAG. When seen together, these measures demonstrate the government's increased commitment to small and medium-sized growers.

Reflecting on these changes, Edgardo García, ATC's secretary general, said that the new law improved "the alliances of the revolution" by more clearly distinguishing "between friends and enemies of the revolution." The 1981 law, he noted, left untouched capitalist estates with holdings below the 850-1700 acreage limit, even though they were intentionally underutilized by anti-Sandinista growers. Conversely, he contended that the government was obligated to defend the interests of landless peasants who supported the revolution, even if that meant alienating capitalist producers.

UNAG, the most autonomous of the country's mass organizations, also greeted the 1986 reform law enthusiastically. Its president Daniel Nuñez said, "We're not worried [about the expropriation of private lands] for a very simple reason. After six years of revolution, 80 percent of the land is still in private hands, and only 20 percent in the hands of the state. The new law is consistent with a mixed economy and political pluralism." But Rosendo Diaz, the president of the opposition Union of Nicaraguan Agricultural Producers (UPANIC), representing the majority of the country's large producers, had a sharply contrasting opinion. "This is a law to make Nicaragua's lands state property and to transform the peasant into a peon of the state."[40]

An end to peasant land invasions was one intended effect of the new law supported by all sides. UNAG felt that the broadened law plus its guarantee of government/owner negotiations gave landless peasants more land while protecting landowners against spontaneous land invasions. The ATC's García agreed, noting that peasant land takeovers are often counterproductive. He pointed out that it was more efficient for one farm to employ 50 workers than to have that farm subdivided into plots for five landless peasants.

Investing for the Future

At the same time the government was reconsidering its agrarian reform priorities, questions were also being asked about the advisability of investing in capital-intensive projects. Despite efforts to increase credit to small farmers, most of the government's investment funds had gone to large-scale infrastructure and production projects. Between 1982 and 1985, MIDINRA directed an investment drive that was unprecedented in the country's history. It decided that the country's best bet for economic growth and increased agricultural production was to increase the technology and infrastructure available to the state sector. Under this development strategy, the state agricultural sector was to be the country's most dynamic source of capital accumulation while the peasant sector was expected to decline in economic importance.[41]

During the first six years of the revolution, fully half of the government's investment budget went to a handful of projects. These included two large dairy farms, a tobacco production scheme for the Bulgarian market, a deep-water port in Bluefields to facilitate agricultural expansion in the country's eastern half, a hydroelectric plant, an African palm plantation to produce vegetable oil, an ambitious plan to produce corn on highly mechanized and irrigated Pacific coast property, and a poultry complex. Nicaragua stood out as the only Central American nation investing in a new tomorrow for its agricultural sector. The level of development was comparable to the expansion of the road network in the 1950s and the surge in cotton production in the 1950s and 1960s.

These large-scale agricultural projects were conceived when the country counted on more international financing and did not face military aggression. The closure of the U.S. market, the drying up of external financing, and the U.S.-backed *contra* war with its attendant economic costs combined to put a stop to new large investments and undermined the government's ability to finish those already started. MIDINRA was obligated to redefine its development strategy. Simpler, less costly production methods, which did not require external inputs and could be applied to both agroexport and basic food crops, were given increased consideration.

The government's loss of support in rural areas also contributed to a reevaluation of its development strategy and goals. The emphasis on state farms and the limited scope of agrarian reform were largely responsible for the reduced rural loyalty. Moreover, peasant frustration with Sandinista policies helped the *contras* to weaken allegiances in remote areas.

The other important factor convincing the Sandinistas to pay more attention to individual producers was the rising importance of UNAG. As the revolution developed, the limitations of the state sector became increasingly obvious. It was overextended, overly bureaucratic, and often inefficient. All the while, UNAG was demonstrating an alternative path toward agricultural development. In the face of foreign exchange shortages, UNAG forged its own links of support with sympathetic foreign governments and humanitarian organizations. It showed the government that it was a dynamic and important sector that had to be heeded. Not only did small growers produce 85 percent of the country's beans and corn but they were also a major source of beef and coffee. While these growers were often less productive than larger growers, it was not because they were an inherently backward sector. UNAG insisted that, with more government technical and infrastructural assistance, small growers could become an engine of economic growth for the entire society. Moreover, UNAG demonstrated that its members could become a strong source of political support for the revolution.

A Problem of Balance

A tough and continuing problem for the Sandinistas has been their attempt to simultaneously achieve national food security through greater grain production while simultaneously increasing production of agroexports. Soon after the revolution, the new government promised to put the nation on the path toward food security and balanced agricultural production. It hoped to mechanize and modernize basic food production in a drive to make Nicaragua "the granary of Central America." In practice, however, more attention was given to the agroexport sector.

The guerrilla war had succeeded in ousting Somoza and ending repression. Yet, it did not extricate Nicaragua from its position as an underdeveloped nation that was overly dependent on a few agroexports. The Sandinista leadership was acutely aware of the economic and political constraints of the agroexport economy, and immediately took measures to give Nicaragua more economic independence. These included reducing the country's dependence on U.S. trade, and investing in agroindustries which would process its agricultural produce for domestic markets.

The war, however, had left the country devastated and bankrupt, giving the new government little room to fully explore new development strategies. The immediate priority was to put foreign exchange in the national treasury thereby assuring foreign lenders that it would soon have the capacity to meet payment schedules. Having no mineral wealth, there seemed no alternative but to pump up agroexport production. The government hoped that renewed agroexport production would not only ease the balance-of-payments and external debt crunch but also give the country the investment capital it needed to diversify the economy.

This urgency to expand agroexport production was reflected in the government's agrarian reform program. Priority was given to the state farms that produced agroexports rather than to small farms which were thought to be less efficient. There was also a concern that land grants to campesinos would cause a shortage of farmworkers needed to pick coffee and cotton. The desperate need for foreign exchange affected relations between the government and capitalist producers. Eager to keep up pre-revolutionary production levels, the government attempted to provide the incentives and technical assistance demanded by large agroexport growers. It wanted to build their confidence in the new mixed economy, and was careful not to institute an agrarian reform that would reduce this confidence.

Obstacles to Development

During the first few years of the revolutionary government, the economy did exhibit strong economic growth. Both basic food and agroexport production had approached or surpassed pre-revolutionary levels. Consumption increased, food prices were the lowest in the region, and food imports were less necessary. By 1983, however, a series of domestic and international obstacles began to cloud Nicaragua's vision of a healthy national treasury and national food security. Despite the government's efforts to provide the capitalist sector with a secure place in the economy, most large growers were wary about making new investments and many intentionally decapitalized or slowed down production. Talk about socialism and the government's priority commitment to workers and peasants even made the small sector of "patriotic" producers uneasy.

The U.S.-directed war of destabilization also undermined the government's plans for agricultural development. The *contras* targeted farms, grain silos, agricultural machinery, and farmers themselves. They aimed to slow down agricultural production in the hope of destabilizing the government and undermining its popular support. Production levels of both agroexports and basic grains declined as a result of this aggression. In one Nicaraguan town, the *contras* burned all six grain silos, leaving the residents to pick through the charred ruins for kernels of corn they could salvage. As part of its defensive war against the *contras*, the Nicaraguan army evacuated thousands of campesino families living in war zones, further decreasing production of corn and beans.

The war absorbed resources that could otherwise have been used to promote agricultural production, and obliged the government to adopt the slogan: "Everything for the Combatants, Everything for the War Fronts."

Defense spending, which accounted for over 7 percent of government expenditures in 1981, soaked up over 50 percent of the national budget in 1986.

The shooting war represented only one side of the U.S.-sponsored destabilization campaign. The U.S. economic war against Nicaragua started with the cancellation of wheat credits in 1981. Subsequent blows included the termination of sugar quotas and successful attempts to block all international assistance from the World Bank, International Monetary Fund (IMF), and Inter-American Development Bank (IDB). After 1981, the United States terminated all development assistance, import/export insurance, and commodity credits to the Sandinistas. The assault against Nicaragua's agricultural economy culminated in 1985 when the Reagan administration declared a total trade embargo against Nicaragua. Besides the array of politically motivated attempts to destabilize and isolate the Nicaraguan economy, the country also suffered from the general weakening of agricultural commodity prices in the 1980s.

Other agricultural and food supply problems, however, were the direct result of the government's own policies. Rather than embarking on a concerted campaign to improve the technology and infrastructure available to small producers, the government concentrated on developing state farms and an agroexport production economy. While credit was available to peasants for the first time, the small farm sector's needs for technical and marketing assistance were largely ignored. The demands of the peasantry for individual land grants were also bypassed until recently.[42]

Further complicating the situation for peasants were the low prices they received for their corn and beans. As a way of keeping the more vocal urban residents content, the government tried to keep the cost of staple foods low. Yet, in doing so, it inadvertently lowered the production incentive for growers. As a result, many farmers simply cut back on production. Deepening food shortages persuaded the government in 1984 to raise prices paid to producers of basic grains and later to completely liberalize the marketing of corn and beans (which had been strictly controlled by government agencies). The government hoped that the absence of price controls on basic foods would spur increased production and thereby reduce food shortages and the troublesome black market.

The Challenge of Agrarian Reform

In Nicaragua, the course of agrarian reform, while still not a major success story for the revolution, demonstrated the flexible and pragmatic nature of the Sandinista leadership. From being an essentially conservative plan to bolster the dominant agroexport economy, the reform changed in 1985 to become more responsive to the needs of the peasantry and small-scale agriculture.

In the 1979-1984 period, there were many similarities between the Salvadoran and Nicaraguan reforms. Both programs targeted the most inefficient estates and examples of semifeudal land tenure while encouraging medium-size capitalist tracts. The two programs also demonstrated similar social and economic biases against the peasantry, and limited distribution to this sector.[43]

Since 1985, however, the paths of the two reforms have sharply separated. While the Salvadoran program has languished, the Nicaraguan program has become more dynamic. In marked contrast to the reform in El Salvador, agrarian reform in Nicaragua grew more responsive to demands from below (peasants and small farmers) and less concerned about guaranteeing land security for the agrarian bourgeoisie. In El Salvador, peasant organizations supporting the reform lost their political leverage while capitalist growers benefited from increased attention and financing from the government and AID.

Other major differences between the two reform programs include the following aspects:

* The Salvadoran reform required beneficiaries to compensate expropriated landowners while the Nicaraguan reform required no such payments by beneficiaries (although the government does itself compensate former landowners).

* There was no campaign of military repression associated with the Nicaraguan reform.

* The Salvadoran reform enjoyed generous financial support and technical assistance from the United States while the Nicarguan reform suffered from a U.S.-directed campaign of economic destabilization.

* The Nicaraguan reform counted on more consistent government and military support.

* The program in El Salvador fell far short of its projections while the one in Nicaragua went significantly beyond its stated goals and is still expanding.

Probably the most important difference between the two reform programs was that in Nicaragua the reform opened up a debate about the appropriate balance of agroexport and basic food production and the appropriate place of small and large producers in the economy. This debate, while not yet resolved in Nicaragua, has not even been broached by other Central American governments.

The course of the Nicaraguan reform illustrates the difficulties faced by underdeveloped countries that wish to establish an economically and politically independent path toward development. The options of these countries, even ones as strongly committed to the poor majority as Nicaragua, are severely limited by their historical role of producing low-priced commodities for foreign markets. The economic structures and social relations established by the agroexport system run deep through Nicaraguan society. The challenge that the Nicaraguan agrarian reform faces is to design land tenure and land use patterns that support both large-scale and small-scale production. The recognition that peasant producers need not be an inefficient or backward sector of the agricultural economy is a necessary first step toward meeting that challenge.

Table 11

Land Reform in El Salvador and Nicaragua
Some Comparisons

El Salvador	Nicaragua
Compensation	
Repayment over 15-30 years for tax value of expropriated property.	No repayment required.
Participation	
Design of program imposed by Washington, with no participation of peasants. Only US-backed peasant associations included in implementation of the reform. Other campesino organizing repressed.	Reform was part of platform of Sandinista guerrillas. Government promoted formation and growth of two organizations of small farmers, peasants, and rural workers. These groups sucessfully pressured government to extend reform and suggested land for expropriation.
Rentals	
Reform gave tenants right to title to small rented properties. Less than one-fifth actually received titles, and one-fourth were evicted. Virtually all lands affected too small for subsistence.	Reform reduced rents by as much as 85 percent. Renters assured of sufficient land to earn guaranteed minimum income.

El Salvador	Nicaragua

Credit

Reform sector starved for credit. Because of lack of clear titles and other equity, beneficiaries are required to pay highest interest rates.

Reform sector given priority for lowest interest rates. Total credit increased ten-fold for small farmers.

Govt. Assistance

Technical and marketing assistance practically nonexistent for reform sector. No attempt to improve living and working conditions.

Government has organized a national marketing system for small farmers and made serious effort to provide agricultural extension services for entire reform sector. Has received international recognition for its efforts to improve health services, education, and nutrition of rural population.

Landless

Land reform did not address problems of landless.

Landless population benefited from reform by large increase of steady employment offered by state sector. Landless workers were incorporated into cooperatives.

Prospects

No more advances in the land reform expected. Program abrogated by 1983 constitution and subsequent decrees. Attacks on reform sector will continue and will drive many beneficiaries off land. Mounting debt will also weaken and reduce size of reform sector. Reprivatization of cooperatives is a strong possibility.

Agrarian reform is an ongoing process. Expropriations are continuing but slowing down. Land titling continued at brisk pace through 1985. Although slowed down by war, reform sector expected to increase productivity and efficiency. The balance among state, cooperative, and private independent production will change to include more cooperative ownership.

Chapter Seven

Campesino Rebellion: Guatemala, Honduras, and Costa Rica

We are barefoot, but we are many. We plant, weed, cut, grind, transport and ship sugar cane. We do the same with cotton, coffee, and the products made in the factories. We produce the riches that the landowners and all the powerful count, enjoy, and waste. Therefore, when we stop working, the wealth that they enjoy stops as well. Without us, they are nothing.

This is a lesson we must never forget: that we are many and we have a great force in our hands, while the landowners are few and without us can do nothing.

—From the Guatemalan peasant magazine
De Sol A Sol, July 1980

Agrarian reform programs—even the most superficial measures—are usually enacted in response to the struggle by campesinos themselves for rural justice. In Nicaragua, it took a revolution to institute a land redistribution program. In El Salvador, the moderate agrarian reform program is a desperate attempt to pacify landless campesinos and preempt a revolution. Pressure for land has forced the governments of Guatemala, Honduras, and Costa Rica to adopt piecemeal reform projects as a way of easing rural tension. Ever present in these pacification projects is the Agency for International Development (AID). By directing land-titling and colonization projects and backing conservative rural associations, AID attempts to coopt peasant ·movements and redirect land distribution programs away from broader struggles for political and economic power. But campesino rebellion continues to spread as the problems of landlessness and rural unemployment deepen.

Guatemala

During the ten-year period of representative democracy from 1944 to 1954, campesino organizing flourished in Guatemala. Demands by Indian peasants for more land resulted in an agrarian reform program that expropriated the idle land of the elite and the United Fruit banana company. For the first time, many campesinos saw the potential for a better life. Both democracy and agrarian reform in Guatemala were cut short by the 1954 military coup. The new regime headed by Colonel Castillo Armas evicted the nearly 100,000 beneficiaries of his predecessor's land distribution program.

Since 1954, agrarian reform has been judged synonymous with revolution by the country's military rulers and oligarchs. Successive Guatemalan regimes with the help of AID have addressed the problem of rural landlessness through the government's Institute for Agrarian Transformation (INTA). "We don't have agrarian reform any longer in Guatemala," quipped one INTA official, "We have agrarian transformation."[1] Over 30 years of "agrarian transformation" has resulted in increased concentration of land ownership, a deepening of the agroexport system, and growing numbers of landless peasants.

With AID funds, INTA has sponsored several land-titling and colonization programs over the past 30 years. The first colonization program involved the settling of landless peasants on a piece of land in the South Coast region given the government by United Fruit after the Armas coup. Most colonization projects since then have taken place in isolated areas like the Northern Transverse Strip and the Peten. The military and other powers-that-be have supported colonization projects as a way to clear land for ranching and to secure better government control over the region.

One such colonization project currently underway is the AID-sponsored Small Farmer Development Project to resettle Indian families in the Playa Grade area of the Northern Transverse Strip. The project has helped pay for the construction of roads into this remote region and has been used by the army as a base for its pacification program of "development poles" and "model villages." The colony of Playa Grande is a militarized zone with an AID-financed infrastructure.

Land and Landlessness

In a 1962 pastoral letter, the Catholic Bishops of Guatemala described the life of the campesinos in their country:

> On the plantations, peasants are submerged in conditions that hardly permit them to avoid death by starvation. Besides the conditions of their work, they live collectively in wooden shacks, without light, without windows, without interior walls for privacy, without adequate sanitary systems in situations closely resembling concentration camps rather than the homes of free human beings.[2]

Since the Guatemalan bishops made that statement, conditions in rural Guatemala have worsened as the result of the country's highly skewed land ownership patterns. Even AID, which has fostered the country's agro-export system with U.S. economic aid, says the land tenure situation is "more serious than in any other country of Central or South America."[3]

Over the last few decades, the average size of *minifundios* (small farms) has dropped 20 percent. Farms with under 3.5 acres represent 54 percent of the total number of holdings but only four percent of farm acreage. AID calculates that at least 8.5 acres of non-irrigated land is necessary to support one family. Over 400,000 farms, most of them in the Altiplano, fall short of that threshold; and about 425,000 farmworkers have no land at all. At the opposite end of the spectrum, farms with 1100 acres or more account for just 1 percent of the total number of farms but absorb 34 percent of the country's cultivated land. In the fertile provinces along the Pacific and Altantic coasts, the proportion of land represented by these large farms rises to over 50 percent.

Guatemalan campesinos have not forgotten their brief taste of freedom and progress under Arbenz. In the face of increasing incursions by large cattle ranchers in the 1960s, *ladino* (non-Indian) small farmers in the northeastern provinces of Zacapa, Chiquimula, and Izabal supported the region's first guerrilla movement. Aided by U.S. counterinsurgency advisers, Colonel Carlos Arana Osorio crushed the rebellion, in the process earning the epithet "Butcher of Zacapa." Arana was given a large cattle ranch by the government as a reward for his brutal counterinsurgency campaign and went on to become president of Guatemala.

The next upsurge of rural resistance occurred in the Highlands and the adjoining Northern Transverse Strip. The military regime, aided by foreign loans and investors, began an ambitious plan to develop the agricultural frontier during the 1970s. Roads were built into formerly uncharted regions, opening up isolated areas for cattle ranching, oil development, and hydroelectric projects. In 1975, the Guerrilla Army of the Poor (EGP) announced its presence in northern El Quiché by assassinating a hated rancher, José Luis Arena Barrera, nicknamed "The Tiger of Ixcán" by Indian campesinos.

It was not until three years later, when the army and landowners joined together to repress the land-hungry Kekchí Indians in the northeastern corner of the Northern Transverse Strip, that Indians threw their support to the new guerrilla resistance led by EGP. On September 29, 1978, the army massacred over a hundred Indians who had gathered in the town of Panzos to demand clear title to the land they were farming. Rich ranchers, coveting the same land, called the military in to the area claiming that the peasants were invading their lands. After the Panzos massacre, the ranks of the EGP swelled with angry campesinos.

That same year, Indian campesinos formed a national peasant organization called the Committee for Campesino Unity (CUC), which set out to organize the country's exploited seasonal workers. In January 1980, CUC occupied the Spanish embassy to protest government repression directed by then-president General Lucas Garcia, one of the country's largest landowners. The army burned down the embassy killing 39 people. Undeterred, the next month CUC led a national farmworkers' strike on the South Coast that arrested the cotton and sugar harvests and forced the government to increase the minimum wage from $1.12 to $3.20 a day.

Rigoberta Menchú, CUC's international representative, now supports the guerrilla struggle as the only hope for her people. Both her mother and father were cruelly killed because of their support for CUC, and her two sisters joined the guerrilla army. Menchú said that through labor organizing and dialogue with the guerrillas, her family and friends began to better understand the common plight of campesinos in Guatemala:

> We began thinking that our enemies were not only the
> landowners who lived near us, and above all not just the

landowners who forced us to work and paid so little. It was not
only now we were being killed. They had been killing us since
we were children, through malnutrition, hunger, and poverty.
We started thinking about the roots of the problem and came to
the conclusion that everything stemmed from the ownership of
land.[4]

The four major guerrilla organizations that direct the armed resistance
in Guatemala rely primarily on campesinos for membership and support. In
1982, the guerrilla armies joined to form a common front called the
Guatemalan National Revolutionary Unit (URNG). As part of its
political platform, the URNG promised "true agrarian reform, giving land
to those who work in an individual, collective, or cooperative fashion."

It was not until Vinicio Cerezo Arévalo became president in 1986 that
some kind of government-instituted agrarian reform became possible in
Guatemala. Few dared even to speak publicly about the need for agrarian
reform during the decades of direct military rule that preceeded 1986, when
an elected civilian government took power. During his campaign for
president, Cerezo promised the large landowners that he would not enact
an agrarian reform program. But pressure from the rural and urban landless
population forced Cerezo to opt for conservative land distribution.
Cautious not to precipitate a coup, Cerezo called his program to distribute
unused government land "rural development," not agrarian reform.

Rebellion on the South Coast

After more than three decades, agrarian reform is once again a hot issue in
Guatemala. Peasants are marching on the capital to demand land redistribution, the military is concerned that the expanding landless population
will join the leftist guerrillas, and the large landowners threaten to resist
even the most superficial changes.

The campesino movement for agrarian reform began in Nueva
Concepción, located in the province of Esquintla on the country's fertile
South Coast along the Pacific Ocean. Spray-painted now on the walls of
the parish hall in Nueva Concepción are right-wing death threats and the
slogan, "No a la reforma agraria." Nueva Concepción reeks of pesticides.
It is a dusty town surrounded by vast expanses of cotton and sugar
plantations, which used to be a banana-growing region before plant disease
forced United Fruit to abandon its plantations.

In 1986, soon after Cerezo became president, Father Andrés Girón,
the parish priest of Nueva Concepción, sparked a national campesino
movement to demand that the government institute an agrarian reform
program. As part of this campaign, Girón led a five-day march to the

National Palace in May 1986 to ask that the Cerezo government redistribute lands to the landless and near landless.

The march and Girón's call for an "integral agrarian reform"—words that almost no one has publicly spoken in Guatemala for many years—were like lighting the fuse on a keg of dynamite. The padre's demand for agrarian reform spread hope among the country's landless population and sparked vicious denunciations by the major growers' association UNAGRO. Mounting campesino pressure for land redistribution put the Cerezo government in a difficult position. While he recognized the need for measures to address land-tenure inequities, Cerezo had promised the country's elite he would not initiate any agrarian reform.

It is not surprising that the current peasant movement was born in Nueva Concepción, where the country's land use and ownership problems are particularly evident. Here, 37 percent of the land is used for cattle ranching, 45 percent for cash crops (mainly sugar and cotton), and only 15 percent for basic foods.[5] Peasant farming has been progressively squeezed out of the picture in the South Coast. Since 1950, the land area devoted to subsistence farming has decreased at an annual rate of 2.5 percent while the area given to agroexports has increased at an annual rate of 5.7 percent.[6]

Nueva Concepción is a gathering point for the seasonal farmworkers that come to the South Coast each year to cut cane and pick cotton. The minimum wage of $3.20 per day is rarely paid, and lately there are not enough jobs for the hundreds of thousands of farmworkers that pass through the area. Political violence in the Highlands caused at least 100,000 Indians to move to the South Coast, adding to the area's permanent workforce of landless peasants. Since 1983, desperate farmworkers have offered to work on plantations just for food. Recent cutbacks in cotton production have deepened the misery around Nueva Concepción.

Girón helped organize the Peasant Movement Association mainly to help the landless campesinos in his parish, but the movement quickly spread throughout the South Coast and up to the Highlands. The movement spurred the government to come up with several proposals to redistribute some public land and to accelerate a Commercial Land Markets program sponsored by AID. Neither program is highly regarded either by the campesino movement or by the landed elite.

At best, there is probably only enough public land to accommodate one-third of the country's landless population, and government proposals only speak of distributing a small fraction of this public land. Responding to the Cerezo government's modest proposals, Father Girón said the "peasant movement wants, not just a few farms, but the South Coast because here is the land wealth of Guatemala." The fiery priest added,

"The rich have already eaten; now it is the poor's turn to eat."[7]

The Commercial Land Markets program concerns private holdings. But instead of expropriating idle land or setting an acreage limit on private farms, this program simply buys land commercially and then turns around and sells the land to small farmers, albeit at reduced interest rates. It is managed by an AID-funded private organization called the Penny Foundation and directed by a large landowner. Additionally, rather than using the land to grow basic foods, the new owners are obligated by AID to grow nontraditional crops for export.

The National Agricultural Union (UNAGRO) and the Coordinating Committee of Agricultural, Industrial, and Financial Associations (CACIF) are hostile even to these token land redistribution programs. Business and agricultural leaders argue that even the most limited reform programs are dangerous since they raise the expectations of land-hungry campesinos. Big agricultural operators point to a series of land invasions by land-starved peasants as evidence that this new talk of agrarian reform is causing an alarming amount of rural unrest.

Girón, the Peasant Movement Association, and other Guatemalan peasants have reacted angrily to the slow pace of the government's efforts to meet their demands for land. At a large demonstration in Nueva Concepción, Girón said, "We are tired of false promises of officials and politicians. We want land and agrarian reform now."[8] President Cerezo does not support agrarian reform, said Father Girón, "because he is under pressure from the private sector and the military."[9]

Landlessness is an urban as well as a rural problem. Unable to support themselves in the countryside, campesino families have flooded into urban areas, living in shanty towns that ring Guatemala City. So serious is the housing deficit in the capital that the number of families that need housing is now larger than the number of families that have decent shelter. On the very day that Cerezo was inaugurated, 10,000 squatters occupied public lands in Guatemala City demanding that the new government grant them title to the land and supply them with services—a request denied by Cerezo.

AID warns that the landless population is open to "violence and politicization" by the left, and the military is also concerned that landless peasants will incorporate into the ranks of the guerrillas. Yet the intransigence of large landowners, including those army officers who own vast estates, obstructs the institution of even the most modest agrarian reform program. The elected government of Vinicio Cerezo has created a small opening for discussion of agrarian reform. Cerezo, however, has failed to stand behind the peasant movement and has been careful not to anger the oligarchy.

Hunger and desperate living conditions have sparked the renewed demands for agrarian reform. But there is widespread concern that the demands by rural and urban Guatemalans for land will soon be met with the same kind of repression that marked past military regimes. As one conservative newspaper columnist noted, "[Father Girón], instead of obtaining land for his followers to cultivate, could be getting them land for their tombs."[10]

In Guatemala, the chance for an agrarian reform program was lost in 1954. Under present conditions, even with a moderate civilian government, a real agrarian reform program that confronts the rural power structure is virtually impossible. Attempts to address rural tension through colonization programs, distribution of unused government land, and a commercial market program do almost nothing to reduce the power of the oligarchy and do little to meet the demands of landless campesinos. Short of a miracle, it seems that the kind of agrarian reform that is now necessary can only come from a direct and violent confrontation with the military and economic elite.

Honduras

The construction of a new U.S. military base at Palmerola in 1983 brought international attention to the Comayagua Valley in central Honduras. Up the road from the base, a new community in the valley also merits attention. A group of 65 families belonging to the Ivan Betancourt Campesino Group are working, as one of them puts it, to "reclaim" land left idle by Oswaldo López Arrellano, the former Honduran president and chief of the armed forces. The peasants have claimed the land under the Honduran agrarian reform law which targets idle land for redistribution, and are using it to harvest corn, chile, and beans.[11] They have named their cooperative after a priest who was killed by ranchers following an earlier land occupation.

Their task has not been an easy one. The national police have evicted them on several occasions, in one instance burning their one-room homes to the ground. Before the land occupation, many of the campesinos had been working as temporary farm laborers making about $2 a day. Several families had been forced to leave their homes to make way for the military base.

"We want you to see what hard workers we are," said Pedro Archuleta, a lively old campesino wearing a weathered straw hat full of holes. "Our rough hands have known many years of planting, weeding, and harvesting. Our backs are used to bending over many fields. We are not complaining. That is just the life of a campesino. We only want what the law says we should get, land like this which nobody else uses. We are Honduran campesinos, and we give this land life. We are ready to stay here and die if necessary," asserted Archuleta, "because we have nowhere else to go. We have tried many other routes to find work and to feed our families, and this has to be our last stand."[12]

Another member of the Betancourt cooperative, José de la Cruz Velenzuela said, "the man who owned this land wants us to leave so that he can let 100 cattle graze here. They put cows here when we can't afford clothes. Feed 100 cows and let 100 Christians die."[13]

Peasant Movement Pushes Agrarian Reform

The 1954 strike by banana workers sparked peasant organizing throughout Honduras. A main target of peasant associations has been the idle land of banana companies. During the 1950s, only about 10 percent of the plantations of United Fruit and Standard Fruit were being cultivated. Groups of peasants began to illegally occupy the unused lands, but many were subsequently evicted by the banana companies to make room for new herds of cattle.

Peasant pressure for land and the emphasis of the Alliance for Progress on agrarian reform persuaded the Honduran government in 1962 to announce a small land distribution program. The country's first land reform program was limited to the settlement of individual families rather than cooperatives. Despite its narrow scope, large landowners (notably United Fruit) felt threatened and together with hardline military officers brushed the program aside in 1963.

Evictions became common during the 1960s and 1970s as the cotton and cattle industries reached out for land occupied by small, powerless campesino families. The land-grabbing resulted in tense and often bloody confrontations between the landowners and indignant peasants. To gain more strength, Honduran workers and peasants forged alliances with several national institutions including the church, university, and political parties.

Emboldened by this support, several peasant organizations organized a massive "hunger march" in 1973 to protest the country's skewed land ownership patterns and military repression. The march precipitated the downfall of the traditional military government, and one of the first actions of the new military government of Oswaldo López Arrellano was to reorganize the national agrarian institute (INA) and issue a decree authorizing the distribution of idle lands. The new agrarian reform bill especially enraged cattle ranchers because it redefined "underutilized land" in a way that seriously threatened the extensive cattle operations in Olancho and other provinces.[14]

The 1975 agrarian reform law recognized that landless campesinos have a right to gain title to uncultivated land. It allows landless farmers to request public or private land that is neither being cultivated nor used as cattle pasture. If the INA and the courts determine that the land is indeed not fulfilling what is known as its "social function," it is turned over to the petitioning farmer.[15] The agrarian reform law was remarkably progressive when compared with the token agrarian reform programs enacted by other Central American countries. Nonetheless, it did fall far short of the kind of agrarian reform that truly challenged the economic and political structures keeping the rural majority destitute and powerless.

The 1975 agrarian reform set in motion a new peasant movement to demand land. But the INA has not kept up with the petitions for land, and the peasant associations have charged that it has bowed to pressure from the large landowners to obstruct the full implementation of agrarian reform.[16] Since the date of the country's first land reform programs only 10 percent of rural Hondurans have benefited, leaving as many as 150,000 families without land. At that rate, it will take over 60 years to distribute the country's idle land to the rural landless.[17]

Esteban Enriquez of the National Campesino Union (UNC) places the blame for the slow pace of land reform on bureaucratic red tape. "The legal paperwork to get idle land through the agrarian reform," he complained, "takes five years or more. The long wait gives landowners time to start using the land, and the courts usually refuse to give the land to the campesinos." If they haven't started using the land, Enriquez charged, the landowners rely on "their influence and bribes."[18]

Usually, INA only actually distributes land in cases involving government holdings or when a peasant organization is extremely well organized. Otherwise peasant claims get lost in the bureaucracy. "We have discovered that the only way to get the land is to take possession of it physically in what we call *recuperaciones de tierra,* [recoveries of idle farmland]," noted Enriquez. "In Honduras, we are the agrarian reform."

Even when peasants do get land, they usually do not get the follow-up help they need. Over 90 percent of those peasants who received land during the 1970s never received any credit or technical assistance[19]—leading, according to an estimate by one expert, to a desertion rate as high as 75 percent among reform beneficiaries.[20]

Throughout the spotty history of Honduran land reform, one constant has been organized campesino pressure for more land. When the government does enforce agrarian reform, it is frequently following pressure from campesino federations like the UNC. Honduran campesino women feel the need for land at least as strongly as the men. Victoria Sandoval, of FEMUCH, the organization of Honduran women, said:

> Nobody should forget that women support the land occupation more than anyone. After all, who gets up at three or four in the morning to make the tortillas for the days of the land recoveries? Some of the men might not agree that women should be speaking out. But that doesn't worry us. We have struggled as hard as the men, and probably suffered more because we have to take care of our children, too."[21]

In January 1983, a group of nearly 40 women from a rural area known as Caratasca occupied idle land on which they started growing corn, beans, and tomatoes. "Last year my baby died because I was too poor to feed her properly," said one of the women in the Caratasca land recovery. "I don't want any more of my children to die. So I decided to join this land occupation. Maybe now we will all have enough *masa* (corn meal) for our tortillas." Another women, Katarina Montoya, explained that the land, which was owned by a *rico* in Tegucigalpa, had been left idle for many years. "When land is left unused," she said, "it is wrong in a country like ours with so many poor people without any land at all."[22]

Washington Skirts Issue of Landlessness

AID is well aware of the potentially explosive nature of rural Honduras. Over $230 million in U.S. economic aid is pumped into Honduras each year. But AID has not been willing to use this aid as leverage to demand that the Honduran government proceed with a more rapid and profound agrarian reform.

AID is the largest foreign contributor to the Honduran agrarian reform program. But instead of furthering land redistribution, AID funds a land-titling program that mostly benefits coffee growers, who are among the most conservative Honduran farmers.[23] Under the program, farmers who already have land are given official title to the land, a move which helps them obtain credit. According to the UNC, the land reform institute spends 90 percent of its budget handing out legal titles to those who have been working their plots for many years.[24]

The other main focus of AID in rural Honduras is a program to encourage the increased production of nontraditional agroexports like cucumbers and broccoli. At a time when Honduras has to import over 100,000 tons of grains each year, AID is putting millions of dollars into projects that convert farmland previously used to grow corn and beans into land devoted to agroexport production. Not too far from the land occupied by the Ivan Betancourt Cooperative is one such AID project involving Castle & Cooke and local businessmen. AID claims the project has created employment for hundreds of farmworkers, but it fails to report that virtually all those employed picking cucumbers are women and children working for less than $2 a day.

Another AID project in Honduras funded Food-Pro, a subsidiary of the food giant Unilever (British/Dutch corporation), to employ mal-nourished campesinos in planting snow peas, broccoli, and cauliflower for export to the United States. In the fields marked by a sign bearing a familiar AID logo, farmworkers are paid less than the Honduran minimum wage.

AID funds are also pouring into a program managed by the American Institute for Free Labor Development (AIFLD) to provide "political training" to an AIFLD-associated peasant organization in an attempt to counter the growing militance of campesino organizing in Honduras. Such training stresses the necessity of working within the law and warns campesinos against associating with leftist organizations. AIFLD also distributes a conservative newspaper for campesinos called *El Avance*, which benefits from donations by the right-wing Olin Foundation.

Many peasant leaders are now questioning the priorities of their own government as well as the merit of the expanded U.S. military presence in their country. To make way for a U.S. military training center at Trujillo along the Atlantic coast, an entire community of campesinos were evicted from their farms. And closer to the Nicaraguan border, 92 peasant families were told to move to make way for the expansion of the Aguacate air base, which is now used by the *contras*.[25]

In 1983, the entire state of Olancho, the scene of numerous land occupations by the UNC peasant union, was declared a counterinsurgency zone. Assisted by U.S. advisers during a U.S. military maneuver in that region, the Honduran military swept through the state in a drive to wipe out a small band of guerrillas. Peasant leaders, some of whom were arrested during the counterinsurgency sweep, accused the military of using the occasion to intimidate the peasant population.

One campesino leader, Teofilo Trejos, said that it was "ridiculous" that there is not more money to help the rural poor "since there is plenty of money to build military airports, construct ports, and buy arms. Here you have the spectacle of military maneuvers that cost millions of dollars in the very zones where peasants are dying of hunger."[26]

Campesino "Terrorists"

Standing in his modest office, UNC director Marcial Caballero pointed to the framed pictures of five UNC members who were brutally murdered by large landowners and their security forces. In 1984 alone, hundreds of campesinos were arrested under the Anti-Terrorist Law passed that year. Four were killed, and several others disappeared. Meanwhile, vigilante activity by landowners and their private security forces enjoys the approval of the powerful National Association of Growers and Cattlemen (FENAGH), which has labeled the peasant unions "enemies of private property."

Campesinos in Honduras emphasize that their demand for idle land falls within the guidelines of the agrarian reform law. But the severe reaction by the national police authorities and landowners has discouraged many campesinos. "They're forcing us to go to the mountains," said Caballero, "We're not guerrillas, but if people keep being beaten and jailed, they're leaving us only one alternative."[27]

Randy Stringer, an international rural development expert, told the *Christian Science Monitor* that, "If attention is not paid to the landless or the land-poor in this country, then just get ready for another Salvador there. It may take five years, it may take 10 years, but it will happen."[28]

Although strong and fairly sophisticated, the peasant movement in Honduras is badly divided along organizational and ideological lines. Divisions among the major campesino organizations are exacerbated by attempts of the two main political parties to gain their allegiance, through promises to more quickly enforce the agrarian reform law.

Peasant organizations, particularly those that lead land invasions, have been terrorized by ranchers and security forces, but the level of repression has not yet approached that seen in neighboring Guatemala and El Salvador. The country's relatively weak oligarchy, and the ability of campesino leaders to gain a national hearing before the military, the church, and the political parties explain the lack of extreme polarization seen elsewhere in Central American society. But this absence of intense class conflict may be a thing of the past as land invasions increase, the economic crisis grows, and the country becomes more politicized.

Costa Rica

While rural unrest is still far below the level of conflict seen in other Central American countries, the signs of increased polarization are everywhere in the Costa Rican countryside. "A time bomb is ticking" in rural areas, says Rogelio Cedeño, a leader of the moderate Confederation of Democratic Workers (CCTD). He says that "the nation's democratic tradition is in jeopardy because of the government's refusal to heed the call of rural Costa Ricans for the distribution of idle farmland."[29]

Although, Costa Rica does have a higher percentage of medium-sized farms capable of supporting a family than any other Central American nation, land ownership is highly concentrated and becoming more so all the time. Just one percent of the farms cover 36 percent of the arable land—a proportion comparable to Guatemala. Over half of the farms are regarded as too small to support one family, and landlessness has tripled in the last 30 years. The number of farms covering over 500 acres actually increased from 1955 to 1973 while the area in small farms (under 50 acres) decreased during the same period.[30]

Over 60 percent of rural Costa Ricans do not have land.[31] Many of them work on the banana plantations of the Atlantic coast, pick coffee on the central mesa, or labor as hired hands on the far-flung ranches of the northwest. Unemployment is rising fast in Costa Rica. About 25 percent of rural Costa Ricans are now unemployed.

The agroexport system is not providing the number of jobs it did only a few years ago. With prices down and world supply high, growers have cut back production. On the day the banana boat comes in, unemployed men in Puerto Limón line up along the docks hoping for a job loading bananas. But the banana business is hiring fewer and fewer people these days. After a long strike in 1984, United Brands announced that it was shutting down (and selling to the government) its banana operation on the Pacific coast. The banana companies are also switching to African palm production which requires considerably less labor.

Providing somewhat of a counterbalance to the inequities in land ownership and rural unemployment are Costa Rica's educational and social services systems, which result in Costa Ricans ranking among the most literate and healthy of Latin Americans. The government has until recently preferred to solve land conflicts and labor struggles through mediation and the provision of government services. Since the onset of the economic crisis in the late 1970s, however, rebellion and repression have become more common-place in the Costa Rican countryside. The government has proved less willing to consider the demands of angry campesinos. Instead of negotiating a solution, the government has called out the security forces to break up strikes, evict squatters, and arrest protesting small farmers.

Schools and health clinics in rural areas and the ability to vote in regular elections may have produced a better life for Costa Rican campesinos and small farmers, but they have not eased land concentration and landlessness. In the last few decades, the increase in agroexport production, particularly the expansion of the beef business, has worsened land concentration and landlessness in Costa Rica.

The existence of an extensive uncultivated agricultural frontier has supplied a partial release for rural tensions. Peasants pushed off their lands by cattle ranchers often cleared new plots of land in isolated areas. The government's agrarian institute, assisted by AID, has also used the agricultural frontier for colonization projects that have resettled small numbers of landless peasants.

Costa Rica does have a toothless agrarian reform law on its books. The 1961 "Lands and Colonization Law" mentions the need for "avoiding the concentration of land" while stressing the nation's "respect for private property." In the first 22 years of this "land reform," only 16,000 landless peasants benefited—being placed as part of colonization projects in isolated jungle regions and on government land grants.[32] The U.S. government also funds and sponsors land-titling programs for small farmers without clear title. Since most of the farms receiving titles were tiny plots, the titling program has only served to reinforce the inequitable division of land in Costa Rica.

Rise of Precarismo

For the past 20 years, unemployed farm workers and displaced farmers have been occupying idle land in Costa Rica. At first, the occupations occurred only in the country's most isolated and undeveloped regions, but in the last decade—as the quantity of frontier land shrunk—campesino groups began to cultivate land in the country's agricultural heartland. Since 1980, land occupations have numbered a hundred or more each year. The land occupiers are known as *precaristas*, or those with precarious land tenure. At least one out of every six rural families in Costa Rica is now a *precarista*.[33]

A 1984 occupation by several hundred families attracted the attention of the Catholic Church—which, while often providing the impetus for campesino organizing efforts in neighboring countries, had traditionally avoided social issues in Costa Rica. The families claimed the idle land on a 24,000 acre estate called Alturas de Cotón, on which only 500 acres were being cultivated. When the Rural Guard moved to evict the *precaristas*, sympathetic residents of a nearby town blocked roads to obstruct the police. Some 700 villagers were arrested by the Guard, and one *precarista* died in the scuffle. The local bishop declared the land occupation "a sign of the unjust land distribution."[34]

The *precaristas* are not the only ones adopting a more militant stance. In September 1986, more than a thousand small farmers gathered in the capital city of San José to protest the government's elimination of price subsidies for basic grains. Under pressure from AID and the IMF, the Arias government had cut government support of grain prices. In response, small farmers belonging to the Atlantic Small Producers Union declared that they could not continue to profitably produce basic grains at the market price. They charged that increasing quantities of U.S. food aid, sent in an attempt to economically stabilize the government, have lowered market prices for local crops.

In what is becoming a pattern in Costa Rica, the Civil Guard broke up the demonstration with tear gas and clubs, claiming that the campesino movement was being manipulated by a leftist terrorist group trained in Nicaragua and Libya. Accusations about foreign involvement in destabilization efforts are based on unsubstantiated information supplied by the U.S. State Department. Fleeing the assault by the security forces, the campesinos of the small producers union took refuge in the national cathedral—a situation that only a short while ago would have seemed likely only in countries like El Salvador and Guatemala, not democratic Costa Rica.

Police repression is coupled with a rise in right-wing paramilitary groups directly linked to the government's Intelligence and Security Division (DIS) and the security forces. Groups like the Northern Zone Democratic Association and the Reserve are closely linked to large cattle operators in the Guanacaste province and the area along the Nicaraguan border. They serve the dual purpose of assisting the *contras* and operating an unofficial rural intelligence and paramilitary network. The most visible and influential organization of this type is the Free Costa Rica Movement, which maintains ties with the World Anticommunist League and paramilitary organizations in Guatemala.[35]

These rural paramilitary groups, encouraged by the U.S.-sponsored militarization and politicization of Costa Rica, see increasing campesino militancy as the beginning of a revolutionary insurgency and aim to repress it before it spreads. However, there has been no evidence that land takeovers and growing dissatisfaction in rural Costa Rica are related to anything other than hard times and landlessness.

The Costa Rican political and economic elite have charged that rural strikes and land occupations are "communist inspired." However, Mitchell Seligson, a scholar who studied the Costa Rican peasantry, calls the land occupations a kind of "spontaneous land reform." The squatters themselves do not see *precarismo* as a political movement. They have limited their goals to land acquisition, and have not even demanded widespread agrarian reform. According to Seligson, the power of the large landowners is too great for any significant land redistribution to take place anyway: "The coffee aristocracy, in alliance with other land interests, is not likely to let the squatter movement get out of hand."[36]

As their frustrations mount, however, the rural poor are likely to increase their organizing efforts—and may soon see themselves as a national political force. Fearing the worst, a prominent politician remarked in 1984: "I prefer having a peasant owning a plot of land to having him be a guerrilla."[37] But the spirit of compromise that has characterized Costa Rica in the past is rapidly disappearing as austerity measures and a U.S.-directed political and economic agenda take hold.

Social Injustice, Not Marxism

The rebellion of campesinos in Guatemala, Honduras, and Costa Rica is firmly rooted in the conditions of their everyday life. Land invasions and hunger marches are acts of survival, not, as the local elites and Washington imply, evidence of communist agitation. Guatama Fonseca, a Christian Democratic politician and former labor minister of Honduras, summarizes the feelings of many Central Americans about the nature of rebellion in this region:

> Those who attribute the present upheaval in Central America to communism are simply ignorant of how 80 percent of the people in the region live. The only thing the peasants know is misery. They have no land, no homes, no work, no income, no food, no medicine, no legal help, no social services, no schools, no water, no light, and no rights. It is injustice, not Marxism, that is the source of revolution.[38]

Campesino rebellion stems from the land and hunger crisis in Central America. But limited land distribution and food aid programs (examined in the next chapter) do not go to the roots of this rebellion. In Guatemala, such programs have failed to confront the economic and political power structures that keep peasants poor and repressed. In Honduras and Costa Rica, AID-backed agrarian reform programs have helped prevent wider rural upheaval but have not addressed the continuing causes of rural impoverishment. As landlessness and rural poverty increase, more militant and revolutionary movements seem inevitable.

Chapter Eight
Food Security: Obstacles and Solutions

During the Somoza period, the Nicaraguan economy was structured to complement the U.S. economy, based on its interests and not ours—meat for Puerto Rico, wood for building houses in Louisiana, cotton for U.S. soldiers' uniforms in Korea, a sugar industry to make up for the quota they took away from Cuba. Today, however, with the revolution, Nicaraguans can begin to decide something as basic as what to produce.

—Nicaragua's Minister of Agriculture,
Jaime Wheelock

Food security is the other side of the land and hunger crisis. Simply put, food security refers to both the availability of sufficient food and the ability to acquire it. In a rich agricultural region like Central America, food

155

security should be easily within reach. Yet, as seen in previous chapters, that is not the case. Instead, food security is now a more distant hope than it was 30 years ago, and in most countries is moving further out of reach every year. Land is more scarce for peasants, per capita food production is declining, unemployment rates are soaring, and fewer people can afford the minimum food basket.

Food security requires a national food system that satisfies the basic food needs of even the poorest social strata. In third world countries where foreign exchange is in short supply, achieving food security implies that the domestic agricultural system supplies most of the population's nutritional needs. The maintenance of equitable and secure trading relations to complement domestic food production is another essential component.

Food security is a precondition for economic and political stability. Without this fundamental security, nations face difficult import choices and are confronted by serious political challenges. Food security is also a moral imperative, for the right to eat is as basic as the right to live.

Looking at the Central American crisis through the prism of food security helps one understand how deep-rooted the crisis really is. Seeing the region this way also brings the solutions to the land and hunger crisis into better focus. This chapter first examines the domestic and international obstacles to food security and then discusses possible solutions.

Domestic Obstacles to Food Security

The main domestic obstacle to food security is the dual structure of the agricultural economy in which a narrow elite uses the best land for agroexport production, forcing peasants to subsist on small marginal plots or as landless seasonal workers. This economic system is closely tied to and protected by a political/military power structure which staunchly resists political and economic reforms. This entire political economy stands in the way of food security.

Redistribution of land and a radical change in politics are necessary if the region is ever to be food secure. However, even if those steps are taken, the domestic path toward food security is strewn with other persistent obstacles. Most of these problems have to do with the ambiguous role assigned to small-scale growers. On the one hand, the economy depends on the peasantry for most basic food production and for the cheap labor it provides to the agroexport system. On the other hand, these small producers are treated as an impossibly backward sector and have been neglected by government technical assistance, education, credit, and infrastructural support programs.

As a result of this neglect, the small-farm sector is mired in the past and is not as productive as it could be. The steel-blade of their machetes is often the only thing that distinguishes today's campesinos from their predecessors slaughtered by De Vargas and his conquistadors. While today's peasants are tightly integrated into the modern political economy, they remain isolated from the government services that large-scale producers rely on.

It is not that peasants resist change, they just cannot afford it. Expenditures by peasants to improve production, even the purchase of a bag of fertilizer, necessitate their families going without food for several days or forcing one of their children to drop out of school. The government denies them credit because they do not have collateral and are therefore not deemed credit-worthy. For most peasants, the chances of purchasing a tractor, individually or as part of a cooperative, are as remote as their chances of riding in an airplane.

Small farmers also suffer from the lack of government services and the absence of efficient marketing systems for basic foods. The typical small farmer has never received credit, cultivates without the benefit of irrigation, is never able to consult with an agronomist, and lives in a region where unmaintained dirt roads make travel difficult. Governments channel technical assistance and credit to large growers primarily because of their political alliance with agroexporters and their concern with generating foreign exchange. It is also simpler to deal with a small group of large growers than with a large group of small growers who are usually extremely isolated.

Throughout Central America, there is a strong need for an integrated food distribution system that would cut food losses, eliminate parasitic middle buyers and sellers, and deliver better quality food to consumers. Such a system would involve rural dispatching markets, bulking centers, and farm cooperatives. Yet, currently, small farmers are generally on their own. Few of them have their own vehicles, and are consequently forced either to transport their produce to market by rural buses or to pay the exorbitant rates charged by private truck drivers called *intermediarios*. The inefficiency and income loss resulting from the lack of better distribution systems can be seen during the five-hour drive from Tegucigalpa to San Pedro Sula in Honduras. Campesinos stand in front of tiny roadside stands holding up samples of their oranges, papayas, watermelon, bananas, or pineapples. Only one kind of fruit is available at each stand, and the stands are grouped together by type of fruit. Along one stretch of the road are rows of banana stands, and a few miles up the road the watermelon stands start appearing.

With a pickup truck, peasants could gather quantities of each fruit and then market them together. But these peasants will probably have access to a vehicle only if they become members of cooperatives that provide collective marketing services. Afraid that their produce will rot if it sits there any longer, the individual growers eventually sell their produce at bargain prices to the *intermediarios*, who take it to market in their pickup trucks or trailers.

Lack of organization presents another major obstacle for small farmers. The leading producers in the agroexport sector have powerful associations that facilitate the marketing of their produce, all the while exerting pressure on the government for more public support and lower taxes. The interests of small growers are not represented by the leading national associations of growers and ranchers. As a result, small growers often pay higher taxes and do not benefit from the incentives and price breaks that large growers win from corrupt, unrepresentative governments.

Individually, small farmers cannot afford agricultural inputs to improve their harvests: an irrigation system to prolong their growing season, a tractor to plow their land, or a truck to take produce to the market. But working together as an organized group, they probably would be able to afford these improvements and be in a stronger position to demand better prices for the food they produce.

The same holds true for seasonal workers. Farmworker unions could demand higher wages and better working conditions, benefiting society as a whole—because the increased wages would expand national markets for both agricultural and manufactured goods. A cohesive group of small farmers and rural workers would present a powerful force capable of challenging the traditional power structure and agro-export system. That fact is not lost on the armed forces and larger growers of Central America, who have fought—often violently and brutally—attempts by farmworkers and small farmers to organize. State-sponsored associations that impose leadership and programs on local communities have also undermined grassroots organizations.

The low price of basic foods is another persistent stumbling block to food security. At first, it would seem that cheap food is exactly what these poor countries need. But low prices reduce the incentive to produce for the local market. The low prices paid for their corn and beans discourages small farmers from producing marketable surpluses of these basic grains. Even when there is a large domestic demand for basic foods, large growers have little reason to switch to basic food production since export crops fetch higher prices on the international market.

Several interconnecting factors contribute to the low prices farmers receive for basic foods on the domestic market. The main factor is historical. Cheap food and cheap labor are the pillars that have held up the agroexport system. To keep their profit margins high while keeping the region's commodity prices competitive on the world market, large growers pay farmworkers below-subsistence wages. Together with food grown on their tiny plots, peasant families can scrape together a meager living. The increasing number of landless farm laborers cannot even do this much. It is this landless sector that is often the most volatile and the prime target of the repressive force of Central American militaries.

The peasantry's lack of political power also keeps food prices low. Larger growers have the political clout to force governments to keep taxes and interest rates low but the producers of basic grains carry little political weight. As pointed out above, attempts to organize to increase their power are usually dealt with harshly by state security forces.

An increasingly determining factor in keeping grain prices low is the influx of cheap food imports. Over the last 30 years, Central American governments have increased grain imports as local food production declined. Imported food worsens the "cheap food" problem because grain exports from foreign countries are generally subsidized by the exporting government. Due to U.S. government price-support and export-subsidy programs, U.S. transnational corporations can ship large quantities of grains to Central American countries at prices below the levels sustained on local markets. The influx of cheap imported food, therefore, makes it ever more difficult for domestic growers to continue providing basic foods for internal consumption. This situation makes food security the victim of a vicious circle in which declining food production is offset by increasing food imports, which in turn cause further declines in internal food production.

The agricultural policies of Central American governments are often in direct conflict with the needs of small producers. Governments try to keep food prices low in order to reduce the pressure for wage increases. The importation of cheap food on easy credit terms prevents food shortages and keeps the urban masses supplied with relatively cheap food—without the necessity of overhauling the entire agricultural system. In the 1970s, when the region's economy was still growing and foreign loans were easing the balance-of-payments crunch, this strategy worked relatively well. However, negative economic growth rates, cut-offs of foreign loans, and debilitating debt payments in recent years have made this reliance on commercially imported food a less desirable option of late. The flow of tremendous quantities of U.S. food aid has at least temporarily averted a severe food shortage. But food aid, like commercial imports, keeps local market prices artificially low and discourages local food production, so that this short-term, band-aid solution becomes a long-term obstacle to food security for Central America.

Domestic obstacles to food security and broader-based economic development have to be considered in terms of the entire political economy. Development programs sponsored by political and economic elites are usually self-serving measures that perpetuate and fortify the dual structure of agriculture. Closely linked to the internal impediments to food security is an economic quagmire of international obstacles.

International Obstacles: Trading Against the Tide

Even when third world residents succeed in establishing popular political control (as they did in Nicaragua in 1979), they face an array of international obstacles that frustrate development plans. Most of these are directly related to the uneven, unjust nature of global trade and capital accumulation. Closely connected to the economic obstacles are the political ones. Colonial or neocolonial powers (the United States in the case of Central America) often take military measures or undertake covert operations to ensure that less powerful nations remain within their orbit of influence.

No Foreign Exchange, No Food Security

Foreign powers have molded Central America into a region that exports largely unprocessed commodities to the world's capitalist market. Imposed on the region was an agricultural economy designed to satisfy foreign tastes, not local appetites. Approximately 85 percent of its exports are unprocessed agricultural products.[1] These commodities are subject to wide price fluctuations. While the corporate traders thrive on this instability through their informed speculation in global commodity markets, Central American nations have a difficult time maintaining economic stability.

Global commodity trading takes place within the framework of uneven development, meaning that the industrial world benefits at the direct expense of Central Americans. The primary agricultural commodities from Central America have experienced a decline both in their share of the world market and in their real price, while the costs of manufactured imports to the region have rapidly increased. The prices that Central American agroexports realize on the world market fluctuate widely from one year to another but the long-term trend has been steadily downward.

But what do the fortunes of agroexports have to do with food security? Couldn't these countries just produce all the corn, beans, and rice they need first, and then use the leftover land and resources to produce export crops? It is certainly possible for basic grains to be given more of a priority in regional agriculture, but at the same time Central Americans desperately need foreign exchange. Without it, campesinos cannot buy the blades for their machetes. Without it, there is no fuel to transport food, no modern irrigation systems, no fertilizer to improve corn yields, no tractors to prepare the fields, and no money to buy food items not produced locally. Without it, there is no way to import food in times of shortages.

Foreign exchange is an essential ingredient for food security and development, but the need to acquire it does not preclude having more balanced agricultural systems. The necessity of acquiring large sums of foreign currency could be reduced if luxury imports were more restricted and the flow of private capital better regulated. More appropriate use of technology, reduced dependence on chemical pest control, and the development of more local industries would reduce the need for foreign exchange.

TNCs and the Terms-of-Trade Gap

The global reach of TNCs is a mighty obstacle in the path of food security. TNCs hold sway over the international commodity markets. These global titans grab a giant share of profits from the region's exports. They are the ones that small nations depend on for their fertilizer, agrochemicals, farm machinery, and high-yield seeds. In the globally interdependent capitalist market, there is no escaping the tentacles of the TNCs.

TNCs also bear direct responsibility for the distorted food system in Central America. These corporations benefit not only from the cheap production of agroexports but also from increasing trade in food imports. Peasants who grow basic foods are pushed off their plots to make room for large producers who grow bananas, coffee, cocoa, tobacco, and other export crops for foreign consumers. Firms like Cargill and Continental then profit from the region's need to import increasing quantities of corn and wheat.

In the last 20 years, the TNCs have moved into the region's agro-industry. The new food system they are imposing encourages the consumption of imported products with little nutritional value. Advertising campaigns have convinced many Central Americans-to switch from cheaper and more nutritious foods like tubers, maize, roots, legumes, and tropical fruit drinks to Coca Cola, Hardee's hamburgers, french fries from McDonald's, and Bimbo bread. Some of the same TNCs that benefit from cash-crop production are also involved in marketing processed foods locally. R.J. Reynolds, for example, produces or purchases at very low prices, bananas, tobacco, and coffee from Central America. At the same time, the corporation provides Central American consumers with unnutritious foods like crackers, candy, canned vegetables, and soft drinks. Central American countries suffer coming and going because of the domination of international trade by TNCs and industrial nations. The higher purchasing power of the developed world determines that local growers produce for those who can pay the most. Central American consumers who would like to eat more meat are outbid by pet owners in the United States. Development agencies like AID insist that the region's economic salvation lies in increased agroexport production because of its comparative advantage due to cheap labor. However, when countries do increase their export cropping they find that the United States and other industrial countries are raising protectionist barriers against beef, sugar, tobacco, and other commodity imports. Product refinement for export is not a solution either, since there's no hope in finding markets in developed countries for processed commodities like ground coffee and milk chocolate because of prohibitive trade barriers and strong domestic lobbies.

While the United States is steadily adopting new protectionist measures to promote domestic industries, its foreign aid agency (AID) insists that Central American countries tear down what few tariff walls they have and completely open up their economies to world trade. Yet the openness of the region's economy to international trade has already had a devastating effect on local food production and has stymied the development of local manufacturing and agroindustries.

Debt Crisis Worsens Chances for Food Security

Lower commodity prices and shrinking markets for export crops mean rising debts. Because third world countries are forever falling behind in their balance of trade, they have to apply for larger and larger loans to pay their bills. During the 1970s, international banks plied Central American governments with development loans whose payments are now coming due with a vengeance. Meanwhile, the cost of manufactured imports is rising dramatically, and interest rates on international loans are getting steeper.

Since 1975, Central America's external public debt has increased at an average annual rate of 25 percent. To meet their yearly debt obligations at present, the Central American nations would have to set aside over one-quarter of all income earned from exports. So grave is this debt crisis that each time a child is born in Central America she or he inherits a per capita debt of $782— twice as much as most Central American campesinos earn in an entire year. The debt crisis has grave consequences for food security. Instead of having the flexibility to use foreign loans and aid for development projects to improve the region's food-producing capability, Central American governments are fettered by the reality that an increasing portion of these funds are flowing back to the industrial nations as debt payments. A study by the U.S. Department of Agriculture concluded that "a staggering accumulation of international debt over the past decade has created the potential of a food crisis."[2] In Central America, as in other parts of the third world, that food crisis has already arrived.

Yet it is not just this staggering debt that is worsening the region's food crisis. To enforce debt repayment, the International Monetary Fund (IMF) has obligated countries to affect "adjustment programs." These programs try to squeeze more wealth out of financially strapped nations through austerity measures that keep wages low and the price of goods high. The IMF also pushes indebted countries to increase incentives for new agroexport production and further decrease services offered to those farmers whose products do not earn coveted foreign exchange. The landed elites usually welcome IMF adjustment programs because it is the poor majority that is forced to "adjust."

It is exceedingly difficult for third world countries to evade the constraints on their development imposed by international finance, the world market, and the agribusiness TNCs. Central American nations also have to consider the power of industrial countries, mainly the United States, to overthrow or destabilize governments which those industrial nations disagree with politically. As demonstrated in Guatemala in 1954, Cuba in 1959, Chile in 1973, and more recently in Nicaragua, the United States often attempts to block efforts by Latin American nations to pursue independent development strategies. Since the proclamation of the Monroe Doctrine in 1823, the United States has sought to advance its economic interests and political hegemony under the guise of promoting democracy and protecting Latin American nations from foreign aggression. The costs of returning a wayward country to the U.S. fold frequently far outweigh the economic benefits of trade and investment in that one country. However, the political and economic independence of one country, like Nicaragua, is taken as a threat to U.S. hegemony in the entire region, therefore justifying the price of counterrevolution and intervention.

Assessing the Solutions

There is no dearth of proposed solutions to the land and hunger crisis in Central America. Economic, technological, social, humanitarian, and political varieties are continually offered and tested in the region. An entire development business revolves around providing solutions to hunger and agrarian problems. AID is the lead development agency in the region but the World Bank and the Inter-American Development Bank (IDB) also claim to be solving the land and hunger crisis and putting Central America on the road to food security. Most of the solutions being offered, however, are "top-down" solutions that tend to reinforce the very obstacles to food security we have just discussed.

False Gifts from Foreigners

Since the end of World War II, foreign aid has been the remedy favored by the United States and former colonial powers to spur economic development in the third world. The focus of this foreign economic aid has changed numerous times during the last four decades. Like styles, though, discarded development philosophies often come back into fashion. Yet no matter what style or strategy, the primary intent of economic aid has been to increase global trade and investment opportunites. In Central America, this has been done essentially by strengthening the agroexport system. Closely related to the global trade and investment objective is the aim of some foreign aid programs to keep third world countries politically stable.

Foreign economic aid is either bilateral (from one government to another) or multilateral (contributions of many governments channeled through an international financial institution). In Central America, AID is the main source of bilateral assistance and most multilateral aid comes from the World Bank and the Inter-American Development Bank (IDB).

One of the first internationally initiated development strategies concerned the diffusion of technical assistance so that third world countries could "catch-up" to the agricultural advances of the industrial world. Another early focus involved the deployment of foreign consultants to establish planning departments and agricultural ministries. At the same time that foreign aid was bolstering the social infrastructure, it was also funding the expansion of the material infrastructure of development: roads, docks, bridges, and dams. The idea was that once this infrastructure was in place and a country's agroexport system primed with technical assistance and credit, its economy would "take-off" on the same development path followed by more "advanced" nations.

Initially, Central American countries did experience steady rates of economic growth, but by the 1960s it became apparent to the foreign development experts that economic growth was not trickling down to the poor majority. The numbers of destitute and malnourished people were increasing at the same time the economies of Central America were

Table 12

The Challenge of Food Security

Obstacles	Solutions
Domestic	
1. Land concentration and domination of agroexport system.	1. Agrarian reform.
2. Government neglect of small-farm sector.	2. Government recognition of importance of small-farm sector for national food security and economic development; extension of credit and technical assistance.
3. Lack of campesino organization.	3. End to repression of rural organizing and government support for grassroots decision-making.
4. Lack of infrastructure for basic-foods production and marketing.	4. Increased government support for national food system that emphasizes food security.
International	
5. Low and fluctuating prices for agricultural commodities.	5. International commodity agreements and formation of associations of exporting nations.
6. Dependence on only a few cash crops for foreign exchange.	6. More agroindustrual development and diversification.
7. Increasing external debt.	7. Renegotiation and cancellation of debt burden.
8. TNC control of world agribusiness.	8. Regulation of TNC investment in agricultural production and local food processing industries, state marketing of exports, commodity agreements, and cartels of exporting nations.
9. Political and economic power of larger nations, particularly the US.	9. Diversification of trade, regional alliances, and association with other non-aligned nations.

"developing." This realization did not change the basic thrust of development aid—that of increasing economic growth by promoting the agroexport system—but it did persuade foreign donors to support more redistributive and social impact projects. The clearest example of this was the Alliance for Progress, which hoped to politically stabilize Latin America through rural development programs and ameliorative reforms.

In the last two decades, rural development programs have been a major focus of development aid. Concern about political unrest in rural areas led AID to fund project categories like "small farmer development," "integrated rural development," and "farm-to-market rural roads." These projects aim to create a petty bourgeois class of agroexport producers who will exert a conservative and politically stabilizing influence in rural areas. Anthony Cauterucci, AID director in Honduras, explained that, "Over the long term we are looking at moving subsistence-oriented agriculture toward high commerical value agriculture and at linking campesinos to the export process."[3] When AID talks of campesinos and small farmers, it is in fact referring to the upper strata of peasantry and not the large majority of below-subsistence peasants.

Some rural development programs are directed more at poverty alleviation than at actual economic development. These projects provide the rural poor with food, medical assistance, government services, and sometimes land as a direct way to ease rural tensions. In general, however, rural development projects do not address the domestic obstacles to food security but keep the peasantry marginalized from political and economic power. These programs are introduced into rural areas as a substitute for agrarian reform programs that would truly develop and empower the small farm sector.

The most recent trends in development aid include "private-sector support" projects that encourage new investment by private entrepreneurs and support the "privatization" of public-sector corporations and services. The Caribbean Basin Initiative (CBI) and other economic aid programs introduced by the Reagan administration operate along these lines by providing subsidies and incentives to U.S. investors to launch new agroexport ventures involving nontraditional crops. A case in point is AID's support for a 450-acre project in Guatemala in which a group of right-wing Cuban-American investors produce melons and feed grain on land that once supported basic food production. U.S.-sponsored development projects like this one are happening throughout the isthmus, and are essentially counterproductive.

In the last 30 years, over $10 billion in international economic aid has been injected into Central America. Both the CBI and the recommendations of the Kissinger Commission have resulted in rapid increases in the level of foreign aid flowing to Central America. Between 1980 and 1986, AID spent more than $3 billion in the region singlehandedly, and it is projected that another $8 billion in economic aid will be pumped into Central America by the end of the decade.

Despite these vast sums, life for the rural and urban poor has not improved. Instead, conditions for the poor majority have deteriorated. Income and consumption levels have declined, and the region is less food secure than it was before it began receiving the "benefits" of foreign aid. Still, it would be wrong to label development aid as the colossal boondoggle it seems to be. Economic aid has "failed" to reduce poverty and hunger not through ineptness, but because broad-based development and food security were never the main objectives of foreign development programs in the first place.

From the initial technical-assistance diffusion projects to more recent rural development and private-sector support projects, the main, (although often unspoken) goal of foreign economic aid has been to strenghten global trade and capitalist investment. In Central America, economic aid has served to bolster the agroexport system's role as a source of cheap commodites for the world market. Foreign aid has facilitated this by providing agroexporters with infrastructure, agricultural credit, and technical assistance.

Rural development projects, while supposedly geared toward assisting small farmers, actually serve to prop up the dual structure of agriculture. As Susan George, author of *Ill Fares the Land*, puts it, many of the projects proposed by international aid agencies are directed toward "helping people to make do with less rather than aiding them to obtain more."[4] AID's rural development projects in Central America fit this description perfectly. Many AID projects tell small farmers they can make do on their tiny plots by increasing agrochemical purchases and by producing vegetables for export. AID's agricultural projects have increased the region's tobacco, vegetable, shrimp, and citrus exports but have done little to expand domestic food production.

Rural development projects are not, by definition, inappropriate or unneeded. Central American campesinos do need agricultural credit, technical assistance, and information about birth control. But the main beneficiaries of AID's agricultural programs are usually medium-sized to large farms whose owners can take the risk involved in utilizing agricultural credit and technical assistance programs. When those at the bottom of the society are neglected, however, rural development projects serve to reinforce the unequal distribution of land, wealth, and power. Regretfully, the entire thrust of most international development aid has been to change things from the top, rather than directly supporting campesino groups that are struggling from the bottom up.

That most economic aid furthers uneven development and capital accumulation is the sad result of viewing Central America from the lofty perch of those at the top. Such aid flows through the very political and economic elites responsible for inequitable land and income distribution. It promotes investment by TNCs without regard for national development priorities, builds dependency on imported food and technology, and pushes increased exports as the main solution to the region's problems.

Recently, the "development" thrust of U.S. economic assistance has been overshadowed by more blatantly political objectives. Over 75 percent of U.S. economic aid is not targeted for individual projects, but rather flows into the general coffers of recipient governments as a way to guarantee their political allegiance and keep their economies from collapsing. Thus, instead of a plan to truly assist economies sorely in need of development, the short-term goals of economic and political stabilization have become the major focus of Washington's foreign assistance strategy in Central America.

The Technological Fix

Rather than address the structural obstacles to food security, the industrial world and its TNCs have offered Central America a dubious technological fix: agricultural modernization. Modernization advocates argue that larger doses of farm machinery, agrochemicals, high-yield seeds, "scientific" farming practices, and biotechnology will increase production without the need for land redistribution. The modernization solution initially focused exclusively on large-scale production but has lately stressed the modernization possibilities of small-scale farming too.

The technological fix to world hunger came into vogue in the 1960s with the Green Revolution, whose proponents hailed the use of high-yielding seeds and increased agricultural technology to produce larger harvests of basic grains. State-of-the-art farming did increase yields but world hunger did not go away. Green Revolution enthusiasts—like AID, the World Bank, and the Rockefeller Foundation—ignored the obvious fact that people who are hungry do not have the purchasing power to buy food. The lack of land and income—not food shortages—were the major reasons for hunger and malnourishment.

Two decades after the Green Revolution broke ground, world hunger has worsened. The failure of the Green Revolution did not, however, mean the end of the enthusiasm for the modernization solution. Advocates of modernization proclaimed the arrival of a Green Revolution for small growers. While small producers can certainly use technical assistance, the mini-Green Revolution has neither increased basic food production nor improved the lot of the peasantry in Central America. The technical package of seeds, fertilizer, and pesticides is too expensive for most of the region's small farmers, and those that do have the start-up money for these inputs choose to produce high-priced agroexports, not low-priced basic foods.

A salient problem of the modernization solution is that it ignores the basic wisdom of many traditional agricultural practices. While high-yield seeds may produce more under ideal conditions and with plenty of irrigation, fertilizer and pesticides, these "ideal" conditions rarely exist for small farmers. Locally grown seed may not produce as much but it is often better suited to local conditions and, because it is not an expensive import, is less risky. Peasants do not produce record yields but they are usually very efficient given their lack of inputs and the poor soil conditions under which they operate.

Technological modernization increases the need for imported supplies and machinery, frequently luring farmers into debt while draining national foreign exchange reserves. Once hooked on this "quick-fix," farmers are forever dependent on foreign TNCs for the tools of their livelihood and the all-important spare parts without which their entire farming operation comes to a halt. Other problems concern the huge amounts of expensive, non-renewable energy that are required for high-tech agriculture and the fact that capital-intensive production is imprudent in countries with high rural unemployment rates.[5]

Yet modernization continues to be pushed onto Central America and other parts of the third world by foreign governments, globetrotting TNCs, and international aid agencies. While third world countries welcome agricultural modernization, its success depends upon making supplies and machinery available to the poorest sectors, and modernization should never be viewed as a substitute for land reform and decisions on appropriate food production.

In fact, in nations with unequal land ownership, modernization will likely increase the gap between rich and poor, since the former can more easily afford the costs of modernization. The high costs of increased agricultural technology should be closely scrutinized by countries committed to agrarian reform and food security. The complete package of capital-intensive agriculture is clearly inappropriate for the labor-rich and capital-poor third world. Rather than more technology and increased inputs, small farmers that produce basic foods need information on inexpensive and risk-averting ways to improve production through such practices as organic farming, mixed cropping, and biological pest control.

Agrarian Reform

Changing the patterns of land tenure has long been offered as a solution to the economic and political problems faced by Central American countries. Redistributive reforms do have a role in combatting rural landlessness, increasing basic food production, and making more intensive use of available arable land. But most agrarian reforms fall far short of confronting the agroexport economy, resulting only in cosmetic changes.

The reforms funded by AID are mostly administrative programs designed to release social tension and forestall leftist revolutions. They are limited to treating the social consequences of the agroexport system rather than confronting the system itself. Land needs to be redistributed in Central America. However, if agrarian reform is to help ensure food security it has to go beyond redistribution to include more effective government support for the peasantry, higher prices for basic foods, and measures that alter the dual structure of agriculture. Another essential component of successful agrarian reform is the engagement of campesinos in the planning and implementation of land redistribution and agrarian transformation. This broader concept of agrarian reform is one that almost no development agency would espouse and is likely better described as agrarian revolution.

Food Aid to the Rescue

Food assistance is neither a temporary nor long-term solution to the region's food problems. Instead of furthering food security, food aid aggravates food security problems. Food aid undermines local food production, allows governments to postpone reforms that would increase local food production, and props up unpopular regimes.

The United States is the major source of food aid to Central America, and Washington likes to give the impression that this food feeds the hungry and reduces malnourishment. In fact, very little of U.S. food aid to Central America can even remotely qualify as "humanitarian" assistance. Most food shipments are used to cover budget deficits of allied governments, ease balance-of-payments crises, and support pacification programs. Less than 20 percent of food assistance is actually distributed free to poor people in Central America.[6]

Most U.S. food aid is distributed under the PL480 or "Food for Peace" program, which is administered by the Agency for International Development (AID). The main intent of the program, has not been to feed hungry people but to unload unmanageable surpluses of food. Congress created the PL480 program in 1954 to support the country's farm industry. The program does this by buying surplus commodities from U.S. farmers and shipping them to non-commercial foreign markets. The program has also been used to create commercial markets for U.S. commodities. Once hooked on concessional food imports, countries become a steady market for commercial agricultural exports on a paying basis. According to the founding legislation, the PL480 program was to be used "to improve the foreign relations of the United States." In Central America, it is this political objective which accounts for the current flood of U.S. food aid into the region. AID acknowledges that food aid programs in Central America "increase sometimes substantially the magnitude of the total assistance package we are able to offer governments and thus increase our ability to influence their decisions."[7]

Before U.S. food aid started flowing to Central America in the 1950s, the region was largely self-sufficient in basic foods. That does not mean that everybody had enough food, only that there was adequate domestic food production to cover the effective demand of those with purchasing power. Imports of both U.S. commercial and concessional food came at a time when per capita food production was beginning to decline, mainly as a result of the agroexport boom and the consequent displacement of small farmers.

In terms of relieving the U.S. market of surplus commodities, the PL480 program has been very successful in Central America. Today, Central American nations annually import from the United States about 900,000 metric tons of grains and feeds, about 500,000 tons of which is wheat. Wheat can only be grown in a few areas of Central America, but much of the rest of U.S. food imports could readily be grown within the region if there was greater emphasis on food security. Each year, for example, Central American countries import over 100,000 tons of corn from the United States.

Food aid constitutes an increasing portion of U.S. agricultural exports to Central America. The rise in U.S. food aid, however, is not due to the increased hunger and malnutrition in the region; rather, this aid is a function of politics. It was not until 1979—the year of the Nicaraguan revolution, when Washington felt its hold on the region slipping—that Central America started receiving enormous quantities of U.S. food aid. PL480 food aid from 1980 through 1985 was 2.3 times the amount delivered in the previous 27 years of the program.

Most food aid—over 80 percent—is given directly to Central American governments in the form of concessional credits for U.S. food. This government-to-government food aid is known as Title I. The recipient government then sells Title I food on the local market, and the proceeds from the sales are used for either the government's general budgetary support or to cover specific government programs. Not only does Title I food help generate local currency but it also saves governments from spending scarce foreign exchange to import food. The food does not go to hungry Central Americans but to those who can afford to buy bread or vegetable oil at their local stores.

This critique of the Title I program is not drawn from a Marxist textbook; it comes from the U.S. Department of Agriculture (USDA) itself, which concluded in 1985 that "PL480 food commodities, placed on the open market of a recipient country, will not, in general, be evenly distributed throughout the population. PL480 food shipments increase the average daily caloric intake for the highest income groups considerably more than for the poor."[8]

Title II programs distribute what is often called "humanitarian" food aid. It is given mainly to private voluntary organizations (PVOs) and to the UN's World Food Program (WFP), and less frequently to governments for distribution to the poor and malnourished. It is distributed free to participants of supplementary feeding programs or to displaced and refugee populations.

However, Title II food is also handed out in exchange for labor in Food-for-Work development projects sponsored by the local government or military. Instead of fulfilling a humanitarian purpose, this food is being used to support counterinsurgency and counterrevolutionary wars. In Guatemala and El Salvador, Title II food is distributed as part of pacification programs designed to increase military control over rural populations. Soldiers often hand out the food at the same time they are lecturing peasants about the need to defend the "fatherland" against "commmunist subversives." In Honduras, right-wing PVOs like Friends of the Americas parcel out food allotments to families of the *contras*.

Food aid often acts as a disincentive to the production of basic grains. Imports of cheap and free U.S. food depress prices realized by local growers. In the aftermath of the 1976 earthquake in Guatemala, the influx of foreign food "knocked the bottom out of the grain market in the country for nine to twelve months," according to the director of one relief agency.[9] The earthquake, while causing extensive property damage and loss of lives, did not destroy the corn crop, but foreign food donations made it impossible for local growers to sell their corn at profitable prices. The deluge of U.S. food aid in recent years has elicited angry outcries by farmers throughout Central America. In Costa Rica, peasants demanding a halt to U.S. corn imports and an end to the government's austerity program were attacked by police during a 1986 demonstration. Dairy farmers in both Costa Rica and Guatemala have protested U.S. programs to dump U.S. milk products on their local markets. "It's illogical that a country which has enough capacity for local consumption and for export should be receiving AID donations," said one angry Costa Rican farmer.[10]

In the late 1970s, Catholic Relief Services in Guatemala advocated that all food aid stop "because of the dependency it creates and resignation it produces."[11] The dependency issue is a crucial one, wheat being a prime example. When the United States began experiencing a wheat surplus in the 1950s, Central Americans were hit by a barrage of advertising that advocated more wheat consumption. Commercials and billboards falsely claimed that bread was nutritionally superior to corn-based tortillas. Companies such as Pillsbury, Cargill, and General Mills quickly set up mills in each country to process U.S.-supplied grain.

Before long, many Central American consumers, especially those living in the cities, were changing from tortillas to white sandwich bread, thereby adapting their taste buds to a basic grain that does not grow in the tropical climate of Central America. In the early 1950s, Costa Rica was importing about 5,000 tons of wheat each year; today it imports 20 times that amount. The region has become dependent on wheat flour imports from the United States, subjecting Central America even further to domination by the United States economically and politically.

Again, a trenchant analysis comes from a U.S. government source, this time the General Accounting Office (GAO): "The U.S. direct food aid program has allowed governments to postpone essential agrarian reforms and needed agricultural investment. In addition, it has helped depress prices. Food aid has also shifted public tastes, especially those of urban consumers, away from locally grown foods toward imported ones. In the long run this increases demand for imported foodstuffs."[12]

Washington has also taken advantage of a little known export guarantee program (called GSM-102) to support its political agenda in Central America. Under this program, the U.S. government guarantees payment to TNCs for commercial food exports to countries like El Salvador that could otherwise not afford to import many U.S. agricultural commodities. The Central American nation turns around and sells this food (whose price to them has been subsidized by the U.S. government) using the profits to generate critical balance-of-payments revenue. In the first 25 years of the guarantee program, only $16 million in commodity insurance was issued for exports to Central America. As the political situation became more critical, Washington expanded its guarantees substantially. From

1980 to 1984, $290 million in commodity guarantees were authorized—almost 20 times more than in the entire previous history of the program.

Food aid and commodity programs are an often overlooked part of the U.S.-sponsored attempt to maintain the economic and political inequalities in Central America. This injection of aid disrupts local markets and allows politicians to postpone making needed changes in the agricultural system. Food aid is also setting up Central American countries for a hard fall. The extraordinary sums of food assistance have made Guatemala, El Salvador, Honduras, and Costa Rica dangerously dependent on political and economic conditions in the United States. There is no guarantee that Washington will be able to continue pumping over $120 million in food aid and over $60 million in commodity guarantees into the region year after year. About half of U.S. agricultural exports to Costa Rica and El Salvador come under the PL480 program. The withdrawal or termination of this largesse would cause severe economic dislocations and food shortages throughout the isthmus.

Controlling Population Growth

High population growth rates are sometimes considered to be the main reason for poverty and hunger in the third world. It is certainly true that population is increasing faster than the pace of economic growth and food production. It would be erroneous, however, to say that population growth causes poverty and hunger in a region that is more sparsely populated than many food-secure regions of the world.

The connections between population and hunger are complex. The history of development does show, however, that poverty causes increased population growth—not the other way around. Family size generally declines only when living standards begin to improve and members of a society have some control over the resources they need. An extensive study of 64 countries by the World Bank found that when the income of the poorest group rose by 1 percent the fertility rate dropped by nearly 3 percentage points.[13] Improved health care, better nutrition, adequate wages, social security systems, and pension plans make it realistic for couples to consider limiting family size. In Costa Rica, which has a social security system and better health services than elsewhere in the region, birth rates are lower. Recent changes in Nicaragua may also influence the future birth rate. As one Nicaraguan woman commented: "Since they started the new clinic and we get good free medical care, fewer children die now. My husband agrees that we should have only two other children and try to keep them in better health with the help of the clinic."[14]

International efforts to increase awareness about birth control have helped Central Americans gain better control over their lives. Yet population growth in Central America is unlikely to slow substantially until there is better health care and better distribution of land and income. Because of high infant mortality, parents have many children to ensure that some will survive to contribute economically to the family.

In the countryside, children are a major economic resource. From the age of four, campesino children haul water, collect firewood, and look after the livestock. A study of the relationship between land and population in El Salvador by Stanford University professor William Durham found that by the time Salvadoran children are seven or eight, they begin to earn more than they cost their families.[15] Later as adults, children also compensate for the lack of a social security system by caring for their aged parents.

Relative to many other parts of the world, Central America is not overpopulated. The population density of Central America is roughly comparable to the states of New York or Maryland. The Land Tenure Center in Wisconsin reported that "if land were more evenly divided in El Salvador [the most densely populated of Central American countries] . . . the land could easily accommodate the 4.7 million people who live there."[16]

Another way to evaluate the food production constraints brought on by population is to look at per capita cropland statistics. In terms of the amount of cropland per person, Central America is actually less densely populated than the world average. In fact, countries like Honduras and Nicaragua could be considered underpopulated. People not having enough land on which to grow the food they need would not be a problem if land were more evenly distributed and put to better use, and if more government services were available to small farmers. About 25 percent of all arable land in Central America is left idle by large landowners, and land currently used as pasture is more than twice that of land currently cultivated. Combined with the large amounts of forest land that is potentially exploitable (about one third of total land area), there are many possibilities to expand cultivation of food crops to meet the needs of the current and future population of Central America.

In the end, achieving environmentally and economically sound rates of population growth is not an educational issue but a fundamentally political one. The rise of political leadership committed to food security and meeting the population's basic needs would do more to solve land scarcity and overcrowding in cities than any imaginable educational campaign. Political changes can make the difference between famine and plenty. The best example of this is China, a country plagued by famine before their revolution. Although China has only half as much farmland per capita as

India, hunger is rare in China but prevalent and worsening in India. High population growth is not the root of hunger in Central America; its origins lie, instead, in the callous maldistribution of land and income.

Hungry for Change

The roots of rebellion are burrowing deeper into Central America. The landless call for land redistribution, the malnourished demand a better diet, and the poor want a just share of national income. Thus the dual structure of agriculture upon which the agroexport system is based is facing domestic and international threats to its continued stability.

Meanwhile, the standard modernization and development strategies are being replayed without much success. Neither the Alliance for Progress, the Green Revolution, nor the Caribbean Basin Initiative have addressed the root causes of the land and hunger crisis. These top-down development strategies have moved the region no closer to food security. Instead, they have contributed to the rationalization of the agroexport system and Central America's extreme class divisions.

A centuries-old economic and political system has left most Central Americans in desperate poverty, ready for new solutions. But before nations can begin to decide something as basic as what they want to produce and for whom, unjust agrarian structures must go. The agrarian transformation needed in Central America involves a thorough land reform program. It requires a sweeping revision of the region's food system, with an overhaul of the whole network of relationships determining production, marketing, processing, distribution, consumption, import, and export of food. The need for national food security, rather than the demands of a small exporting elite, must guide economic decision making. If land is more evenly distributed and put to better use, Central Americans can be guaranteed a good diet and a decent living. The great quantities of idle arable land and the vast amounts of pasture land could then grow more basic grains, fruits, and vegetables for Central Americans.

Campesinos encouraged to join together in production and food-processing cooperatives could make the small-farm sector a dynamic part of the regional economy. Independently, workers in the cities could produce low-cost consumer goods desired by the rural population. Peasants would be able to buy these goods by virtue of their sale of increasing amounts of staple and semi-processed foods to city residents.

If more of the region's economic surplus were channeled into investments for the social good, small farmers would benefit from new infrastructure and increased government assistance. Extensive regional cooperation in agriculture would also benefit Central Americans. The processing of primary products in an enlarged agroindustry would both augment employment and decrease dependency on the industrialized countries. Expanded regional food trade would reduce the foreign exchange crisis and brighten prospects for food security in Central America.

Solutions like these will not come easily or peacefully. The land and hunger crisis is both the cause and the symptom of a general breakdown of political and economic systems in the region. To remove the domestic and international obstacles to food security requires more than token reforms. In Central America, it is far too late for political or economic tinkering. The land and hunger crisis cannot be solved merely by modernization remedies, development aid, or redistributive reforms. Neither can the crisis be circumvented by U.S. political stabilization programs that shore up economies with financial aid, prop up governments with false "democratization," and prime the forces of repression with military assistance.

This is the autumn of the patriarchs, the oligarchs, the generals, and the imperialists in Central America. The old order is tottering, but it will not fall without a final push. Yet removing the old guard is only part of the solution. For the land and hunger crisis to be resolved, the region's political and economic leaders need to create a system of food security—one that meets the basic food needs of even the poorest social strata, satisfies most nutritional needs from domestic production, and maintains fair and secure trading relations to complement internal food production. The task is not an easy one, but neither is it an impossible one.

FOOTNOTES

Chapter One: The Justice of Eating

1. Juan Antonio Aguirre, "Agriculture in Central America in the Year 2000," *Desarrollo Rural en las Americas*, Vol. XII, No. 2, Mayo-Agosto 1980, p. 81.

2. In Central America, agriculture employs from one-third to two-thirds of the workforce in each country. Despite new industrialization, agriculture still employs almost 4 times as many workers as industry.

3. From the film on Dr. Charles Clements, "Witness to War: An American Doctor in El Salvador."

4. United Nations Environment Program, *Genetic Resources: An Overview* (Nairobi: United Nations, 1980), p. 24.

5. David Browning, *El Salvador: Landscape and Society* (London: Oxford, 1971), p. 16.

6. Small and medium-sized farms in the region produce: between 68 percent and 96 percent (depending on the country) of the basic grains (except rice), between 59 and 93 percent of the vegetables, and between 46 and 65 percent of the fruit. CEPAL, *Istmo Centroamericano: Los Sistemas Alimentarios de las Canastas Básicas*, (Mexico City, March 1981).

7. Of the four million hectares of fertile land in Central America, 83 percent belongs to large farms producing for export. This estimate for land use in 1970 is from CEPAL: *La Pobreza y la Satifacción de Necesidades Básicas en el Istmo Centroamericano* (Mexico City, March 31, 1981), p. 29.

8. Jacobo Schatan, *La Agroindustria y el Sistema Centroamericano* (Mexico City: CEPAL, 1983), p. 46. Central America now has more than 1.5 million landless rural workers: Confederación Universitaria Centroamericana (CSUCA), *Los Trabajadores Temporeros en la Agricultura Centroamericana* (San José, 1983).

9. John Weeks, *The Economies of Central America* (New York: Holmes & Meir, 1985), p. 102.

10. Interview by author near Palmerola, Honduras, July 1984.

11. AID, *Land and Labor in Guatemala*, 1982; UN, "Realidad Campesina y Desarrollo Nacional," No. 5, 1976; Carmen Diana Deere, "A Comparative Analysis of Agrarian Reform in El Salvador and Nicaragua,"

in *Development and Change*, Vol. 13, 1982, p. 3; Schatan, op. cit., p. 47. Information derived from CIERA statistics prepared by Peter Marchetti and Solon Baraclough; Beatriz M. Villareal, *El Precarismo Rural en Costa Rica: 1960-1980* (San José: Papiro, 1983), pp. 25-26.

12. Schatan, op. cit., p. 38.

13. Interview by author, San Marcos, Guatemala, June 1984.

14. Alain de Janvry, *The Agrarian Question and Reformism in Latin America* (Baltimore: Johns Hopkins University Press, 1981), pp. 151-173.

15. For a good discussion of this process of proletarianization see de Janvry, Ibid.

16. SIECA, *Compendio Estadístico Centroamericano* (Guatemala: 1957 and 1981).

17. USDA, *World Food Aid Needs and Availabilities, 1984,* (Washington, July 1984).

18. See "Less Developed Countries May Offer Opportunities for Export Business" in *Farmer Cooperatives*, February 1982, pp. 12-17.

19. *Boletin Informativo Honduras (CEDOH)*, December 1983, p. 9; CEPAL, "Grado de Satisfacción de las Necesidades Básicas en el Istmo," (Mexico City), 1982.

20. Tropical Agricultural Research and Training Center (CATIE), "Improving the Small Farm Production Systems in Central America," (Turrialba, Costa Rica), 1982, p. 1.

21. The relationships among income, land, and hunger are especially clear in El Salvador. Between 1961 and 1975, the average income of families with small farm plots increased 12 percent. This contrasts with an over 120 percent increase in income for large landholders during the same period. Tommie Sue Montgomery, *Revolution in El Salvador: Origins and Evolution* (Boulder: Westview, 1982), p. 30. Montgomery cites Salvador Arias Penate, "Las Perspectivas del Desarrollo Agropecuario en Relación con la Tenencia de la Tierra," *ECA*, No. 379, May 1980, p. 457.

22. See reports for various countries by CEPAL, "Estudios Económicos de América Latina," 1982. Most staple foods doubled in price during the 1970s, and during the 1980s there have also been sharp increases in food prices. In Guatemala, the price of beans tripled between 1978 and 1982, forcing many poor families to eliminate this source of protein.

23. IDB, *Economic and Social Progress in Latin America, 1978,* (Washington).

24. Programa Regional del Empleo para América Latina y el Caribe (PREALC), "Diagnóstico de las Estadísticas y Bibliografía en Centroamerica y Panama," (Santiago), 1979, p. 10.

25. AID, *Country Development Strategy Statements: Data Abstract*, 1982.

26. *Boletín Económico*, No. 9, (Guatemala), September 1982, p. 2.

27. University of Central America, San Salvador, "La Fase III de la Reforma Agraria y Las Condiciones de Vida de Sus Beneficiarios— Seminario Permanente Sobre la Economic Nacional del Departamento de Economía," (San Salvador); *Proceso*, (El Salvador) September 12, 1983, p. 9.

28. Schatan, op. cit., p. 63. The FAO estimates that 1250 calories are needed to maintain normal bodily functions and metabolic rates. See "El Hambre en Honduras" in *Boletín Informativo Honduras (CEDOH)*, October 1984.

29. James P. Grant, *The State of the World's Children 1982-83* (London: Oxford University, 1983), pp. 29-31.

30. Interview by author with Marijka Velzeboer, Tegucigalpa, September 1984.

31. INCAP, "Vigiláncia Epidemiológica de la Desnutrición," Annex II, 1978, p. 15. Cited in Institute for Food and Development Policy, "Guatemala: Hungry for Change," Food First Action Alert, March 1983.

32. Pan American Health Organization (PAHO), "The Inter-American Investigation of Mortality in Childhood," (Washington: 1971).

33. "Children's Energy Crisis," *New Internationalist*, March 12, 1983, p. 3.

34. PAHO, op. cit.; *New Internationalist*, March 12, 1983, op. cit.

35. AID, *Congressional Presentation FY85, Latin America and the Caribbean*, Vol. II, p. 88.

36. Grant, op. cit.

37. Ibid.

Chapter Two: The New Plantation

1. IDB, *Social and Economic Progress in Latin America*, 1983.

2. IDB, *Economic and Social Progress in Latin America*, 1981.

3. David Browning, *El Salvador: Landscape and Society* (London: Oxford, 1971), p. 205.

4. Vera Kelsey and Lilly Osborne, *Four Keys to Guatemala* (New York: Funk & Wagnalls, 1939), pp. 58-59.

5. William C. Thiesenhusen, "How Agriculture has Effected Social Change in El Salvador." Paper prepared for delivery at the University of Wisconsin, February 2, 1984.

6. Thiesenhusen, op. cit., p. 13.

7. Eldon Kenworthy, "Is El Salvador a New Vietnam?" *In These Times*, March 23, 1983, p. 16.

8. CEPAL, "America Latina y la Economía Mundial del Café," (Santiago) 1982. Figures are from 1977.

9. Interview by author, Quezaltenango, May 1984.

10. *El Salvador Bulletin*, December 1983.

11. Testimonies compiled by Global Justice, Albuquerque, New Mexico, 1984.

12. Ibid.

13. CEPAL, *The Transnational Oligopoly in the Coffee Industry*, (Santiago) 1982, p. 10.

14. Ibid., p. 6.

15. "Bananas had their origin in Southeastern Asia . . . reached Africa at about the beginning of the Christian era . . . [and] from Africa the banana was carried to the Americas in 1516 and became so well established in a short space of time that some of the early travelers thought it was an indigenous plant." Charles B. Heiser, *Seed to Civilization* (San Francisco: W.H. Freeman, 1973), pp. 158-160.

16. Walter Truett Anderson, "The Real Domino Theory in Central America: An Ecological Disaster in the Making," *Pacific News Service*, August 1984.

17. Steve Lewontin, "Outpost of the Banana Empire," *Honduras Update*, July 1984, pp. 4-5.

18. Philippe Bourgeois, "Racism and the Multinational Corporation: The Ethnicity of the Labor Force on a Subsidiary of the United Fruit Company in Limón, Costa Rica and Bocas del Toro, Panama", *Mundo Indígena*, Fall 1984, p. 3.

19. Ibid.

20. EDUCA, *El Universo Bananero en Centroamerica* (San Jose) 1977, p. 19.

21. Edelberto Torres-Rivas, *El Desarrollo de la Agricultura en Centroamerica*, (San José: Documentos de Estudios, CSUCA, 1982), p. 61.

22. Elisabeth Burgos-Debray, (ed.), *I, Rigoberta Menchú* (London: Verson, 1983), p. 22.

23. Ibid., p. 41.

24. Information from summary report of the Conference on Land Tenure in Central America. Presented by Washington Office on Latin America (WOLA) at Johns Hopkins University, March 23, 1981, p. 22. Also see Figueroa Galvez and Julio Alfonso, *El Cultivo Capitalista del Algodón* Guatemala: Universidad de San Carlos de Guatemala, 1980). The authors cite government figures that show that cotton producers spend almost three times as much on inputs as they do on wages.

25. Torres-Rivas, op. cit.

26. Ibid.

27. Calculations from data supplied by Granillo Bonilla and Rina Amelia, Universidad Centroamericana José Simeon Canas, "La Modernización del Cultivo del Algodón, Causas, y Consequencias," (San Salvador), 1980, p. 32; El Salvador differs from other Central American producers in that a large portion of its cotton (about 20 percent) is used internally to produce textiles and clothing for the regional market. *Mesoamerica*, Vol. 2, No. 1, January 1983, p. 9.

28. Galvez and Alfonso, op. cit.

29. For an excellent description of pre- and post-revolutionary cotton production in Nicaragua, see CIERA and INIES, "El Subsistema del Algodón en Nicaragua," (Managua), 1983.

30. Information obtained from the Instituto de Investigaciones Económicas, (San Salvador: Universidad de Centro America).

31. Interview by author with John Bellamy, Export Director, Asociación de Azucareros, August 1984.

32. Hearings Before the Subcommittee on Inter-American Affairs, House

of Representatives, *Toward a Strategy of Inter-American Development*, March 3, 1969.

33. See statement of the Nicaraguan Foreign Ministry in Tony Anderson, "Reagan Embitters Nicaragua by Cutting Sugar Imports," *Multinational Monitor*, June 1983.

34. See "Agriculture: Quotas Boost Sugar Earnings," in *Washington Report on the Hemisphere*, February 21, 1984, p. 7.

35. Ibid.

36. Comment to author by an anonymous Costa Rican near San Jose", March 1982.

37. Robert C. West, "Recent Developments in Cattle Raising and the Beef Export Trade in the Middle American Region," in *Proceedings of the 42nd International Congress of Americanists* (Paris: Societe des Americanistes, 1977), Vol. I, p. 399.

38. *Ambio*, No. 1, 1981, op. cit.

39. Figures from the United States Department of Agriculture.

40. Norman Myers, "The Hamburger Connection: How Central America's Forests Become North America's Hamburgers," *Ambio*, No. 1, 1981; SIECA, *Compendio Estadistico Centroamericano* (Guatemala), 1975, 1983.

41. *Pacific News Service*, August 1984, op. cit.

42. *Ambio*, No. 1, 1981, op. cit.

43. Robert Williams, *Export Agriculture and the Crisis in Central America*, (Chapel Hill: University of North Carolina Press, 1986) pp. 77-94.

44. Oftentimes the United States will enforce food-quality requirements when U.S. farmers and ranchers holler for reduced imports. The requirements are relaxed again when the domestic market becomes undersupplied.

45. Williams, op. cit., p. 117.

46. Jaime Biderman, "The Development of Capitalism in Nicaragua: A Political Economic History," *Latin American Perspectives*, Winter 1983; Jacobo Schatan, *La Agroindustria y el Sistema Alimentario Centroamericano* (Mexico: CEPAL, 1983), p. 47.

47. James D. Nations and Daniel I. Komer, "Rainforests and the Hamburger Society," *Environment*, April 1983.

48. UNCTAD, *World Commodity Trade: Review and Outlook*, (Geneva: United Nations, 1983).

49. Fidel Castro, *The World Economic and Social Crisis* (Havana: Publications Office of the State, 1983), p. 62.

50. Derived from FAO, *The State of Food and Agriculture 1983*, (Rome: 1983), p. 28.

51. SIECA, "Estructura del Volumen y Valor de Importaciones de Agroquímicos," (Guatemala: 1984).

52. United Nations, *UN Yearbook of International Trade Statistics, 1983* (Geneva: United Nations, 1983).

53. *Farmline*, May 1982, p. 7.

54. *FAO Trade Yearbook, 1981.*

55. An Overseas Development Council report showed that more stable commodity prices for the third world would have resulted in $15 billion in economic gains if they had been instituted ten years ago. Jere R. Behrman, *International Commodity Agreements: An Evaluation of the UNCTAD Integrated Commodity Program* (Washington: Overseas Development Council, 1977), Monograph No. 9. Cited in George, op. cit., p. 40. Stable and higher commodity prices would mean increased imports by Central American nations and reduced external debt. Commodity agreements and better terms of trade might not mean more food for the hungry of most nations, but they would allow all governments to plan better. In the case of governments committed to food security, such arrangements would bring direct benefits to the population.

Chapter Three: The Land of the Oligarchs

1. *Multinational Monitor*, May 1981.

2. Aristotle, *Politics*, Sections 1279-81.

3. For an analysis of this dynamic, see: John Weeks, *The Economies of Central America*, (New York, 1985) pp. 15-16.

4. Ibid.

5. Marc Herold, "From Riches to 'Rags': Finanzcapital in El Salvador, 1900-1980," (unpublished manuscript, University of New Hampshire, 1980) p. 22.

6. David Browning, *El Salvador: Landscape and Society*, (London: Oxford, 1971) p. 223.

7. John A. Booth, "Toward Explaining the Regional Crisis in Central America," *Mesoamerica*, March 1983.

8. Instituto de Investigationes Económicas, "Visión Global de la Concentración Económica en El Salvador," (San Salvador), 1984, No. 039, Listado 2. This study found that there are 1,309 individuals with declared capital over a million *colones* (about $400,000) that fall within 114 family groups.

9. Ibid., p. 30.

10. Quoted in Kenneth J. Grieb, "The United States and the Rise of General Maximiliano Hernández Martínez," *Journal of Latin American Studies*, No. 3, November 1971, p. 152.

11. *Diario Latino*, November 24, 1977. Quoted in James Dunkerley, *The Long War: Dictatorship and Revolution in El Salvador* (London: Junction Books, 1982) p. 113.

12. Tommie Sue Montgomery, *Revolution in El Salvador* (Boulder: Westview, 1982), p. 55.

13. Caesar Sereseres, "The Guatemalan Legacy: Radical Challengers and Military Politics," 1983. University of California; Rand Corporation. Paper presented to *Study group on U.S. Guatemalan Relations*, School of Advanced International Studies, Johns Hopkins University.

14. Susanne Jonas and David Tobis (eds.), *Guatemala* (Berkeley and New York: NACLA, 1974), pp. 210-251.

15. Thomas Anderson, *Politics in Central America* (New York: Praeger, 1982) p. 36.

16. Ibid, p. 37.

17. Juan C. Arancibia, *Honduras: Un Estado Nacional?* (Tegucigalpa: Editorial Guaymuras, 1984) p. 36.

18. The two leading political parties, the Liberal Party and the National Party, have made only feeble attempts to represent the interests of campesinos and workers. The Liberal Party in the early 1980s oversaw the increased militarization of Honduras and the spread of repression against peasant and leftist dissidents. The National Party, traditionally the more conservative political party, offers absolutely no hope for those who seek to turn around the country's political direction.

19. Interview by author with U.S. Commercial Attaché, Tegucigalpa, April 1982.

20. Arancibia, op. cit.

21. *La Tribuna*, December 13, 1985.

22. Mitchell A. Seligson, *Peasants of Costa Rica and the Development of Agrarian Capitalism* (Madison: University of Wisconsin, 1980) p. 13.

23. Lowell Gudmundson, "Costa Rica Before Coffee: Occupational Distribution, Wealth Inequality, and Elite Society in the Village Economy of the 1840s," *Journal of Latin American Studies*, Vol. 15, Part 2, November 1983.

24. Samuel Z. Stone, *La Dinastía de los Conquistadores: La Crisis del Poder en la Costa Rica Contemporanea* (San José: Editorial Universitaria, 1975).

25. Oscar Arias Sanchez, *Grupos de Presíon en Costa Rica*, (San José: Editorial Costa Rica, 1983) p. 94.

26. José Luis Vega Carballo, "Costa Rica: Deterioro Política y Crisis Económica." in Donald Castillo Rivas (ed.), *Centroamerica: Más Allá de la Crisis* (Mexico: Programa Editorial de la Sociedad Interamericana de Planificación, 1983) p. 171.

27. Dennis Gilbert, "The Bourgeoisie," in Thomas Walker, ed. *Nicaragua, The First Five Years* (Boulder: Westview, 1985) p. 164.

28. George Black, *The Triumph of the People*, (London: Zed, 1981), p. 90.

Chapter Four: International Connections

1. Food and Agriculture Organization (FAO), World Conference on Agrarian Reform and Development, INF. 3, "Examen et analyse de la réforme agraire et du développement rural dans les pays en voie de développement," (Rome) 1979, p. 112-13. Cited in Susan George, *Ill Fares the Land* (Washington: Institute for Policy Studies, 1984), p. 10.

2. Interview by author with Director of the American Chamber of Commerce, Guatemala, June 1984.

3. Contract with Tela Railroad Company, a United Fruit subsidiary. Cited in CEPAL, "Bargaining Position and Distribution of Gains in

the Banana Exporting Countries, Especially Honduras and Panama" (Santiago de Chile) 1982, p. 9.

4. Letter from H.V. Rolston to Luis Melarra, Manager of the company in San Pedro Sula, first published in the review *Vanguardia* of October 20, 1949, in San Pedro Sula. Cited in Ibid., p. 11.

5. Richard H. Immerman, *The CIA in Guatemala: The Foreign Policy of Intervention* (Austin: University of Texas, 1982), p. 71.

6. Frank Ellis, *Las Transnacionales del Banano en Centroamerica* (San José: Editorial Universitaria Centroamericana, 1983), p. 364.

7. Ibid., p. 366.

8. The three TNCs have 74 subsidiaries spread across the isthmus. Honduras alone hosts 31 subsidiaries of Castle and Cooke and United Brands. Information from CEPAL, "Bargaining Position . . . ," op. cit., p. 22.

9. Ibid., p. 115.

10. Luis Valverde Obando, "Empresas Multinacionales y su Relacion con los Empresarios del Sector Bananero en Costa Rica," *Ciencias Sociales*, No. 19, 1980, pp. 53-67.

11. CEPAL, "Bargaining Position . . . ," op. cit., p. 115.

12. Ibid., p. 116.

13. UPEB (Union de Paises Exportadores de Bananao), "Estudio Sobre Empresas Transnacionales," 1977.

14. CEPAL, "Bargaining Position . . . ," op. cit., p. 62.

15. Ibid., p. 135.

16. CEPAL, "America Latina y la Economia Mundial del Cafe," (Santiago de Chile), 1982, p. 1.

17. CEPAL, "The Transnational Oligopoly in the Coffee Industry and the Case of Colombia," (Santiago de Chile), 1982, p. 7.

18. The United States imports 35 percent of the world's traded coffee. West Germany, the second largest importer, buys about 10 percent. As a region, Western Europe accounts for 45 percent of coffee imports. See Shamsher Singh et al., *Coffee, Tea, and Cocoa: Market Prospects and Development Lending* (Baltimore: Johns Hopkins University, 1977).

19. A few TNC traders—ACLI International (owned by Cargill), Volkart (family-owned firm in Switzerland), and J. Aron (owned by Goldman Sachs financial services corporation)—handle most of the developed

world's coffee trade. ACLI, which controls about 10 percent of the global coffee market, also stands among the top five in the cocoa trade. The trading companies buy huge shipments from Central America. One large multi-commodity trader, Saks International (Netherlands), purchases 25 percent of its U.S. coffee imports from El Salvador, while ACLI International relies on Guatemala for about 10 percent. Smaller traders depend almost entirely on coffee from one producing country. The U.S.-based firm Sierra Bravo Corporation, for instance, gets 97 percent of its coffee from Guatemala. See: Frederick F. Clairmonte and John Cavanagh, "Corporate Power in Selected Food Commodities," *Raw Materials Report*, Vol. 1, No. 3, pp. 21-39.

20. CEPAL, "America Latina . . . " op. cit., p. 23.

21. CEPAL, "The Transnational Oligopoly . . . ," op. cit.

22. Ibid., p. 95.

23. Ibid., p. 59.

24. Since 1980, the amount of coffee exported to non-ICO members has doubled. Costa Rica, for example, produces about 20 percent more coffee than its ICO quota. It ships this coffee to countries outside the ICO agreement, such as South Africa and Israel, at prices substantially below ICO rates.

25. CEPAL, "The Transnational Oligopoly . . . ," op. cit., p. 53.

26. Ibid., p. 50.

27. Frederick Clairmonte and John Cavanagh, "Cotton Trading: Futures for the Few," *Development Forum*, July 21, 1978.

28. UNCTAD, "Fibres and Textiles: Dimensions of Corporate Marketing Structures," (Geneva), 1980, p. 19.

29. UNCTAD estimates that just 35-40 textile TNCs dominate world textiles in both developed and underdeveloped countries.

30. Robert G. Williams, *Export Agriculture and the Crisis in Central America* (Chapel Hill: University of North Carolina Press, 1986), p. 39.

31. *Development Forum*, July 21, 1978, op. cit.

32. The six tobacco trading companies are Universal Leaf Tobacco, Debrill Brothers, Transcontinental Leaf Tobacco, Export Leaf Tobacco (subsidiary of BAT), and two subsidiaries of Imperial Tobacco Leaf (Kulenkampff and A.C. Monk). United Nations, UN Center on Transnational Corporations, *Transnational Corporations in World Development*, (New York), 1983, p. 216.

33. Clairmonte and Cavanagh, *Raw Materials Report*, op. cit.

34. *Raw Materials Report*, Vol. 1, No. 3, op. cit., pp. 21-39.

35. Williams, op. cit., p. 107.

36. Keith Schneider, "Looking Abroad to Fill Our Bellies," *New York Times*, August 3, 1986.

37. Williams, op. cit., pp. 103-104.

38. Ibid., p. 109.

39. Interview by author, San Marcos, Guatemala, June 1984.

40. ROCAP, "Project Evaluation Summary, Part I, Project #596-0097, Agribusiness Employment-Investment Protection," (Guatemala), 1983, p. 3.

41. AID, *Regional Strategy Statement 1986.*

42. Interview by author, San Marcos, June 1984.

43. Laurie Becklund, "Snow Pea Debacle Leaves Guatemalans Out in Cold," *Los Angeles Times*, September 6, 1984.

44. ROCAP, op. cit.

45. Interview by author with Noel García, Guatemala City, May 1984.

46. Resource Center Compilation of Corporations, 1985.

47. TNCs dominate and control the local food processing industry through their use of international patents. In Guatemala, for example, foreign firms own 86 percent of the patents for food processing. *SIAG*, July 1985.

48. Williams, op. cit., p. 44.

49. Aleman de Desarrollo, "Inversiones Extranjeras en el Sector Industrial de Costa Rica," (Berlin), 1982.

50. CEPAL, Jacobo Schatan, "La Agroindustria y el Sistema Alimentario Centroamericano," (Mexico), 1983, p. 66.

51. Interfaith Center on Corporate Responsibility, Batya Weinbaum and Henry Frundt, "New Foods for the Hungry," 1978.

52. CEPAL, Schatan, op. cit.

Chapter Five: Chemical Craze

1. A survey of tombstones in a Honduran cemetery showed that only 60 percent of the deaths were recorded with the government.

2. International Labor Organization, "Guide to Health and Hygiene in Agricultural Work," (Geneva), 1979, p. 94.

3. World Health Organization, Technical Report Series No. 634, "Safe Use of Pesticides," 1979.

4. Interview by author, August 1984.

5. ICAITI and UNEP, "An Environmental and Economic Study of the Consequences of Pesticide Use in Central American Cotton Production," (Guatemala), 1977, p. 88-91.

6. Ibid., p. 195.

7. See "Poisons and Peripheral People: Hazardous Substances in the Third World" in *Cultural Survival*, Vol. 5, No. 3, Summer 1981, p. 4.

8. David Weir and Mark Schapiro, *Circle of Poison* (San Francisco: Institute for Food and Development Policy, 1981).

9. Interview by author with AID official, Guatemala City, May 1984.

10. Instituto de Ciencias Ambientales y Tecnología Agrícola (ICATA), *"Perfil Ambiental de la República de Guatemala"* (Guatemala: ICATA, 1984), p. 64.

11. World Health Organization, op. cit.

12. One estimate indicated that a mere 12 TNCs will control over 75 percent of the world market by 1990. The United States accounts for 35 percent of the world pesticides production, followed by West Germany (19 percent) and Great Britain (16 percent). See "The Agrochemical Industry" in *TIE Europe*, No. 15, May 1983.

13. Shelley A. Hearne, *Harvest of Unknowns: Pesticide Contamination in Imported Foods* (New York: Natural Resources Defense Council, 1984), p. 21.

14. U.S. Bureau of the Census, "U.S. Exports, Schedule B, Commodity by Country", Report FT 446, Calendar Year 1982, (Washington), 1983, p. 181.

15. Alexander Bonilla, "Pesticides: Exportation and Importation of Contamination," (San José: unpublished paper, 1983).

16. *Shell in Agriculture*, February 1981.

17. Testimony of Albert H. Meyerhoff, Natural Resources Defense Council, before the Subcommittee on Department Operations, Research, and Foreign Agriculture, Committee on Agriculture, House, April 6, 1983.

18. Ibid., p. 6.

19. Loans from AID can be used to buy unregistered, restricted, or banned pesticides. Prior to a 1975 lawsuit, AID had financed the import of chemicals like heptachlor, chlordane, loptophos, dieldrin and parathion into Central America. The subsequent prohibition on the use of AID funds to purchase chemicals only extends to agricultural projects under direct AID control. In reality, most AID money for small farmer assistance is in the form of loans for credit that flows through intermediary financial institutions. Bert Printz of AID's environmental affairs division admitted that AID does not control the use of funds because they are "indirect acquisitions." This means that, for example, in Guatemala, there will be no restrictions on pesticide purchases with the $9 million of AID's $16.5 million dollar program in 1986 that is earmarked for agricultural credit.

20. *Chemical Marketing Reporter*, December 24, 1984.

21. The notifications are sent once a year after the first shipment of the restricted chemicals arrives in the importing country.

22. GAO, "Better Regulation of Pesticide Exports and Pesticide Residues in Imported Food is Essential," (Washington), 1979, p. 31.

23. Forty percent of all U.S. pesticide exports were shipped to Central America during this period; Sean Sweezy and Ranier Daxl, "Breaking the Circle of Poison," (Institute for Food and Development Policy: A Food First Research Report, 1983), p. 2.

24. Thirty years ago, only two insect species were resistant to synthetic pesticides, but today well over 400 species have developed resistance to the chemicals that were created to kill them (See: John E. Davies, Virgil H. Freed, Fred W. Whittemore, eds., *An Agromedical Approach to Pesticide Management* (AID: 1982), p. 65). Along with the organochlorines, growers started using the even more toxic organophosphates like parathion. The organophosphates have the advantage that they degrade faster than the organochlorines, but their high toxicity makes

them more hazardous for farmworkers. The organophosphate parathion is 60 times more toxic than DDT. In the 1970s, an estimated
one-fifth of the world's parathion was applied in the small country of El
Salvador. GAO, op. cit., p. 8.

25. P. Belli, "An Inquiry Concerning the Growth of Cotton Farming in
Nicaragua," Ph.D. dissertation, University of California, Berkeley,
1968. Cited in Institute for Food and Development Policy, Food First
Research Report, Sean Sweezy and Ranier Daxl, "Breaking the Circle
of Poison," 1983, p. 2.

26. Andy Feeney, "Breaking the Circle of Poison," *Environmental Action*,
April 1984.

27. P. Belli, op. cit.

28. FAO, L.A. Falcon and R. Daxl, "Informe al Gobierno de Nicaragua
Sobre Control Integrado de Plagas de Algodonero," (Managua), 1977.

29. Roberto Chediak, Tami Bensekry, Patricia Mora, Esther Lopez, and
Juan Carlos Del Bello, "Desarrollo de la Infrastructura y Capacidad de
Planificación en Ciencia y Tecnología," June 1983, p. 77.

30. Ibid., pp. 78-92.

31. Ibid., p. 159.

32. Material on Guaymi workers from unpublished paper on Guaymi
Indians by Philippe Bourgois, Stanford University, Department of
Anthropology.

33. "Report of the National Bipartisan Commission on Central America,"
(Washington), January 1984, p. 77 (popularly known as the Kissinger
Commission). Efforts to control malaria and eradicate its host mosquito
during this century have been highlighted by two breakthroughs. Dr.
William Gorgas, a U.S. army surgeon, set about draining swamps and
screening worker housing during the construction of the Panama
Canal. Within two years, the death rate from malaria decreased 80
percent. After World War II, the second breakthrough came with the
success of spraying chemicals like DDT and dieldrin in areas infested
with malaria-carrying mosquitoes. At one point, the World Health
Organization thought that malaria could be eradicated once and for all
with pesticides. However, repeated use of pesticides, especially in
cotton, caused mosquitoes to gradually develop resistance to the
chemicals. Government health teams were forced to turn to stronger
and far more expensive chemicals. Propoxur costs 20 times as much to
provide the same level of protection formerly guaranteed by DDT. The

extra costs in malarial control resulting from resistance have been described as "perhaps the most significant economic consequence of pesticide use in cotton." (ICAITI, op. cit., p.150). As malaria-bearing mosquitoes developed resistance to all four classes of synthetic insecticides, the incidence of malaria began to rise again, until infection rates had multiplied to previously unknown levels by the mid-1970s. Also contributing to the rise in malaria has been the extension of irrigation systems (which breed mosquitoes) into the cotton regions.

34. Derived from data in Pan American Health Organization, *1983 Annual Report to the Directors*.

35. ICAITI and UNEP, "An Environmental and Economic Study of the Consequences of Pesticide Use in Central American Cotton Production," (Guatemala), 1977, p. 127.

36. Georganne Chapin and Robert Wasserstrom, "Agricultural production and malaria resurgence in Central America and India," *Nature*, September 17, 1981, p. 182.

37. ICAITI, op. cit., p. 2.

38. Interview by author, IGSS Hospital, Escuintla, August 1984.

39. Interview by author, September 1984.

40. David Weir, "The Boomerang Crime," *Mother Jones*, November 1979.

41. Testimony of Vincent A. Gallagher, *Regulation of Pesticides*, op. cit. p. 107.

42. Interview by author, August 1984.

43. Interview by author with member of cotton production cooperative near León, August 1984.

44. Interview by author, August 1984.

45. SIECA, *Compendio Estadístico, 1981*. Figures for 1979.

46. Chediak et al., op. cit., p. 8.

Chapter Six: Agrarian Reform and Revolution, El Salvador and Nicaragua

1. See John Weeks, *The Economies of Central America* (New York: Holmes & Meir, 1985), pp. 18-19.

2. For an excellent discussion of the political and economic purposes of agrarian reform, see: Alain de Janvry, *The Agrarian Question and Reformism in Latin America* (Baltimore: Johns Hopkins University Press, 1981) pp. 202-223.

3. Laurence Simon, and James Stephens, Jr., *Pacific News Service*, 1981.

4. Roy Prosterman and Mary Temple, "Land Reform in El Salvador," *AFL-CIO Free Trade Union News*, June 1980, p. 1.

5. Peter Shiras, *Food Monitor* January-February, 1981.

6. Roy Prosterman and Mary Temple, "Agrarian Reform in El Salvador", *AFL-CIO Bulletin*, July 1980.

7. *New York Times*, March 13, 1980.

8. *AFL-CIO Free Trade Union News*, op. cit., p. 4.

9. *AFL-CIO, Free Trade Union News*, June 1980.

10. Shiras, op. cit., p. 169.

11. *Washington Post*, October 3, 1983.

12. *Multinational Monitor*, May 1981.

13. *Central America Report*, November 4, 1983.

14. Interview by Deb Preusch with Tom King, August 1984.

15. John D. Strasma, *Some Financial Aspects of the Consolidation of the Agrarian Reform in El Salvador*, Final Report to AID, El Salvador, January 1985.

16. AID, Regional Inspector General for Audit (Latin America), "Agrarian Reform in El Salvador: A Report on its Status," 1984.

17. AID, "Agrarian Reform . . . ," op. cit.

18. Castellanos Cea Campos y Cia., "Reporte de Observaciones y Recomendaciones Sobre el Control del Programa," (San Salvador), July 1983, pp. 15-19.

19. *National Catholic Register*, February 27, 1983.

20. Laurence R. Simon and James C. Stephens, *El Salvador Land Reform 1980-81, Impact Audit* (Boston: Oxfam, 1982).

21. *In These Times*, July 11, 1984.

22. Simon and Stephens, *El Salvador Land Reform . . .*, op. cit.

23. *New York Times*, June 30, 1984.

24. *Time*, June 4, 1984.

25. Nola Reinhardt, "Agro-Exports and the Peasantry in the Agrarian Reforms of El Salvador and Nicaragua," in William Thiesenhusen, ed., *Searching for Agrarian Reform in Latin America* (forthcoming from Allen Unwin Publishers).

26. AID, "El Salvador: Agrarian Reform Accomplishments," June 20, 1985.

27. Reinhardt, op. cit.

28. Robert G. Williams, *Export Agriculture and the Crisis in Central America* (Chapel Hill: University of North Carolina Press, 1986) pp. 133-134.

29. Jaime Biderman, "The Development of Capitalism in Nicaragua," *Latin American Perspectives*, Winter 1983.

30. Williams, op. cit., p. 166.

31. Joseph Collins, *Nicaragua: What Difference Could a Revolution Make?* (San Francisco: Institute for Food and Development Policy, 1985) pp. 22-26.

32. These points of the FSLN's agrarian reform program were paraphrased from "The Historic Program of the FSLN." See *Sandinistas Speak*, (New York: Pathfinder, 1982).

33. Information from Peter Marchetti, S.J., director of INIES in Managua.

34. Joseph R. Thome and David Kaimowitz, "A Half-Decade of Agrarian Reform in Nicaragua," in Thomas Walker, ed., *Nicaragua: Five Years Later*, (Boulder: Westview, 1985).

35. Interview by author, February 1981.

36. Juan O. Tamayo, "Land Reform Wins Support, Despite Snags," *Miami Herald*, September 16, 1984.

37. Central American Historical Institute (CAHI), "The Nicaraguan Peasantry," September 1985.

38. *Mesoamerica*, June 1986.

39. *Miami Herald*, January 1986.

40. CAHI, "Agrarian Reform Undergoes Changes in Nicaragua," *Update*, February 7, 1986.

41. Eduardo Baumeister, "State-Rural World: A Changing Relationship," (Managua: Centro de Investigación y Estudio de la Reforma Agraria, 1986).

42. For a provocative discussion of these issues, see: Forrest D. Colburn,

Post-Revolutionary Nicaragua: State, Class, and the Dilemmas of Agrarian Policy (Berkeley: University of California Press, 1986).

43. See Reinhardt for an excellent comparison of the two reforms.

Chapter Seven: Campesino Rebellion: Guatemala, Honduras, and Costa Rica

1. Interview by author, May 1984.

2. Pastoral Letter of Catholic Bishops of Guatemala, August 1962.

3. AID, *Land and Labor in Guatemala: An Evaluation*, 1982.

4. Elisabeth Burgos-Debray, (ed.), *I, Rigoberta Menchú* (London: Verson, 1983), p. 116.

5. SEGEPLAN, *Agricultura de Exportación, Población, y Empleo en la Costa Sur*, 1984.

6. Ibid.

7. *Central America Report*, July 18, 1986.

8. *Latin America Weekly Report*, August 7, 1986.

9. *Enfoprensa*, June 27, 1986.

10. *Central America Report*, July 18, 1986.

11. Interview by author with members of Ivan Betancourt Community, August 1984.

12. Ibid.

13. *New York Times*, December 3, 1985.

14. Robert G. Williams, *Export Agriculture and the Crisis in Central America* (Chapel Hill: University of North Carolina Press, 1986), p. 128.

15. Private estates of 1,200 or more acres are subject to expropriation. Landowners are compensated for improvements on the land.

16. *Mesoamerica*, May 1983; *Inforpress*, January 26, 1984.

17. Diego F. Alvarez, "La Reforma Agraria del Gobierno Militar y las Perspectivas en el Gobierno Constitucional," *Alcaraván*, (Tegucigalpa) February 1981, p. 6.

18. Interview by author, August 1984.

19. *Alcaraván*, February 1981, op. cit.

20. Estimate cited in address by William C. Thiesenhusen at conference on Asia Development Model and the CBI, September 28, 1984, p. 4.

21. Interview by author, August 1986.

22. Interview by Deb Preusch with members of Caratasca land occupation community, March 1983.

23. *Mesoamerica*, September 1983.

24. *Central América Report*, July 17, 1985.

25. Williams, op. cit., p. 181; *Latin America Weekly Report*, July 20, 1984.

26. *Mesoamerica*, September 1983, op. cit.

27. *Latin America Weekly Report*, June 29, 1984.

28. *Christian Science Monitor*, December 23, 1985.

29. Abelardo Morales, "Democracia Rural Cede Terreno al Latifundio," *Aportes*, (San José), May/June 1984.

30. Mitchell A. Seligson, "La reforma en Costa Rica, 1942-1976: La evolución de un programa," *Estudios Sociales Centroamericanos*, Enero-Abril 1978; *La agroindustria y el sistema alimentario centroamericano* (CEPAL, 1983).

31. AID, *Country Study: Costa Rica FY 1980*.

32. *Quarterly Economic Review*, Supplement 1984.

33. Beatriz M. Villarreal, *El Precarismo Rural en Costa Rica* (San José: Editorial Papiro, 1983), p. 25.

34. *Inforpress*, July 19, 1984.

35. Jean Hopfensperger, "Costa Rica: Seeds of Terror," *The Progressive*, September 1986.

36. Mitchell A. Seligson, *Peasants of Costa Rica and the Development of Agrarian Capitalism* (Madison: University of Wisconsin, 1980), p. 165.

37. *Latin America Regional Report*, September 21, 1984.

38. Interview by staff of Institute for Food and Development Policy with Guatama Fonseca, 1984.

Chapter Eight: Food Security—Obstacles and Solutions

1. This refers to all exports shipped out of the Central American region.

2. Mathew D. Shane and Mervin J. Yetley, "Debt Situation Sets the Stage for a Food Crisis," *Foreign Agriculture*, January 1985.

3. AID, *Honduras: Progress Under U.S.-Honduras Economic Cooperation*, August 1984.

4. Susan George, *Ill Fares the Land* (Washington: Institute for Policy Studies, 1984), p. 57.

5. An attempt to feed the world population a North American diet using U.S. production technologies would exhaust known petroleum reserves within eleven years. Susan George, *Ill Fares the Land* op. cit., p. 27.

6. USDA, *Food for Peace, 1984 Annual Report on Public Law 480.*

7. AID, *Regional Strategy Plan for Latin America and the Caribbean*, December 1983, p. 25.

8. USDA, Sovun Tun and Mervin J. Yetley, "A New Method to Assess Effects of Food Supply Shocks on Consumption in Developing Countries," (Washington), 1985, p. 13.

9. Alan Riding, "U.S. Food Aid Seen Hurting Guatemala," *New York Times*, November 6, 1977.

10. *The Tico Times*, March 22, 1985.

11. Caritas de Guatemala, "Segundo Informe y Evaluación del Programa Promoción y Nutrición," July 1978 to January 1979, p. 98. Translated by Tony Jackson.

12. GAO, "Disincentives to Agricultural Production in Developing Countries," (Washington), 1975, p. 117.

13. World Bank, *Population Policies and Economic Development*, (Baltimore: Johns Hopkins University Press, 1974).

14. Oxfam America, "Hunger and Population," *Facts for Action* No. 17, p. 3.

15. William Durham, *Scarcity and Survival in Central America* (Stanford: Stanford University, 1979).

16. William C. Thiesenhusen, "How Agriculture Has Effected Social Change in El Salvador," (Paper delivered at University of Wisconsin, February 20, 1984), p. 18.

Appendix

Statistical Overview of Central America

Social Indicators

	Costa Rica	El Salv	Guate	Hond	Nica	Pan	United States
Population (millions of inhabitants)	2.5	4.9	8.0	4.4	3.3	2.2	230
Population Doubling Time (number of years for population to double at current rate of change)	28	26	22	20	20	33	96
Rural Population (percent of total)	51	58	67	60	43	43	23
Population Density in Agricultural Areas (persons per sq. mile)	190	715	445	125	220	230	—

Health Indicators

	Costa Rica	El Salv	Guate	Hond	Nica	Pan	United States
Life Expectancy (years at birth)	74	65	61	60	62	71	75
Infant Mortality Rate (deaths/1000 live births)	19	53	70	87	43	22	12
Maternal Mortality Rate (deaths/10,000 liveborn)	23	—	96	82	65	73	—
Low Birth Weight Births (percent of births)	---- 12.0 in Central America ----						6.8
Infant Mortality from Infectious/Parasitic Diseases (percent)	11	—	—	32	—	—	1.5
Death Rate from Enteritis & other Diarrheal Disease (deaths/100,000 persons)	26	105	166	49	74	31	13
Physicians (people per physician)	1440	3220	8610	3120	2260	1170	520
Rural Access to Water (percent of households connected to water)	61	5	3	15	6	24	—

Economic Indicators

	Costa Rica	El Salv	Guate	Hond	Nica	Pan	United States
Per Capita GDP as Percent of U.S. Per Capita GDP	15	5	10	5	6	15	100
Per Capita GDP Growth Rate (AAGR, 1961-80)	3.2	1.5	2.4	1.7	1.8	4.5	—
Per Capita GDP Growth Rate (AAGR, 1981-85)	-2.1	-3.4	-3.9	-2.3	2.4	0.4	—
Energy Consumption (kilowatts/per capita)	580	210	220	240	280	730	11630
Cost of Living Index, 1982 (1975 = 100)	383	236	185	191	241 ('80)	156	—
Food Prices Index, 1982 (1975 = 100)	462	231	169	183	292 ('80)	160	—
Balance of Payments, 1983 (Millions $U.S.)	-393	-117	-210	-252	-358	-210	—
Terms of Trade Index, 1985 (1970 = 100)	70	80	76	79	67	82	—

Food Indicators

	Costa Rica	El Salv	Guate	Hond	Nica	Pan	United States
Calorie Intake Per Capita (percent of requirements)	118	94	93	96	99	103	139
Calorie Deficit of Poorest Half of Population (percent of requirements)	8	35	39	32	16	—	—
Protein Intake Per Capita (grams of protein)	60	50	53	52	68	61	106
Absolute Rural Poverty (percent of families who can not afford minimum nutritional requirements)	40	70	60	77	57	55	—

Agricultural Indicators

	Costa Rica	El Salv	Guate	Hond	Nica	Pan	United States
Agricultural Land (percent of land area suitable for agriculture)	30	58	24	37	14	24	—
Per Capita Arable Land (acres per person)	.3	.3	.5	.5	1.4	.6	2.1
Agricultural Labor Force (percent of all workforce)	28	40	58	53	41	34	2
Agricultural GDP (percent of total GDP)	21	26	25	30	26	10	3
Agricultural Output (Agric GDP/Agric Population, 1981-82, $U.S.)	--- $490 in Central America ----						$17,400
Per Capita Food Production Index, 1983 (1969-71 = 100)	99	86	102	86	78	101	118

Sources: Statistical Abstract of Latin America, Vol. 24, 1985; IDB, **Economic and Social Progress in Latin America**, 1986; IBRD, **World Development Report**, 1985; UNCTAD, **Handbook of International Trade and Development Statistics,** 1984 Supplement; CIA, **World Factbook,** 1985; PAHO **Annual Report to the Director**, 1984; ILO, **Yearbook of Labor Statistics**, 1983; ECLA/UN, **Statistical Yearbook for Latin America**, 1983.

Index

207